THE COMPUTER CONSULTANT'S GUIDE

Real-Life Strategies for Building a Successful Consulting Career

Second Edition

Janet Ruhl

John Wiley & Sons, Inc.

New York • Chichester • Weinheim • Brisbane • Singapore • Toronto

Library of Congress Cataloging-in-Publication Data:

Ruhl, Janet.

   The computer consultant's guide : real-life strategies for
building a successful consulting career / Janet Ruhl.—2nd ed.
       p.   cm.
   Includes index.
   ISBN 0-471-17649-4 (cloth : alk. paper).
     1. Business consultants.   2. Electronic data processing
consultants.   I. Title.
   HD69.C6R84   1997
   001'.023'73—dc21   97-5544

Printed in the United States of America

10   9   8   7   6   5   4

_____ Preface

A lot has changed in the five years since I wrote the original manuscript of *The Computer Consultant's Guide*. The Internet has moved into mainstream consciousness, the World Wide Web has revolutionized access to on-line information, and many thousands more white collar workers have been catapulted into entrepreneurship as a result of widespread corporate downsizing.

As a result, computer consulting has become an even more attractive option—not only for seasoned professionals, but even for entry level programmers straight out of college who are now as likely to be recruited by so-called consulting firms as they are by corporate employers. Now, too, computer consulting draws on an increasingly international population for whom Internet access makes it possible to work for clients around the globe.

With this in mind, I've tried to update this edition of *The Computer Consultant's Guide* while doing my best to retain the style and content that have made it so popular with earlier readers. As a result, in this new edition you'll find up-to-date information on the on-line resources that can help your consulting career as well as those that are a waste of time. I've responded to the requests of my many international readers and added more information about business and legal requirements for consulting outside of the United States. I've also included updated information about tax issues and the forms of business available to consultants. I've added more information to clarify consultants' insurance needs and have introduced several new tips, contributed by the working computer consultants whose experience and advice made the original edition of this work such a valuable resource.

But even with these changes, the purpose of this work remains the same. My goal is still to give you the information that will help you form a realistic picture of what consultants do and how they do it, to share with you the mistakes and triumphs of those consultants who have gone before you, and to teach you the business and marketing techniques you'll have to master so that you too can join the ranks of those who have succeeded in their own consulting careers.

Janet Ruhl
JanetRuhl@compuserve.com
http://www.javanet.com/~technion

Acknowledgments

This book could not have been written without the contributions of the multitude of people in the consulting community whose wit and wisdom contributed on the CompuServe Computer Consultants Forum over the past decade you'll find distilled here. This continues to be their book and I'm grateful to have had the opportunity first to write it, and now, to update it.

Thanks are due to the forum's sysops, both past and present, whose many hours of volunteer labor keep the forum running smoothly, including our current Wizop Martin Schiff, former Wizops David Moskowitz and Nick Cvetkovic, current sysops Mark Bayern, Bob Upham, and John Sage, and the many former sysops who have made the forum what it is today, including Paul Ferrara, David Moskowitz, Esther Schindler, Jeff Jacobs, and Dorothy Creswell.

Thanks also to the many forum staffers who have contributed their time and expertise over the years, including attorneys Lance Rose and Frederick Wilf, Ben Moyle, and Sharon Marsh Roberts.

Of course, there would be no forum without our forum regulars. So thanks go out too to the hundreds of people who visit the forum every day or two to share with the world their experience, opinions, suggestions, and ideas, as well as the occasional piece of killer Internet humor.

My heartfelt thanks also to the many thousands of visitors who have visited my site on the World Wide Web, the Computer Consultant's Resource Page, especially those of you who have taken the time to contribute your rates to the Real Rate Survey. Your participation has allowed me to provide much better rate information in this new edition and your e-mail has given me a better sense of what it is you need to know as you pursue your computer consulting careers.

The following are some, though by no means all the people to whom special thanks are due: Peter Atwood, Frank Bosso, John C. Brobston,

Peter Bogus, Carl Brown, Joyce Burkard of the ICCA, Theresa Carey, Richard Cohen, Nick Delonas, Howard Eichenwald, Irvin Feldman, Lawrence Fox, Nannette Geller, John Genzano, Payson Hall, John M. Horeth, II, Richard Herzog, Herman Holtz, Burt Johnson, Mich Kabay, Stephen Kent, Warren Keuffel, Roger Loeb, John Maschi, Rud Merriam, Michael Miora, Richard Morochove, Stu Mulne, Mike Nolan, David and Joanna Ruhl, Jeff Sachs, Wayne Schulz, Michael Stein, Tim Sullivan, Bob Upham, Frederic Wilf, Ed Yourdon, Steve Zilora, and the broker in L.A. who wishes to remain anonymous.

Thanks also to my editor at John Wiley & Sons, Ruth Mills, and to her highly competent staff, whose efforts have helped make this book such a success.

And, of course, grateful thanks go to all the readers of this and my previous computer career books whose positive and enthusiastic feedback has encouraged me to believe that these books do serve some useful purpose.

_____ Contents

Introduction

It's been a hell of a week at work. The boss wants you to spec out a new program by Friday, the users are all over you because of problems with the last system you installed, the network was down all afternoon, and rumor has it that the company is getting ready to start a new round of belt tightening and that this time the ax is going to fall on the computer support areas. Thank God they still let you take coffee breaks.

You get your bagel and extra large coffee and pull out the newspaper for a quick look at your declining stock investments when an advertisement headline catches your eye. It says, "Consulting Is the Pathway to Wealth and Independence!" The subheading adds, "The Average Consultant Bills $125 an Hour." You put down your bagel and read the fine print. Could you get rich in consulting? According to the ad, you can. It's right there in black and white: Computer consulting is the fastest growing branch of consulting today.

How great it would be to be your own boss! A little calculation on your napkin reveals that if you were making $125 an hour full time you'd be earning $250,000 a year—and you didn't even include in your calculations the two weeks you usually take off for vacation!

Almost all experienced computer people have moments like this and wonder how real are the chances of taking their experience and succeeding out on their own. All of us have dreams of leaving behind the tyranny of employers and of entering a world where the only limitations on us are the ones we set ourselves.

But computer people are practical, too, and smart—smart enough to know that there is no easy way to riches. Most of us have figured out that if we are our own boss we also have to meet our own payroll. Most of us know, too, that when you start out, being your own boss means being your own sales force.

The decision to quit a salaried job and begin a consulting career is likely to be the single most significant vocational decision we'll ever make. If we do it right, we can end up independent and financially successful. But if we get it wrong, we may end up facing empty bank accounts, blasted dreams, and the toughest kind of job hunt—one undertaken when we are currently unemployed.

So it would be nice if we could find out a bit about what we would be getting into before we had to make a decision like this. And it would be nice, too, if we could get that information not from people who write "How To" books for a living, or from people who have gotten wealthy giving seminars on how to get rich, but from people who earn their money in the computer consulting business, people who have already encountered the situations we're likely to meet and made the mistakes we're likely to make.

Fortunately, we can.

For more than a decade, people interested in computer consulting have had a unique resource available to them, a place where, no matter where in the world they live, they can come and ask real computer consultants about what they do and get personal answers to the questions they pose. The place is the Computer Consultant's Forum on CompuServe, usually known by its nickname, CONSULT. CONSULT is sponsored by an industry group dedicated to furthering the interests of computer consultants, the Independent Computer Consultants Association (ICCA). Every day visitors to this international computer bulletin board post some 200 or more messages about computer consulting—over 75,000 messages a year. People post questions about the legal steps they must take to begin consulting, about problems they're having with clients, about what software to use for a given application, and about hardware problems that are driving them batty. They post messages about problems they're having with distributors, with vendors, with other consultants. And almost every one of these queries gets answered by one or more of the Forum's more than ten thousand active members.

I've been involved with CONSULT since 1988. Since 1990 I've been a section leader and a sysop. Over the years, as I've read nearly every message posted in the public areas of the forum, I've come away with a sense of awe and admiration for what a bulletin board like this can offer people. Untrammeled by limitations of age, gender, race, or nationality, people on our bulletin board trade only one thing: information. Though they pay significant connect charges for the privilege, members of the on-line consultant community share their expertise with perfect strangers, day after day, often investing significant amounts of their own time and money to help other people out, to track down answers to their problems, and to help newcomers succeed in their own field.

In the following pages you too will have a chance to benefit from the insights and wisdom that have flowed through CONSULT over the past years. In the chapters that follow, we'll look at the questions that are most frequently asked by visitors to the forum and examine the most perceptive, useful, and, at times, controversial responses that the forum's practicing consultants have made to these questions. You'll learn for yourself how over 150 practicing consultants feel about their work, what problems they encounter, which real-world solutions have worked for them, and—just as important—which ones have not. When consultants disagree about a subject, whether it be the need for a written contract or the worth of cold calling, we'll hear from both sides of the argument and leave you to decide which approach makes the most sense to you.

You'll meet computer consultants who have become successful at consulting and some who've lost their shirts. You'll hear from those who indeed bill that legendary $125 an hour and from those who would be happy to be billing anything. You'll hear how they find their clients and what they sell them, what they charge and how they come up with their figures. You'll learn about their headaches and about their payoffs. And you'll begin to get an appreciation for the complexity and richness that computer consulting offers.

But as rich a resource as CONSULT is, the messages posted there cannot tell you everything you need to know to make the best start in consulting. To fill out the picture of what successful computer consulting is all about, I've supplemented forum material with information drawn from in-depth interviews with articulate, successful, long-term consultants who work in a variety of niches. To their experiences I've added my own—that same experience that earned me the invitation to join the CONSULT staff. Like many consultants I've got a few noncomputer degrees—a B.A. in anthropology from the University of Chicago and a master's in history—supplemented by specialized training in computer programming. I put in several years working as a corporate software developer, first at IBM and later at EDS, before striking out on my own as a computer consultant specializing in mainframe programming for corporate clients.

Since 1988 I've written extensively about the realities of computer-related careers, both in my first book, *The Programmer's Survival Guide: Career Strategies for Computer Professionals*, and in the many articles I've published over the years in *Computerworld*, *Datamation*, and other trade press journals. Finally, since preparing the first edition of this book, I've given seminars for beginning consultants, set up a popular computer consulting Web site, and formed my own small press, TECH-NION Books, through which I published *The Computer Consultant's Workbook*. In the course of all these activities I've interviewed dozens of headhunters, executives, and consultants of all types, and I've been privileged to hear from thousands of other working computer professionals. The tips and information that they've shared with me have continued to broaden my own understanding of the field.

I cannot promise that what you read in the pages ahead will make you rich. But I can guarantee that it will keep you from wasting your time and repeating the common mistakes that almost all new consultants make. It should clarify for you, too, the real questions you'll have to face in deciding whether you're ready to begin consulting: whether you've got the skills you need to do the work and whether you've got the gumption it takes to find your clients. If after you've studied these issues you decide that you aren't ready to start consulting now, this book will still be of value, because it will give you the information you need to begin educating yourself now, so that you can consult successfully in the future.

A note on the names used in this book: One of the things that experienced consultants know about consulting is that the way you appear to others is as important to your long-term success as the quality of the work you do. With this in mind, I've been very careful to protect the privacy of the consultants whose expertise I've drawn on. Though almost all of the material I've drawn on was posted in messages on a public computer bulletin board, I have made it a policy to cite consultants by name only when repeating statements that reflect well on them. I have also, occasionally, edited messages for spelling and grammar. When I've wanted to quote a statement that might cast doubt on a consultant's competence or perhaps offend a consultant's client, I've used the remark anonymously. When in doubt, I've erred on the side of not using the consultant's names. Therefore there are several consultants whom I've quoted in the following pages whose names appear nowhere in the book. I regret not being able to credit them, but trust that they posted their messages in the hopes of helping others and offer their unattributed remarks in this spirit.

1

WHAT DO COMPUTER CONSULTANTS DO?

Who are these computer consultants? Where do you find them? What do they do for a living?

Statistical information about computer consultants is difficult to find. Many of the organizations that represent consultants refuse to make publicly known the number of their members, or any information about their earnings or specialties, claiming that this is competitive information that their membership doesn't want released.

But intriguing statistics do surface from time to time. In 1992 *Computerworld* announced the results of a survey of its readership. Of the leading trade paper's 629,000 readers, some 112,149 identified themselves as consultants and an additional 52,375 people said that they offered contract DP services, suggesting that at the time, more than one in four *Computerworld* subscribers was involved in some form of computer consulting. By 1996, *Computerworld* reported that this ratio had grown to one in three—a ratio that may well hold true of the computer profession as a whole.

To learn a little more about the characteristics of computer consultants, let's look at the results of a survey of 162 active members of the Independent Computer Consultants Association (ICCA) that was taken at one of the group's annual conventions. Although this is a small sample, it is an instructive one, as it is made up almost entirely of computer consultants who were doing well enough financially to attend a relatively expensive consulting-related business event.

According to that survey, these ICCA consultants were experienced: 75 percent were over thirty years old and 69 percent had been in the computer field for at least five years before beginning consulting. These consultants were well educated, too. Eighty-one percent had a four-year college degree, one third had a master's degree, and 4 percent had a Ph.D. It's interesting to note, however, that the degrees most of these consultants brought to their computer work were earned in noncomputer-related disciplines. Only a quarter of them had computer-related degrees.

When we look at the work these consultants do, we find they cover a lot of territory. While the largest group represented was people who worked with PCs—41 percent of the group—other niches were well represented, too. One-third of the group reported working on mainframe systems, another 10 percent said they specialized in minicomputer work. A full 12 percent of those polled indicated they worked on all three platforms.

These consultants worked hard, too. Fifty-eight percent reported they worked more than thirty billable hours a week. When they were not billing, they were still working. These consultants reported attending seminars and classes and reading significant numbers of trade publications and technical books. And they kept up with technology, too. Half of the group polled reported mastering more than ten new languages, platforms, development environments, or packages since becoming consultants, many of them within the last three years. In the time left over from these pursuits, two-thirds of this group reported putting significant amounts of time into the networking activities necessary for marketing their services.

Why do they do it? Given a menu of motivations to choose from by the pollsters, the largest number of consultants cited "intellectual challenge" as being most important. The next most popular motivations they selected were "flexibility of hours" and "the ability to select projects." Less than one-third of the group rated high income as being very important to them.

Even so, the consultants in the survey, while definitely not rich, were doing well. All but 10 percent of the consultants reported that their companies had gross earnings over $40,000. Thirty-nine percent said they earned over $65,000, and 20 percent reported their companies grossed between $100,000 and $150,000.

WHO IS A "REAL" COMPUTER CONSULTANT?

Before we can look more closely at what it takes to join the ranks of these computer consultants, we'll need to spend some time establishing what a computer consultant really is. This is not as easy as it might seem. As we are all well aware, the term *consultant* has taken more than its share of abuse in the past few years. Once reserved for august experts brought in to advise top managers, we find it used now to describe everyone from the "Nail Consultant" who glues little plastic thingies onto fingernails to the "Lawn Consultant" who poisons grubs. One common joke would have it that a "Computer Consulting Firm" is a euphemism for two fired programmers, and there is some basis in fact for this perception. When MIS executives are fired, they often save face by announcing that they are leaving their companies to "pursue opportunities in consulting." Laid-off programmers frequently resurface as employees of big temporary firms who label them "consultants."

Even computer consultants themselves rarely agree on who is a "real" computer consultant. If you go to any meeting of a computer consultants' networking group and prowl around listening to the conversation, I'm willing to bet serious money that within twenty minutes you'll hear at least one self-identified computer consultant counter another's description of his current project with the sneer, "That's not *real* consulting!"

Forget the PC versus Macintosh wars. Forget the C versus Cobol battles. No topic generates as much heat and as little light within the consulting community as the question of what "real" computer consultants do. Some consultants claim that real consultants never touch code; others assert that real consultants *have* to know how to code. Some argue that real consultants never touch hardware; others can't imagine consulting without hardware sales. Some insist that real consultants deal only with executives and confine themselves to solving strategy issues, while others retort, "Yeah, sure, but I made $120,000 last year as a consultant and all I do is write programs in C++."

Who is right? Whom are you supposed to believe?

The answer is, everyone.

They're all computer consultants—from the people who install off-the-shelf PC software on their neighbor's computer to the folks who earn $2,000 a day telling the CIO how it's done. The more complex computer use gets in our society, the more niches arise that can be filled by bright, capable people with computer skills who are willing to take some risk and parlay those skills into a business of their own.

Higher Risk, More Control, and Greater Competence

So rather than deciding whether people are consultants by looking at the kinds of tasks they perform or the kind of clients they serve, it may be more useful to consider how much risk they take on and how much control they have over the work they undertake. This is one set of criteria that the IRS uses to separate true consultants from employees.

True consultants by this definition are those who have traded the security of a steady job (as specious as it might be in this age of downsizing) for higher pay and the ability to pick and choose what work they will do. Another distinguishing characteristic of such consultants is that they work for a series of clients rather than a single employer, choosing or refusing to work for any particular client according to their own desires, rather than moving from client to client at some supervisor's behest.

Real consultants are able to negotiate the rate they will be paid for every job they take on. If workers' salaries change only when they receive their yearly salary review, it's fair to say they aren't consultants, no matter what their employers may call them.

Finally, the most respected consultants exercise a great deal of initiative when dealing with clients. They make independent decisions about how to approach an assignment they've been given rather than slavishly follow someone else's methodology, and they often bring in their own tools when solving the problems they're presented with instead of relying on the client's materials.

With these criteria in mind you can see that there is a wide continuum of risk and control within the computer consulting community, with some people who call themselves computer consultants working under conditions only minimally different from those of regular employees and others functioning as pure entrepreneurs.

But there's something else that distinguishes a real consultant, something that the people who sell the seminars on consulting success tend to underplay. While most people are capable of assuming risk and treasuring independence, far fewer people, no matter how well intentioned, can meet this second make-it-or-break-it criteria for consulting: *The consultant has to be an expert.*

Consultants must excel at what they do, whatever it may be. Whether you are selling contract coding services or tape backup units, the client's assumption is that you know what you are doing and that you will do it correctly the first time. This, as much as anything else, is what distinguishes a consultant from an employee.

An employee has some leeway. An employee is expected to learn on the job. But a consultant is expected to come into the job ready to perform at a completely professional level. That doesn't mean that consultants never make mistakes. But it does mean that the mistakes they make are the mistakes of an extremely competent person. If you are just learning your trade, no matter how much you bill clients or what services you sell, don't expect others to consider you a "real" consultant.

Risk. Control. Competence. These are the hallmarks of the real computer consultant.

TYPES OF COMPUTER CONSULTING

Now let's look at the services that computer consultants sell to their clients. In the rest of this chapter we'll break consulting down into several clearly defined types of work and describe each in broad terms. Table 1-1 provides an overview. In each section, we'll meet a few real

TABLE 1-1 Types of Computer Consultants

Type	Work Performed	Background Needed
Contract Programmer	Codes, tests, debugs for an hourly rate. May also do design and analysis work.	Salaried employment as a programmer. Excellent technical skills in high-demand languages/platforms.
Reseller/VAR/ System Integrator	Selects and configures hardware and software. Buys wholesale. May run retail outlet or purchase on as-needed basis for client.	Familiar with hardware and software. Extensive contacts in local business community or in a niche industry.
Custom Developer	Develops custom software for clients. May charge fixed bid or hourly rates. Profits from selling upgrades, follow-up releases, and ongoing support.	Knowledge of programming and solid applications expertise. Excellent self-management skills. Entrepreneurial talent.
Expert Consultant	Advises top decision makers on policy or technical direction. Gives lectures and seminars. Frequently quoted in press.	Publication in national media, previous high-visibility executive role in major corporation.
Computer Management Consultant	Project management; provides reports, studies, analysis, and problem solving.	Previous significant management experience in technological field. Visibility in industry. Good network of contacts. Excellent technical skills.
Consulting Firm Employee	Contract programming or project team participation. Paid typical employee salary.	Hired from college with business degree or from other corporations with two or more years' experience.

consultants who've pursued each type of consulting. Keep in mind, though, that while we will describe each of these niches as distinct, in practice most consultants' practices blend the characteristics of several niches. A custom software developer may resell hardware and off-the-shelf software, and a consultant who provides strategic planning for upper management may also do significant amounts of custom database design.

CONTRACT PROGRAMMERS

A large proportion of the people who call themselves computer consultants do contract programming. They write computer programs for their clients and charge them by the hour for this work.

Contract programming isn't glamorous. Indeed, it isn't a particularly well-respected branch of computer consulting, and many of its practitioners adopt a somewhat apologetic, self-deprecating tone when describing what they do. They wish they did more advising. They wish they did more analysis and design, configuration, and planning. When questioned about their work, contract programmers may exaggerate the amount of analysis and design that they do and underplay the number of hours they spend coding and testing.

But contract programming is the meat and potatoes of computer consulting. For every $125 hour billed by a consultant advising high-level executives, it's safe to say that there are at least fifty hours being billed by an experienced contract programmer who spent it coding, testing, or debugging routines in COBOL, FoxPro, or any one of a bewildering variety of specialized computer languages.

While it's certainly true that not all computer consultants are programmers, most of the people who have managed to survive in computer consulting for more than a few years are highly skilled at coding in at least one programming language and quite often in several. The reason for this is that programming is, by any measure, the service that clients most desperately need and are the most willing to pay for.

Clients may be able to get the salesperson at the computer store to advise them for free on what computer to buy; they may be able to find out what they need to know about project management from reading books and attending seminars; but when they run into a situation where they need to have code written to do a specialized task—as most computer users eventually will—they have to find a highly skilled programmer to help them out.

What Contract Programming Is Like

The conditions of contract programming work vary greatly. Some contractors work for a single client for weeks, months, or even, in extreme cases, years. Others provide custom programming services for several clients at the same time. Some work at home, doing their programming on their own hardware using their own software. Others, particularly those who specialize in mainframe work, work on-site, programming on the client's hardware and software.

Contract programming is by far the easiest branch of computer consulting to break into. All that is required to begin is that you have already put in a significant number of years working as a paid programmer and that you be able to show you've had recent on-the-job experience with the software and hardware that is currently in demand in your region. According to several studies, typical contract programmers have had between five and ten years of industry experience before they start consulting.

What You Need to Get Started

Once you decide to start contracting, there is little need for cash outlay, particularly if you are going to be working at a client's shop on the client's equipment. It is easy to determine what to charge, too. There is usually a going rate for each programming specialty and a few conversations with other contract programmers is all it will take to determine what a realistic figure would be for your own skills.

What You Can Earn

To give you an idea of the earning potential of contract consultants, formal and informal rate surveys agree that in the mid 1990s most contract programmers were earning something between $25 and $75 an hour, with the exact figure varying on the computer languages they specialized in, the industry they served, and the part of the country they worked in. These rates may sound lower than that $125-per-hour figure you've heard bandied about as an average rate for consultants. But you must realize that most of these contract programmers were billing those hourly rates thirty, forty, or more hours a week, forty or more weeks a year, year in and year out, making them among the most financially secure of all computer consultants. A 1992 survey taken by a market research group found that the average contract programmer worked 1,700 billable hours a year and grossed $65,000.

How to Find Work

Another plus for contract programmers is that marketing their services is much easier than it is for other kinds of computer consultants. Over the years a whole industry has grown up that is devoted to placing contractors with large corporate clients. A couple of phone calls to a broker or technical service firm (TSF) may be all it takes for a contract programmer whose technical skills are stronger than his or her marketing skills to turn up a viable client.

The Downside of Contract Programming:
Keeping Skills Up-to-Date

All this may sound too good to be true and you may be wondering, where's the catch?

The catch is that the market for contract programming is *intensely specialized*. Clients who have a contract to fill want consultants whose skills are an exact match to their requirements. So unless you have a resume bristling with acronyms indicating languages and operating systems that are currently in hot demand, you may find it extremely hard to find a contract no matter how good your programming skills may be or how much high-quality technical or managerial work you list on your resume. If a job calls for MVS/DB2 skills, only people with those skills will be considered, and your experience with a Unix-based SQL database will do you no good at all.

With the pace at which the technology changes today, this specialization means that it is quite possible for contract programmers to be extremely successful for years, only to wake up one morning and discover that demand for their skills has dwindled to the point where they can't find another contract. As an example, in the mainframe world, batch COBOL contract work was plentiful for a good fifteen years, until it dried up in the early 1990s. Now experienced batch COBOL programmers who lack more specialized skills like CICS and DB2 are finding it difficult to get any contract work at all.

But this problem isn't limited only to the mainframe world. PC programmers must keep up with a dizzying pace of change too. Programmers who used to be able to make a good living coding in nothing but C must now master C++, or perhaps even Visual Basic. They must learn how to develop under Windows 95 and Windows NT, to say nothing of other upcoming environments.

Therefore, contract programming is not likely to be a satisfactory long-term consulting option for you no matter how much you may earn on your early assignments, unless you are willing to do the reading and research it takes to keep up with the industry and are willing to invest in the training it takes to continually upgrade your technical skills on your own.

Meet the Consultant:
Contract Programmer Burt Johnson

Burt Johnson is one consultant who isn't embarrassed to call himself a contract programmer. Johnson's specialty is working with C and C++ applications for the Macintosh and Windows environments. He practices in Silicon Valley where he is able to find many clients eager to pay well for these skills.

Like most computer consultants Johnson works hard. He reports that he often bills sixty or more hours in a single week. To find his clients he relies on a combination of marketing techniques. He sends newsletters on a monthly basis both to old customers and to likely prospects and he uses other common networking techniques. But like most contractors, Johnson has also called on brokers when his own marketing efforts haven't kept his schedule filled, especially in the early years of his consulting practice.

The contract programming Johnson does is by no stretch of the imagination dull drudgework. For one recent project he produced a prototype sports video editor for the NFL using the Sony digital video camera. On another he created an Internet database browser for a major Japanese company.

Johnson's background is typical of many computer consultants. In his forties now, his education includes a B.S./E.E.C.S. degree and an M.B.A. Before becoming a consultant he filled positions as director of software engineering at two companies, including Motorola Computer Systems. Johnson is frank about admitting that one of his earlier attempts at running an independent business did not succeed. But he feels he benefited from what he learned from that failure and believes that it has taught him to be much more careful about contracts, payment, and the other nuts-and-bolts issues related to running a business.

When asked what he likes best about computer consulting, Johnson cites the variety and speed of the projects he works on. He says, "I am able to take on projects and get them done in times that would have been unheard of in a corporate environment and to work on two or three new projects every year." What he likes least, he says, like most consultants, is the need to deal with collecting fees and the other business overhead associated with being an entrepreneur.

SYSTEMS INTEGRATORS/VARS/RESELLERS

The second largest group of consultants in the computer consulting community are those who fall into a loosely defined group that includes people calling themselves "systems integrators," "value-added resellers" (VARs), or simply "resellers." These consultants may not be able to write a line of computer language code, but they do know how to order and configure hardware and software, as well as how to install and customize popular off-the-shelf software packages.

The lines between people calling themselves VARs, systems integrators, and resellers are blurry. In general, people calling themselves resellers tend to sell only hardware and off-the-shelf software, acting like a computer retailer but without maintaining a storefront, while VARs and systems integrators may combine the selling of hardware and off-the-shelf software with more in-depth analysis of client needs. They are also likely to sell training, and may customize the hardware and software solutions they sell. But there's little clear agreement on the precise meaning of these terms, so to keep the discussion simple, we'll just call this whole group "systems integrators."

The Market for Systems Integrators

A small number of systems integrators specializing in systems for the mainframe and minicomputer arena have been in business for several decades, but this niche has really only come into its own with the PC revolution. Nevertheless, contrary to what people unfamiliar with computer consulting might think, those who succeed at selling systems integration services do not usually serve the small business or home computer user market. Mom-and-pop businesses and home computer users, though they might *need* consulting services, can almost never afford to pay the rates computer consultants must charge to stay in business.

The systems integrator's customer base is much more likely to be the sophisticated mid-to-large-size business—one grossing $250K a year or more. This is a business that has already made a significant investment in computers, knows it can expect a worthwhile return on its investment in software and hardware, and is used to paying large sums for other kinds of vendor services. Consultants who know how to serve the needs of such businesses can be very successful.

Niche Specialization

Systems integrators often specialize in a certain niche. They may confine themselves to providing solutions for a single industry, such as chemical manufacturers, or they may specialize in providing software that automates functions like accounting or manufacturing control across industry lines. Ideally systems integrators should have a broad knowledge of competing products that serve their industry and their niche, and they should have an in-depth knowledge, too, of the business needs of their clients.

Increasingly, because of the direction that computer applications are taking, systems integrators need to be knowledgeable about computer networking and cross-platform communications. The task of keeping up with the dizzying speed of change in the worlds of hardware, software, and applications is a daunting one, and it is all too easy for systems integrators who have installed a few successful systems to get complacent and fall behind. Some of the worst horror stories that clients have to tell involve systems integrators who sold them outdated systems that ran on incompatible hardware that ended up, millions of dollars later, on the scrap heap. Because of this, many clients are tempted to go with name-brand integrators, like the computer consulting subsidiaries of Big Six accounting firms, under the sometimes mistaken impression that the size of the firm ensures the quality of their work. Competing with such firms may be the number-one problem encountered by the fledgling systems integrator.

Rates for Systems Integrators

Systems integrators tend to be the consultants who brag about their $125 per hour rate. What they often don't tell you is that they can find only a few billable hours each month. The jobs they find may require only a few hours to be completed, unlike the sustained stints of the contract programmer. Much more of their time is spent on *nonbillable tasks* and a lot more of their money has to be invested in state-of-the-art hardware and software.

Many would-be systems integrators hope to earn money from the markup on selling hardware, but those who have tried this report that it is rare to be able to earn money from hardware sales to make a profit. The competition on price is too fierce for both software and hardware, and hardware is too readily available to the public to leave many clients willing to pay a significant markup for these products. Many consultants who do sell hardware say they do it as a convenience to clients rather than as a profit center. Experienced integrators find that their profits come instead from selling their expertise in putting systems together and from the follow-up business they get for ongoing support and training.

Systems integrators usually estimate their incomes based on having, at best, 1,000 billable hours a year, or half of the available work days.

Breaking In: Marketing and Networking Are Critical

To succeed in systems integration you will need to have much more highly developed *entrepreneurial skills* than are needed for any other kind of computer consulting.

No matter how good your technical skill, you may never get to use that skill if you don't have equally well-developed marketing skills. The kind of systems integration that produces big returns is a tough sell, and you will be competing with large, well-capitalized competitors whenever you bid on a project. Unless you already have built up a network of contacts with managers in the industry or application area that you hope to support, it is very unlikely that you will be able to find much work as a systems integrator at all. Most people who do succeed at this kind of work do it after working for other firms who provide this kind of service, or are themselves professionals in the field they plan to serve who have built a strong reputation in their field and thus begin with a solid network of contacts in place.

Successful systems integrators also tend to be active in professional groups that serve their potential clients, and they tend to be perceived by their business clients as businesspeople with outstanding technical skills, rather than as technicians. Many of the most successful systems integrators come from nontechnical backgrounds. They have been corporate comptrollers, Big Six management consultants, CPAs, or attorneys, before their knack for bossing around computers drew them into systems integration.

No one starts a career as a successful integrator overnight. Like all consulting, it will be a natural outgrowth of what you've already done in the earlier stages of a professional career. Learning as much as you can about the business needs that the technology you want to sell will address, keeping up with that technology, and devoting time to nourish your contacts in the business areas you have chosen to concentrate on will all help.

Meet the Consultant: Systems Integrator Mike Nolan

Mike Nolan makes his living as a systems integrator in rural Berkshire County, Massachusetts, an area better known for vacation homes than big industry. After earning a B.S. and M.S. in mechanical engineering, he put in over twenty years as an engineer working in various locations in the Middle East for a large aerospace company, rising to become manager of engineering for a 180-person department before deciding to turn to consulting.

When he first went into business for himself in the late 1980s, Nolan offered accounting systems to small businesses in his region. Typical projects involved installing networks and accounting software for clients, or modifying and upgrading their existing accounting system.

When I interviewed Nolan in 1991, he reported that he was not yet able to earn what he had as a corporate employee and that it took more hours to earn what he did earn. But he said that he still felt consulting was worth doing, because he found his quality of life so much better than it had been when he was a corporate manager. As he explained it, although he put in longer hours, he had control of those hours, and because he controlled his business, he could make time to do the things he loved to do at home. As he said at the time, "The stresses on me are of my own making, not some corporate or political bullshit."

Contacted again in 1996, Nolan told me that he has seen his business expand to where it is not only profitable for himself, but can employ seven other people. While his business still serves a clientele that includes many smaller businesses, he devotes most of his own time to supporting the accounting systems of a few larger clients—manufacturers with revenues over thirty million dollars as well as a large state agency. However, his employees concentrate on installing and maintaining increasingly complex networks for smaller businesses as well as supporting and customizing accounting and order entry software.

CUSTOM APPLICATION DEVELOPERS

Like systems integrators, custom application developers address a specialized client's business need, but they take a different approach to doing it. While integrators tailor a solution for a client by customizing off-the-shelf software, custom application developers start off with a base system of their own, for example, a generic insurance agency system or a human resources system that they have written. But rather than selling copies of this system off-the-shelf, custom application developers sell each client a highly customized version of this system, one adapted to the client's individual needs.

Because they are able to offer the client a "completely customized solution," these consultants can charge much higher prices for their software than they could if they were selling a one-size-fits-all package. Customized software may sell for $2,000 a module or more, and the developers profit not only from the initial sale, but from a steady stream of upgrades and enhancements that they can also sell the user. It is also possible to earn significant amounts of selling ongoing support services for this kind of software.

Developing custom software and hardware solutions was the third most common service offered by the consultants polled by the ICCA. Sixty-four percent of the group reported offering clients this kind of development services.

This type of consulting can yield enormous profits, but it requires a much greater up-front investment than the other kinds of consulting we've discussed here, because of the need to come up with a stable base system that is flexible enough to be easily modified to provide custom solutions without requiring significant amounts of truly custom programming. Often this kind of consulting is a natural outgrowth of contract programming done for clients where consultants have reserved rights to resell their own code.

To do it you will not only have to have excellent programming skills (or know where to buy them for an affordable amount) but you must know something about software development. Because you will be responsible for ongoing maintenance and enhancements, your long-term profitability will depend on how maintainable your base code is.

Like the systems integrator, you will also need to have finely tuned marketing skills, because it is harder to sell this kind of product than it is to sell contract programming or support for well-known off-the-shelf products. You will have to be able to convince potential clients that you are in business for the long run and that you will stay around to support your product. Needless to say, your product will have to be good because it will be word-of-mouth from happy customers, not glossy ads, that sells this kind of service.

You'll do best at this kind of consulting if you truly enjoy the entrepreneurial side of consulting. You'll be dealing with complex contracts and with a more complex sales cycle than most other computer consultants. Custom developers are also more likely to end up employing others, so to succeed in this area you'll need to have excellent management and business skills and enjoy exercising them.

Meet the Consultant: Custom Developer Michael Stein

Michael Stein is a consultant who has built up a five-person business providing custom database and workflow applications for trade associations, professional societies, universities, and other nonprofits. Out of his work for these kinds of organizations he has developed a suite of products he markets under the name "Members Only." These software products provide membership management, mailing, meeting management, fundraising, and certification. His base system is written in Delphi and uses Btrieve as a database engine, and once sold, his company's three programmers customize these applications heavily for each client.

Like many consultants, Stein came to computer work in a roundabout way. After earning a B.S. in physics at MIT in 1972, he spent a decade as a community activist, working with groups like the Berkeley Free Clinic and the D.C. Community Health Coalition. In the course of this work he became familiar with the needs of the nonprofit groups he now serves.

The projects he does draw both on his industry expertise and his self-taught computer skills. In one early project Stein's company first provided his client, a social action organization associated with a major Protestant denomination, with an analysis of its database needs. When that was delivered, the client asked him to provide the software to meet the needs he'd just identified. The resulting customized contact management, order entry, and subscription software now runs on a forty-station network at the client's Washington, D.C. headquarters.

As his company has grown, so has the size of the projects it undertakes. A recent project involved developing software for Al-Anon/World Service Organization to help it manage its network of Al-Anon groups, its sales of literature and other products, and its subscriptions. His company is also developing membership and meeting management systems for the American Chiropractic Association and several other high-profile nonprofit organizations.

When asked what he likes about consulting, Stein cites "the feeling of autonomy" and "the creative challenges." He adds that he also likes not being caught up in the internal politics of the companies he works for. But he cites one additional factor, one shared by other custom developers: the thrill he gets walking downtown and passing "building after building where I know our applications are running."

THE MULTIMEDIA/WEB CONSULTANT

The explosion of usage of computer multimedia technology in the early 1990s has resulted in the emergence of a new kind of computer consultant, the computer-based multimedia expert. Originally called "desktop publishing experts" or "multimedia developers," with the recent emergence of the Web many of these consultants now bill themselves as "Web consultants" or "Web developers."

These consultants generally bring to their work a background rich in graphic arts experience, as well as a history of employment in media-heavy fields such as advertising, journalism, or printing. And while some self-styled Web consultants may be graphic artists who have only advanced their computer skills to the level of being able to code up simple HTML pages, the consultants most likely to succeed in this niche are those with significant technical skills, who understand computer networking, are comfortable coding Perl and Java scripts, and are capable of designing sophisticated database queries.

Web consultants play a variety of roles for their clients. They must educate them about what the Web can and cannot do for their businesses. They must also help them keep abreast of newly breaking developments in browser and server technologies as well as database access software. Beyond this, they must often keep track of which Internet service providers (ISPs) are reliable, and advise clients on when to use an outside Web-hosting service and when to host their own.

And those are just the technical challenges they face. A good Web consultant must also understand what makes sites work: what goes into designing the content that makes the client's target market do what the client wants them to do at the site. At present this requires excellent writing and marketing skills, as well as a working knowledge of how to apply graphic arts. As the race to turn the PC into an interactive TV nears the finish line, the Web consultant of the next decade will need to add to these skills an advanced understanding of sound engineering, music production, storyboarding, and video production—all while keeping up with the latest releases of operating systems, database server technology, and browser capability.

If you're tempted to enter this niche, the biggest challenge you'll face is its current boom mentality and the influx of people, many with marginal technical and creative skills, who have rushed to cash in on the media-fanned bonanza. Clients stung by hypesters who don't deliver will demand increasing proof of competence from the consultants who survive the inevitable shakeout. So if you want to establish yourself as a true Web consultant, you'll need to commit yourself to getting the continual training needed to keep your technical skills current while you hone your ability to communicate a clear-cut message through imagery, sound, and text. If you can do this, Web and multimedia consulting may indeed provide an elegant career solution for you and others who want to work with computers while using your talents in the creative arts.

Meet the Consultant: Web Consultant Robert Neuschul

Robert Neuschul is a principal of Imagineering Technologies, Ltd., a British Web consultancy. He began his computer career doing IBM mainframe systems design in the late 1970s. In the 1980s he shifted his attention to PCs, and spent five years as technical and strategic manager at Ashmount Research, a British software firm that provides both on- and off-line readers for Compuserve, Cix, Bix, Delphi, and the Internet as well as the long-distance learning capabilities of the Open University, an organization supporting some 200,000 on-line students. Neuschul has also spent several years running a successful film and photographic media practice.

Neuschul's company, founded in 1995, draws on the talents of a number of people expert in everything from chip design to global network management. Together they provide clients with everything from simple page makeup through full facilities management services, or as he puts it, "Anything Web, Internet, or communications related."

A typical recent project involved taking over an existing in-house corporate intranet knowledgebase project for a worldwide legal and financial services company. Neuschul was called in because the project, which already involved over 2,000 Web pages, was taking too long to complete and had already consumed some $400,000. His task was to analyze the existing site, rectify broken links and faulty code, and fix problems caused by the company's use of a bewildering variety of browser releases and display hardware and software.

Having finally gotten the existing system to where it was working properly, Neuschul's next job was to provide the client with a full requirements specification for the next phase of the knowledgebase project and then implement it to complete the site. Throughout the project, his challenge was to retain the cooperation and reduce the animosity of the existing MIS team while taking over their work and completing the project on schedule and on or under budget.

Neuschul is comfortable installing LANs and WANs as well as designing the standout graphics that have earned his site at http://www.

imagine.co.uk a number of awards. He says that he finds his clients through referral, direct networking, and from magazine write-ups of his work.

His advice to anyone thinking of following in his footsteps? "Learn to live without sleep!" "Don't give up!" And, of course, "Keep on learning." And he cautions that "Those who don't understand media in its widest sense will lose out in the marketplace we address."

THE EXPERT CONSULTANT

But don't any computer consultants make a living selling pure advice? Don't some computer consultants sell more than hardware, software, and their own programming skills? What about people like James Martin, Shaku Atre, and Ed Yourdon, those high-level consultants you always see quoted in the trade press? Aren't they what real consulting is all about?

Well, sort of.

There are indeed a handful of people who do make their living as high-profile authorities, and if you read the trade press you already know their names. But they are a very small portion of the computer consulting community.

What confuses the issue is that so many consultants try to *appear* as if they make their living selling high-level advisory services alone. Several years ago when I was asked to write an article about consultants for a computer industry trade journal, the feature editor was very unhappy with my final copy. "I want to hear from real consultants," she said. "You need to interview people who make their livings advising high-level decision makers, not these lower level types who just sell hardware and software."

After the editor supplied me with a list of people whose high-level management consulting had been recently profiled in the computer trade press, I called each one and asked them politely if they could describe their businesses to me. In every case the reply was that they sold their clients systems or software. "What about that high-level stuff?" I asked one of these consultants innocently. "Don't you confer with top executives about corporate strategy?" "Well," the answer came back, "I'm trying to move in that direction, in fact I'd love to move in that direction and I'm doing a lot of marketing along those lines, but for now my clients are a lot more willing to pay for a concrete deliverable."

The reason for this is not hard to understand. Managers find it much harder to justify paying huge amounts for expert assistance in doing the management jobs that they are, after all, being paid to do themselves. Upper management is much less likely to release funds for advice rather than for a simple, concrete deliverable. If they do bring in someone to do high-level consulting, that person is likely to have once been a top executive in a high-profile Fortune 100 firm or someone whose name is, if not a household word, at least one familiar to the readers of *Computerworld* or *PC Magazine*.

Meet the Consultant: Expert Consultant Ed Yourdon

Ed Yourdon is one of the handful of expert consultants whose consulting practice is indeed built around advising top executives on computer-related issues.

Yourdon explains that much of the work he does for his clients is what he calls "insurance" consulting. Companies that are worried about making an expensive mistake want to have a politically acceptable "name"—an expert like himself—come in and tell them that they are right or wrong.

When I interviewed him in 1992, he told me that his recent clients included a large government agency in Australia that flew him in to bounce some technical and strategic questions off him to see if they were going in the right direction for the next several years and a major CASE vendor who wanted him to review a new reverse engineering tool.

Contacted again in 1996 he told me that he now mostly gets called in to do strategic consulting, working with people at the highest levels of IS management. What this really means, he explained with his characteristic dry wit, is that they ask him to help them "transform their organization from brain-dead robots into world-class software ninja masters," and "instantaneously move from RPG and assembler into Java, OO technology, etc."

Yourdon attributes some of his success to having been in the right place at the right time. He studied applied mathematics at MIT in the early 1960s and was able to study with artificial intelligence (AI) guru Marvin Minsky before Minsky became well known. Following graduation Yourdon spent about five years working salaried jobs at DEC, GE, and small software consulting firms, getting solid experience in the then brand-new computer field, before starting his own firm.

But what he points to as the single most important contributor to his success are his many publications, including his classic, *Structured Systems Analysis and Design*. He says, "It's difficult to impress upon fledgling consultants how important it is to have some published credits. A good article in such journals as IEEE or CACM, is sufficient, but nobody seems to be impressed by a couple of articles in the run-of-the-mill trade journals—unless you can say you have a regular column in one of the mags. Once you've published a book, though, you become an instant expert—even if the book is filled with blank pages. The simple truth is that 99 percent of the human race finds it an almost unsurmountable obstacle to write a three-hundred-page treatise on some technical topic."

Yourdon explains that he finds it easy to write books quickly and easily because each book represents a "brain dump" of the seminars and lectures he's given over the one or two years prior to writing the book. Although he is too modest to say it, Yourdon is well known to be a fascinating, entertaining, brilliant, and sometimes controversial lecturer, and this skill has probably been as important to him in achieving success as is his ability to write. Indeed, his kind of world-class speaking and writing skills seem to be a prerequisite for anyone thinking of becoming an expert consultant.

COMPUTER-ORIENTED MANAGEMENT CONSULTANTS

While few computer consultants are likely to attain the level of success of an Ed Yourdon, a small number of computer consultants do build up practices that center on solving management-level problems for their clients.

Typically these consultants fall into one of two groups: One is made up of long-term computer professionals who have put in many years in the trenches mastering a technological niche and leading challenging technical projects. The other is made up of people who discovered the power of software after having mastered some other discipline, for example, accounting or finance. This second group's greatest strength is their understanding of the needs of executives in their original profession. In both cases these people have strong networks of contacts with peers who have risen to positions of corporate leadership and are willing to pay for these consultants' high-level consulting skills.

Unless you are comfortable with the managers you want to advise, speak their language fluently, understand their perspectives, and respect their culture, you are not likely to break into this kind of consulting, no matter how strong your opinions might be on how technology should be managed.

Meet the Consultant: Computer-Oriented Management Consultant Sharon Marsh Roberts

Still in her early thirties, Sharon Marsh Roberts has made the moves needed to position herself as a successful computer-oriented management consultant. She began her business career by earning an M.B.A.

degree and becoming a CPA. After finishing school she hired into a Big Six firm where she worked as an auditor and was initiated into the world of corporate finance.

That experience, focusing as it did on external and internal financial reporting, led to her next position with a two hundred million dollar corporate start-up. Her role there was to help put new financial reporting systems into place. This project familiarized Roberts with a variety of financial software solutions of varying complexity including Lotus 1-2-3 spreadsheets, custom software accounting packages, and one of the two largest general ledger systems in the world—that of McCormack & Dodge.

Roberts says that implementing software for financial reporting turned out to be "a lot more fun" than the financial reporting itself had been. So when her work at the start-up was complete she parlayed her experience there into a job as an internal consultant employed by one of the larger financial service firms in New York City, implementing McCormack & Dodge software for another huge financial client.

Unlike many consultants, Roberts says, "I am not one of those people who always wanted to be an independent consultant or who really sought to be outside of the larger institutions." Roberts was comfortable in the financial services culture and highly successful there in an employee role.

However, as a salaried consultant working for the financial services firm she found that "my predilection for hot projects put me in unique and interesting situations" where she was called upon not only to manage the implementation of technology, but also to manage the tricky task of team building on which the projects' success rested. Eventually Roberts was pulled into independent consulting when a client wanted her to fill a role that the financial services firm was not willing to place her in. At that point Roberts asked to be released from her job at the financial services firm and a few days later began her work for her first independent client.

Since making the break Roberts has continued to consult for medium and large companies in the New York area. Some of her work involves auditing projects in progress. Other assignments involve managing the implementation of new technology.

For example, one of Roberts's recent projects was to provide a technology assessment for a small pharmaceutical advertising firm that was trying to improve communications and workflow management among staffers, a large number of whom were women working from home. Because the company did not have a good history of implementing sophisticated technological solutions, Roberts suggested they avoid trying to install a trendy but complex groupware or Internet-based strategy. Instead she suggested the company begin by installing a much simpler time reporting system. This approach would help them master the methodology involved in implementing more complex systems. As she explains, in making her recommendations "I considered their needs to be as related to team building and management training as technology."

Roberts finds the majority of her clients through networking and referrals, and after three years on her own she sometimes bills as many as 150 hours in a fifteen-day period. She does much of her networking through active participation in professional groups—a characteristic of most management-oriented consultants. In 1997, she became president of the ICCA. She explains that her professional activism puts her in contact with other more technologically-oriented consultants who are able to appreciate where her combination of strong management skills and technical savvy can help them accomplish their technological goals. As Roberts concludes, "It's important to work with people of high technical skills who already are working on better project management. These are the people whose projects will succeed and whom I can benefit."

CONSULTING FIRM EMPLOYEES

Before we leave our survey of the different kinds of computer consulting, we need to look at one last type of consultant, the one whose claim to being a true consultant is without question the weakest of any of the kinds of consultants we've discussed: the consulting firm employee.

Drawn to the computer services marketplace like sharks to fresh blood by reports of the vast amounts to be made selling computer services to corporate clients, the Big Six accounting firms and corporations like defense contractor GE have built up huge computer consulting subsidiaries. These companies use the access to high-level executives that their other businesses give them to bypass the project managers who usually buy computer services and sell their consulting services directly to the company's top executives. The work of these companies' consultants is usually billed to clients at rates ranging from $125 to $225 an hour.

These companies often hire business students direct from college degree programs and they advertise regularly in newspapers for computer professionals with two or more years of industry experience to join their practices. If you'd like to be a consultant but haven't yet got the experience and contacts it takes to become an expert consultant on your own, you may find it hard to resist the thought that hiring in as a consultant with one of these companies could be the big break you've been waiting for.

But it probably isn't.

The first thing you must realize is that these "consultants" are employees of the consulting companies. They are paid an annual salary, not an hourly rate. Furthermore, as an Andersen Consulting spokesperson revealed in a 1991 article in *Computerworld*, the average age of an Andersen Consulting consultant is twenty-five years old. A bit of quick calculation suggests that there are either an awful lot of sixteen-year-olds working for Andersen Consulting to balance out hordes of more experienced people in their thirties and forties, or else most of the clients who pay $125 per hour for Andersen consultants are paying for the services of folks a year or two out of college. Just how such people have become qualified to offer sage advice to executives twice their age I leave as an exercise for the reader.

Independent consultants and programmers who have encountered these consulting company consultants in the workplace report that it is usual for one of a consulting firm's small number of highly experienced partners to sell a project to corporate executives. Only after the paperwork is signed, do the inexperienced fresh-out-of-programming-school troops arrive. The work these young "consultants" do is usually a mix of contract programming—which client employees report they do at the level you'd expect of someone with only a year or two of experience—and implementation of custom and turnkey computer solutions developed by their parent company.

Most sobering is the information that although the services of those twenty-five-year-olds are indeed billed out at those mouth-watering rates, the money goes to the parent corporation whose name on the project is what the client is really paying for, not to the consultants themselves. These salaried consultants are paid salaries that are similar to salaries for other entry-level IS personnel—salaries in the low-thirties range.

If you do sign on to one of these companies fresh out of school, the chances are good that you will end up doing a lot of contract coding and will be expected to put in fierce amounts of overtime. The chances are also good that you, like most Big Six "consultants," will quit for a better job with better training within a year or two, which is the reason why these consulting companies are always advertising for new recruits.

Meet the Consultant: Consulting Company Employee A.J.

A consultant identifying himself only as A.J. showed up on CONSULT a few years ago and posted the following message during a discussion of salaried consulting. His account is typical of what other ex-consulting company employees report. A.J. wrote, "My company charges one hundred dollars an hour for my time, yet pays me only $24,900 a year. They keep saying that the economy is bad so I should be happy that I have a job at all. I just graduated from college in the computer engineering field. I know I'm young, but $24,900 a year for what I do during the day is not fair. No training is provided, yet, of all the clients I have, only one has complained of my inadequacies—the first week at work."

In another five or so years, A.J. may be ready to be a competent computer consultant, but like most people fresh out of school, he needs to put in some time learning the ropes, adding to his skills, learning the client's business and needs. It is a very rare individual who can leap into computer consulting without first absorbing a few years of experience in the field.

COMMON QUESTIONS ABOUT COMPUTER CONSULTING

We'll conclude this overview of computer consulting by reviewing the questions most frequently asked by new visitors to CONSULT and sharing with you the answers they receive.

Q: I'm about to start consulting. I plan to offer my services to home computer users and small business owners who haven't yet bought computers for their businesses. What's the best way to start out?

A: Home computers users can't and won't pay the rates consultants must charge to stay in business and cover their overhead. The best client for your services is one who already has a computer and is running a business large enough to justify spending money on more computer services. Very small businesses rarely fit this profile.

Q: I'm about to graduate college with a degree in computers. I want to start consulting. How do I begin?

A: Unless you've got several years of experience working in some industry behind you, it is usually a mistake to enter consulting straight out of school. It's usually best to spend some years working as an employee, gathering real-world experience, familiarizing yourself with the needs of your clients, and building the network of contacts you'll need to draw on to find your consulting clients.

Q: I plan to start my consulting career by offering backup services to clients. Has anyone been able to pull this off?

A: Although almost all clients need backup services, it is very hard to find companies who know they need such services and are willing to pay for them. Backup services are rarely listed among the services offered by successful consultants.

Q: I've got five years of experience working as a computer programmer but don't have a four-year college degree. Now I'd like to go back to school to help prepare myself to become a consultant. Would getting a computer science (CS) degree be the best way to do this?

A: If you already know how to program, a computer science degree is not likely to enhance your ability to consult. No degree can ensure success, but the programs most highly recommended by consultants are those that train you in running a business and in marketing, and those that sensitize you to issues in business management. A degree in management information science may be a better credential than a computer science degree, as may be a pure business degree.

Q: I am very good at word processing and am the best person in my office when it comes to dealing with computers. I don't know how to program but I'd love to quit my job and use my computer knowledge to support myself. How can I break into computer consulting?

A: It's great that you have aptitude in computer work, but to prepare yourself for consulting you'll need to broaden your knowledge of computer hardware and software beyond the one or two pieces of software you may now be familiar with. The wider your knowledge of solutions available in your niche, the more likely you will be to be able to help clients solve their problems effectively.

Q: I'd like to get some training to prepare myself for consulting. What consulting specialty is now most in demand?

A: It's likely that by the time you finish your training in any currently hot niche, that niche will no longer be anywhere near as much in demand as it is now because thousands of other people like yourself will have responded to its popularity by getting the same training you have gotten. For example, object-oriented programming was very hot in the early 1990s when few people knew how to do it. Now there's a surge of demand for people with experience developing for both corporate intranets and the Internet. However, although you don't hear as much about it, there is always a steady demand for people capable of developing complex business application software using the computer languages preferred by corporate clients, including C, C++, Clipper, Delphi, FoxPro, PowerBuilder, and Visual Basic.

2

ARE YOU READY TO START CONSULTING?

Perhaps the question most frequently asked by people who are thinking of beginning a computer consulting career is, How can I tell when I'm ready to begin? Would-be consultants wonder how much money they need to get started and what level of expertise they must have to succeed. Many wonder whether they should start consulting while still working at their old jobs or whether they must make a complete break.

Starting out right is crucial. A great number of those who begin consulting with the greatest of enthusiasm do not make it through their first year. The reason they fail is all too often that they start without adequate *preparation* and without understanding the *resources* they will need to persevere. Despite what you might hear on TV or read in inspirational business books, there is no magic and little luck involved in entrepreneurial success. You must understand what you are getting into and you must have the skills it takes to do the job.

Because you are considering computer consulting, the skills you will need are demanding ones. You must be able to think like both a *technician* and a *manager*, to function both as a *businessperson* concerned with the bottom line and as a *creative person* concerned with quality and innovation. To top it off you must also be a very good *salesperson*. This last point is crucial. All your other skills will be worthless if you don't have the ability to market them to people willing and able to pay for them.

In this chapter we'll be examining in detail the resources you'll need to back up a venture into consulting. We'll be looking both at *material requirements*, like equipment and money, and at *intangibles*, like personality traits and family support. We'll look at the questions you'll need to ask yourself to determine if you ready to begin consulting. There are several of them and they are all worth serious thought. But unless you can answer the first of these questions adequately, the answers to the rest won't mean a thing, because the first question is, "Where are you going to find your clients?"

WHERE ARE YOUR CLIENTS?

Week after week visitors to the Computer Consultant's Forum post messages containing almost the identical words: "I've decided to become a computer consultant. Now, how do I find my clients?"

Unfortunately, the short answer is, "If you don't already know where your clients are, you aren't ready to start consulting."

It's that simple. Untested hunches about potential client groups won't cut it. You may feel that there should be a huge market out there for your services among small business owners or corporate managers or any number of other vaguely defined groups. But before you count these people, or anyone else, as potential clients you must ask yourself this: Have any of them ever contacted you and offered to pay you to do the kind of work you plan to do as a consultant?

If the answer is no, then you don't yet know where your clients are.

You'll know you've located your potential clients when people are asking you to perform services for them and are offering to pay you for these services. If this isn't happening, then no matter how much you might think that some group of people ought to want your services, there is very little likelihood that they will, and you will have to treat any foray into consulting as a gamble rather than a step in a well-planned career.

If you are ready to begin consulting, your clients will already be coming to you. You may not think of them as clients yet, but they'll be there. Your client is the guy at the user group meeting who asks if you could come in after work some day and see if you can fix the problem with his database that's got him stumped. Your client is the former employer who calls and asks you what it would take to lure you back to work on his system that has never worked as well as it did when you were there. Your client is also lurking behind the contract consultant working on the corporate development project with you who compliments you on your expertise and offers to put a word in for you with the broker he works with if you ever feel like trying your wings.

If people are coming to you and asking for your help with their computer-related problems, you've begun to meet your new clients. *If they are willing to pay you* for your help, then you're getting the sign that you might be ready to begin consulting.

But there is a further consideration: Many beginning consultants find it easy to locate a first client, who gives them a significant amount of work, only to find themselves months or even years later unable to find their second client or a third. This first client syndrome is all too common. Most frequently that first—and last—client is a former employer who lures you back to work with the offer of a high hourly rate and the freedom to make your own hours.

Before you commit to consulting, you must ask yourself not only if you know where to find a first client, but if you can honestly say that you know where you would find *a second and third client*. Hoping these clients will show up is in the same category with hoping you'll win the state lottery. Unless you know where to find your follow-on clients and can begin marketing your services to them now while you are working for that first client, the chances are good you will not be able to sustain a successful consulting practice.

WHAT IF YOU AREN'T READY?

If the answer to the question, "Do you know where your clients are?" is no, then it is wise to accept that you are not ready to start consulting—for now. This doesn't mean that you will never be ready. It means only that you've got some work to do to prepare yourself so that you can eventually make the leap successfully. This book will give you a lot of information that can help you prepare for a future consulting career now. You'll learn how to *start building the network* you'll need and how to put yourself in situations where you'll meet potential clients. You'll get some hints as to *what kinds of skills* are the most useful to consultants, so that you can evaluate any salaried job you might consider taking in terms of whether it can improve those skills. And you'll get a feeling for the kinds of *additional training* that might help you maximize your chances of consulting success.

So there's no reason to jump the gun. Successful consulting careers tend to evolve. It is far better to be dragged into consulting because potential clients are making you "offers you can't refuse," than to rush into it as an escape from an unsatisfactory job situation. It is far better too, if you find yourself suddenly laid off, to put your energy into hunting up a new job rather than waste it in a frustrating and heartbreaking attempt to start a consulting practice that you haven't laid the groundwork for.

PART-TIME CONSULTING

But perhaps there is a way to eat your cake and have it too. If starting out is so difficult, why not moonlight as a consultant for a while without getting rid of your day job until you've built up enough momentum to break free?

This approach does work for some people. Sonny Tobias is one consultant who tried it and made it work. He explains, "What I did to relieve the pressure was to continue working full-time while aggressively networking. When my Rolodex was full of prospects—murky, but prospects nonetheless—I visited a few and offered my services part-time. For about six months, I was pretty busy on evenings, weekends, vacations, and days off, and concentrated on working on skills I wanted to work on. Anyways, I set up shop when I got that 'warm and fuzzy feeling.' "

The consultants most likely to succeed with this approach are those whose consulting is built around *contract programming*, a kind of work that can be done at home in your off hours. The reason that part-time consulting doesn't work for most other kinds of computer consultants is that most other consulting requires you to be on-site during working hours for at least a few hours a week. You need to meet with the client. You need to come in during work hours to do the analysis needed to solve the client's problems. And once you've done any significant amounts of work, you will probably need to be on-call during the day to resolve any problems that come up.

When his system crashes, a client is not going to want to wait until you get home to get the situation resolved. So unless your current boss is one of the few who doesn't mind you taking calls from clients during the hours she's paying for, part-time consulting can be a quick way of terminating your current employment.

Still, some consultants have found ingenious ways to deal with this problem. Part-time consultant Kurt Sussman says that he makes it very clear to his clients that he has a day job. He explains, "Most of the work I do is very involved (real-time lab automation). I let them know in advance that I have a day job and that they're welcome to call me there, but that on-site visits will have to be scheduled in advance. I haven't had to cut and run yet." Sussman charges clients an extra fee for giving out his day-job phone number. "If their problems are critical they'll pay," he says, but this eliminates the problem of his being pestered at work with routine calls.

Another solution successful moonlighters have found practical is to use an answering service who will answer client calls with the consultant's business name, screen the calls, and notify them at their day job when something critical comes up.

The biggest argument against this approach to consulting is that many clients report that they've found part-time consultants unreliable. If things heat up on the day job, such consultants may suddenly find that they don't have the time in the evenings they were counting on for finishing up that code they have to deliver. People underestimate their own need for time off. Very few of us can maintain the same level of productivity in every additional hour we add to our schedules. It may take twice as much work to get half as much done when that work takes place at 3:00 A.M. on a day that started at 6:30 A.M. and included a long commute.

A consultant's most valuable asset is his or her *reputation*. If you enter consulting part-time and get overwhelmed, you may earn a reputation for being unreliable, missing deadlines, or being unavailable when a crisis comes up. In the long run this will make it harder, not easier to build a full-time career in consulting.

HOW GOOD ARE YOUR SKILLS?

Knowing where your clients are is the first step to deciding whether you're ready to start consulting. Without clients you can't be a consultant. But even if you can easily locate clients eager to have you work for them, it is still not certain that you are ready to be a consultant. We'll look now at some additional questions you must answer before making your decision to start consulting. The first of these is: How good are the skills you intend to sell to clients?

The Need for Specialized Skills

Before you make your decision, you need to take a long, critical look at the skills you plan to sell. A successful consulting career can last anywhere from five to twenty years or more. To make it through that kind of period your skills need to be not only top notch, but of a kind that you will enjoy growing and expanding. As employees we are used to learning new things and expanding the scope of our work from year to year. But once you enter consulting you will find that, contrary to what you found as an employee, your scope of work tends to narrow, rather than broaden. In most cases you will be hired to do what you have already done well and you will be pigeonholed by clients as one very specific kind of consultant.

This specialization goes along with being an expert and there is little you can do to buck the trend. Most people who succeed as computer consultants do so by *identifying some expert niche* and filling it competently. They may become database programming experts, or network design experts, or law office automation experts, but to get control of the marketing strategies that are key to surviving in their field most consultants are forced to specialize.

Faced with this strong pressure toward specialization you have to ask yourself this question: How happy will you be doing what your current skills enable you to do for years to come? One big reason for burnout is that many consultants don't give this question enough thought and find that they get sick of doing the same kind of work over and over again. After your initial excitement at doing your own thing wanes, you are still going to have to do it—lots of it. So for you to succeed as a consultant your specialty better be something that you love doing and that you have a pretty good chance of loving ten years down the line.

How Competent Are You?

When examining your skills, you have to be brutally honest about your level of competence. Just being good won't cut it. Ninety percent of all work you are likely to get as a consultant is going to come from word-of-mouth referrals. If your work is just okay, you won't get those referrals. No one is going to say, "You ought to give Joe Schmoe a call. He's a bit of a dim bulb but he gets the work done—eventually."

If the people you currently work with don't consider you a wiz and if you haven't been able to earn the respect and admiration of your peers for the work you do, there is very little chance that you will succeed as a consultant—unless your sole skill is marketing and you intend to join the legion of "consultants from hell," whose superb marketing skills keep them afloat even as they leave a trail of business disasters behind them.

How Experienced Are You?

Even being competent isn't enough. Besides topnotch skills you need experience. If you plan to automate doctors' offices, you should have had experience working with not one or two offices but with at least five. You should know in depth not one but several different approaches to automating such offices, and know, too, why you might choose one solution for one office and another for a different one.

Before you begin consulting you should have already been keeping up with the specialty trade press in this niche for a year or two. You should have a good idea of what the big showstoppers are likely to be in implementing any such system. You should have experience in working with the kinds of people who will use your systems and be comfortable with fielding panicky phone calls from the bluest of blue-haired old ladies.

Likewise, if you are a programmer, it's a good idea to have gone through the whole systems development cycle a few times as a salaried programmer before you begin doing it on your own. Ideally you should have worked on a few projects that succeeded and on a few that crashed and burned, so that you've learned to recognize the early warning signs of project disaster. It would be a good idea, too, to have worked on a variety of platforms and to have reached professional levels of competence in several of the computer languages commonly used in the business environment—not just the LISP or BASIC you learned in college courses.

As a consultant you will indeed be a specialist, but a true specialist is someone who has chosen a few skills to concentrate on out of a much broader collection. Unless you have more than a nodding acquaintance with issues of project management, systems analysis, company politics, and how people function in the workplace under stress, you are not likoly to last long no matter how good the routines that you code or your grasp of how to wire up a network.

If you don't have this kind of experience yet, respect yourself enough to get the training that you need. Spend some time identifying the kind of consulting that you feel you'd be happiest doing. Talk to people who do that kind of work and ask them what they think you should do to strengthen your own skills to prepare for it. Broaden your skills if they are too narrow. Concentrate more on developing a narrower area of expertise if there is nothing you currently excel at. The number of consultants on the market practicing with inadequate skills is the single biggest reason for the public's ambivalence about computer consultants. So to succeed it is vital to ensure that you really are ready to do the job you promise your clients.

How Willing Are You to Learn New Skills?

Finally, when evaluating your skills you must keep in mind that you're working in a field where the technology turns over every five years, so that no matter what it is you've mastered, it's a good bet that in five years it will be obsolete. This means that as a consultant you'll have the additional responsibility of constantly having to upgrade your skills and keep them current.

You will have to evaluate your skills objectively not only when you begin consulting but throughout your consulting career if you are to be able to keep having that career. As an employee the chances are good that your employer has taken the responsibility of helping you grow your skills. But once you become a consultant, if anything, clients will make it harder for you to add to your skills because they will tend to want you to do for them the things you've already done successfully for other clients and will be nervous about having you try something new.

No matter how busy you might be when starting out, it's guaranteed that if you don't *continuously upgrade your skills* you will find yourself in trouble when technology advances beyond what you have mastered. So as part of your final evaluation of your skills you must ask yourself one last question: How good are you at making yourself learn new things and avoiding complacency? If you trust that you can keep up this momentum, then, and only then, you are ready to begin consulting.

THE CONSULTING PERSONALITY

But even the best skills in the world aren't enough to ensure that you can make a go of consulting. You will also have to have a personality well suited to the consulting way of life.

The successful consultant is a person who is *able to handle insecurity and conflict*, the sort of person who thrives on dealing with the unexpected. One way to determine whether you fit that profile is this: Ask yourself how you usually feel during the first two weeks of a new job. Are they your favorite time? Do you love the excitement of coming into a completely new environment, sorting out the people, figuring out what's going on, and building up your own reputation from scratch? If the answer is "Yes," you've got a consultant's personality. If, in contrast, you only start to enjoy a job after you've been there for a while and gotten accustomed to the routine, you may find consulting hellish work no matter how well other people evaluate your performance.

A similar and related test is this: How do you feel about job interviews? If you enjoy the opportunity to match wits with the interviewer and take pleasure in getting across what you have to contribute to a new employer, you'll enjoy consulting. If, on the contrary, you've been known to stay in a job you hated for a year after anyone sane would have left because of how sick you felt when you thought of having to put on that fancy suit and go through the torture of interviewing, you are not likely to succeed in consulting no matter how much you might long for independence.

Consultant Payson Hall suggests another question would-be consultants can ask themselves. "Do you enjoy making systems (human or computer) work, without caring whether or not you get the credit?" Hall points out that the people he's seen who are most successful at consulting are those who would reply with a very strong "yes." He explains that these are people who get their high from *solving a problem* rather than from the *credit* that their solving it earned them. But paradoxically, Hall adds that the person at the other extreme, the one who cares intensely about getting the credit may succeed too, because they are the ones who will go that extra mile to do a job that can earn them that credit. The people who are not likely to succeed, he says, are those who don't really care one way or the other.

Consultant David Olson points out another important personality trait that consultants need, explaining, "I happen to believe that the skill set needed to successfully install a complex system is far more than technical or training skills. Not the least important is an ability to appear—I didn't say *be*—calm when everything looks like it's going down the tubes."

Another important personality trait for consultants is a *strong desire to be in control* of their own career. But people are often quite poor at judging whether they display this trait. Many people think they want to be their own boss when in fact what they really want is to get away from their current boss and find someone they like better to tell them what to do. The truth is that being your own boss is a lot of work.

"Don't jump into the consulting business unless you really want to have your own business," suggests consultant Neal Wurtzman. "Now that sounds all wonderful and everything, and I wouldn't have it any other way—most of the time. But it means being a businessperson first and foremost over being a techie/trainer/whatever. It means dealing with federal/state/local government, getting business, dealing with irate clients, buying your own health/disability insurance, etc . . . etc. . . . etc."

Truer words were never spoken. If you hate dealing with administrivia, you are going to be a nervous wreck running your own consulting business. As a consultant you will be a small business owner and that means you will have to deal with everything from getting appropriate licenses to filing quarterly tax returns on your own, and if you screw up you will find yourself in worse trouble than any employee could ever dream of.

But conversely, if you are indeed strongly driven by the desire to be independent and have more control over your own career, consulting will offer you great rewards, even if to the eye of the outside observer there might be little to be excited about.

Commenting on his sideline consulting business Sigmund Van-Damme notes, "For the past two and a half years I have been doing the exact type of work (Clipper development) on the side as I do at my job. I cannot put my finger on an exact reason why, but the work on the side is exponentially more satisfying." Another consultant explains, "I am currently making a lot less money but having a lot more fun and enjoying myself a lot more." Sentiments similar to these are expressed by almost every successful consultant. The pleasure of knowing that you control your own destiny is without question the single most important payoff for most successful computer consultants.

There is, however, one personality trait that while it may be a real asset to a consultant is also a warning flag for starting a consulting practice, and that is *workaholism*. As a consultant you will find it easy to work sixteen-hour days, every day, and to include midnights, weekends, and holidays in your standard work schedule. No one will tell you to go home, and it is easy to convince yourself that your business will founder if you don't work these kinds of hours. But there is also the potential of failing because of burnout induced by taking on too much work and overwhelming yourself.

Consulting's potential to eat up your time can introduce stresses into your personal life, too. If your tendency is to escape from personal problems into work, you will have to establish some kinds of controls on yourself when you get active in consulting, or you may end up with money in the bank but a personal life that is a disaster.

THE BUSINESS SKILLS YOU'LL NEED

Now let's look at some business skills you'll need to succeed at consulting.

Marketing and Communications Skills

As we've already mentioned, the most important business skills all consultants need to survive are marketing skills. You have to be able to find clients and convince them that you and not someone else can solve their problems. But marketing skill rarely comes naturally to the kinds of people who are drawn to working with technology and to doing the kinds of creative, problem-solving work that most computer consultants enjoy most.

Marketing skills are really a subset of what are generally called communication skills. Successful marketing is very much a result of effective communication. You need to be able to think and speak on your feet in stressful situations. You must be able to produce business letters, reports, and promotional materials that put across a professional image and at the same time get across clear and understandable messages.

Fortunately, unlike personality traits, which can be very difficult to acquire, communications skills can be learned, and indeed, will improve in direct proportion to how much use you make of them. Many consultants attribute their success to membership in organizations like Toastmasters, which force them to practice public speaking, while others swear by seminars like the Dale Carnegie course, claiming they revolutionized the way that they now interact with people in business situations.

Developing your communications skills is very much like developing a set of muscles. If you are serious about consulting, you'd do well to get professional help in developing the finest set of such "muscles" you can.

The Ability to Delegate

Another important business skill is knowing your own limits and knowing when it is appropriate to bring in other professionals to help. Successful consultants recognize that they don't know as much about accounting as a CPA and that it makes sense to draw on the CPA's expertise when it's time to deal with taxes or set up a corporation. Successful consultants know too that it is worth bringing in an expert when crafting agreements involving many thousands of dollars' worth of hardware, software, and services. Yes, lawyers cost money, but the mistakes you are likely to make while attempting to teach yourself intellectual property law on the fly will cost you far more money. Drawing on other people's expertise where appropriate is another form of delegating—a management skill. As a consultant you are a manager—managing yourself. Unless you recognize the need to delegate tasks appropriately you are likely to get snowed under.

On the subject of using professional help, consultant Frank Cook comments, "I don't understand why so many computer consultants are reluctant to seek professional advice from lawyers and accountants. You guys are professionals selling your time. Don't people question paying you to program something that they could do in dBase? Don't you have a set speech explaining how you can do it better and that it'll be cheaper in the long run to use a professional programmer? Well, it's cheaper in the long run to use a professional tax advisor too!"

Computer consultants also need to be able to *recognize the limits of their own specialized computer skills*. They need to know when to call on other people in their field who may have skill sets complementary to their own. Successful consultants network extensively with other consultants, not just to pick up leads to new clients, but because in today's technical climate no one person can master more than a small subset of the overall technology and many projects extend into areas where even the most competent computer professionals will hit their limits. The hallmark of truly competent computer professionals isn't that they know everything, but that they know who to ask when they get outside their own area of expertise.

HOW MUCH MONEY DO YOU NEED TO BEGIN?

Up until now we've been discussing the skills and other intangibles you'll need to succeed at consulting. But what about the tangibles? How much of an investment is needed to succeed at computer consulting? How much of a financial risk do you have to take on to find out if you are cut out for this kind of career?

The good news is that the cash investment needed to get started in computer consulting is minimal. You do not need to find an investor to back you or to hook up with a rich partner. Assuming that you have adequate skills and know where to find your first two or three clients, all that you will probably need to get started is a car, some business clothing, and a phone. Paul Graf reports that he and his wife started their own consulting firm in 1985 with an out-of-pocket investment of $800. By 1990 the firm had offices in three cities and was grossing $800,000. This growth was financed almost entirely out of revenues.

"But what about computer equipment?" you may ask. "Don't I have to go out and spend a few thousand dollars to buy a brand new, state-of-the-art system?"

I hope you really didn't ask this question. If you are really ready to begin doing the kind of consulting that requires a high-powered computer system, I'd expect you to already own one and to have been beating it black and blue in your spare time exercising every piece of software and hardware you could get your hands on long before you thought of taking on paying clients.

You may want to buy a few new toys once you get some revenue coming in, and you may need to buy some special software to allow you to diagnose problems on clients' systems or to let you work on those systems from your home office, but taking the step into consulting should not require a significant investment in new hardware and software. If it does, then you've probably got a lot more training to complete before you're ready to offer your computer skills to clients.

You Can't Buy a Consulting Practice

Alas, there are plenty of sharks out there who make their own livings by convincing desperate people with poor skills that they can buy economic security by becoming a consultant through purchasing the scamster's systems, software, and packaged consultant training programs. But there is no equipment, software, or franchise currently on the market that will let you leapfrog the work it takes to establish yourself as a consultant. I have yet to meet a successful computer consultant who got his start by buying a franchise, paying for a guaranteed client list, or completing a mail-order course. If you find yourself swayed by the pitch of a salesperson selling this kind of program, ask if you can contact a happy purchaser of the program and then ask that person if he'd be willing to show you a client list and let you call and speak with a few of his satisfied clients. The answer you get to these requests should prove illuminating.

Money Management Is Key

The real cash "investment" that you need to start consulting is enough money to get you through the inevitable slow periods you will face in your first few years. Consulting work generally flows in a "feast or famine" pattern. Sometimes you'll have more clients calling than you can possibly fit in, while at others you'll sit idle.

It helps greatly to have enough money in the bank before you begin to keep you from panicking during the inevitable slow periods. It also helps if you are good at *budgeting* the money you have and controlling the impulse to spend it so that you can get the most out of the money you already have. If you are already living life charged up to the limit on a fistful of credit cards, consulting is probably not going to work out for you.

It often takes a few years to establish a consulting practice to the point where you can predict your income with any level of accuracy. Many consultants report that they just squeaked by their first year. Consultant Mark Bayern reports that it took him a good four years until his consulting practice earned him as much as the salary he had previously earned as an employee, though he adds characteristically that "it is much more fun and fulfilling this way."

What can make it particularly hard to manage the money you earn as a consultant is that the amounts clients pay you may seem so temptingly huge. When a client gives you a $10,000 check for a few weeks of work it is easy to get excited and forget you will have to pay at least a third of it to federal and state tax authorities, and that what is left must also cover your health insurance payments and all the other expenses you racked up in the three weeks of unpaid time it took you to land the job in the first place. When you've factored in taxes and overhead, you may well find out that on an hourly basis that check is much smaller than the more modest paychecks you are used to receiving. So you must remind yourself that you won't know whether you are rich or not until you've been in business for a year or two and resist the temptation to spend the money that does come in celebrating your newfound success.

Consulting Can Cause Credit Problems

There is one further painful financial "gotcha" that anyone considering a consulting career needs to be aware of. Once you quit your salaried job and enter consulting, no matter how much money you earn you will find it much more difficult, if not impossible, to take out a mortgage or get other personal loans from your local bank. The guidelines that most lenders use when approving mortgage applicants exclude self-employment income unless the applicant can show tax returns demonstrating that they've been in business for three years or more.

This is true even during boom times, but during credit crunches self-employed people may find it impossible to borrow money even when they have tax returns showing several years of business profitability.

So if you have been planning on buying or refinancing a house, or if you have been putting off buying that new car, and if you will not be able to get the credit you need based on your spouse's income alone, it makes a lot of sense to postpone the decision to move to full-time consulting until after you've gotten the loan.

IS YOUR FAMILY READY FOR CONSULTING?

We've looked now at many of the questions you'll have to answer to decide whether you are ready to get started in consulting. If you are single and live alone, you can skip ahead now to the next chapter. But if you have a family, you're not done yet, because no matter how ready you are to make the change personally, becoming a consultant will have an impact on not just yourself but on your spouse and your children, too. Unless you are willing to let them have some input into the decision-making process, you may find that it is impossible to sustain a consulting career even though you meet all the other criteria we have discussed.

Consulting is more risky than salaried work. No matter how many clients you may have, there's never any assurance that you'll have more when your current projects are complete. You may have no trouble dealing with this, but what about your spouse?

I've seen this situation from both sides, myself. I've made the decision to give up a secure job and become a consultant and I've also experienced having my husband decide to quit a well-paid, secure job with its perks and company-paid benefits to strike out on his own. Believe me, it's much more stressful to be the spouse in this situation than to be the consultant.

As the consultant, you know what is really going on, how likely it is that you'll find more work, and how well you're doing on any current contract. But the consultant's spouse gets what little information he or she has second hand. Your spouse will know you've lost your company-paid health insurance and regular paychecks, but won't know until you bring home a check whether the consulting is really going as well as you say it is.

Consulting may also demand far more hours than a salaried job does. Consultants routinely report working twelve-hour days, and putting in work on weekends and holidays. They may also have clients calling them in the middle of the night with serious problems. If the spouse cannot handle this kind of schedule or finds the insecurity of a consulting income too frightening to live with, the stress can cause serious damage to the relationship.

More than one successful consultant reports that they began consulting only after a divorce freed them from the responsibility of supporting another individual, paying a big mortgage, being tied to living in one part of the country, and having to devote significant hours to maintaining a personal relationship.

But the picture does not necessarily have to be that negative. A consultant who has a supportive spouse may have some significant advantages when it's time to launch a consulting career. Consultant Rudyard Merriam has found this to be true. He explains, "I don't think I would be consulting now if it weren't for my wife. I can consult partially because she has a well-paying job with big company fringe benefits including medical to cover the kids." Other consultants report that their spouses provide encouragement and unpaid office help, and frequently are able to contribute better-developed marketing skills to the business than those possessed by the more technically oriented consultant.

The Consulting Mother

If you are a working mother, you may wonder whether consulting would be a way of making your life more manageable. It may be, but only—as is true with all consulting—if you've taken the time to lay the groundwork for it. And contrary to what some working mothers hope, becoming a consultant will not free you from the need to find adequate day care. Few if any mothers of young children are able to make their living coding serenely while their children frolic at their feet. But if you can find day care that is flexible enough to allow you to work an unorthodox schedule, you may be able to cut down the hours you have to spend away from your children without cutting down your income or ending your professional career.

If you can find reliable day care that allows you to get to client sites during work hours and do your marketing, significant amounts of work can be done out of a home office during the day or in the evenings when expensive day care is not required. The mother who consults will also find that when her children are school-aged, she is more likely than most employees to be able to schedule her work around children's illnesses, capricious school calendars, and irrationally selected school holidays.

But like all working women the female consultant must still put in the extra effort needed to convince the client of her reliability. There are many times when an employee might be able to call in sick where a consultant must show up or face losing the client.

If you would like to start consulting after you start a family, it is essential to lay the groundwork before you go on maternity leave. When you are spending your nights nursing a colicky baby, you are not likely to find the energy needed to market yourself to clients. Ideally, you should try to choose your employers early in your career with an eye to converting them to future consulting clients. A great number of consultants make their start in consulting by doing jobs for previous employers. Working for people who already trust you and have a good idea of your capabilities is a lot easier than selling yourself to strangers, particularly when you have to deal with the additional burdens being responsible for young children imposes.

Many companies have hard-and-fast personnel rules that make it impossible for managers to bring in part-time home-based consultants no matter how good their skills, while others have had excellent experiences with mothers-turned-consultants and will go the extra mile with you to make it work. So if possible, don't waste your time building up a reputation in a company that won't later allow you to work for them as a consultant. Cultivate a network of potential "mother friendly" clients before you need them, and do your best to steer yourself into kinds of computer work that can be done at home. If you can pull it off, you can end up earning far more money for far fewer hours than you would pursuing the alternative course of part-time employment, and you will be able to give your children the attention they need without sacrificing the technical skills that you've worked so hard to attain.

3

SETTING UP YOUR PRACTICE—TAXES, ACCOUNTING, AND LICENSING ISSUES

Once they decide to begin consulting most people wonder what legal requirements they must fulfill before they can begin. They wonder, too, what meeting these requirements will cost them and how complex it will be. Fortunately, there are few formal procedures that beginning consultants must worry about, and even fewer that cost money. But there are some, and we look into them in this chapter, so that you can start off your new consulting practice on the right foot.

WHAT YOU MUST KNOW ABOUT TAXES

Income Tax Withholding

The most important administrative requirement that you must worry about as a new consultant is keeping up with taxes. When you worked as an employee your taxes were withheld by your employer, so that when you received a paycheck it was yours to do with as you pleased. But this will not be the case with money you earn from consulting. Clients will write you checks for the full value of your services and it will be up to you to ensure that you pay the taxes due on that money in a timely manner.

In the United States, the IRS mandates that all self-employed people mail them *quarterly withholding payments* that are based on the amount of income they expect to earn over the course of the year. These payments are due on April 15, June 15, September 15, and January 15. The amount you withhold over the course of the year must be either

(1) an amount equal to what you owed in taxes the previous year or (2) 90 percent of your tax liability for the current year as shown on the 1040 form you eventually file. If you fail to withhold enough to meet one of these two requirements you will be charged significant penalties and interest. This means that it is very important that you begin withholding correctly from the moment that you receive your very first check.

To do this you must be able to estimate your taxes correctly. You can get the federal form needed for filing this quarterly withholding payment, Form 1040-ES, at your post office or the public library, or by calling the IRS's forms line, 800-829-3676. The form includes a worksheet that can help you calculate how much to pay. However, as a consultant you always face the problem that you can't possibly know how much you will be earning over the course of the year. As a result it is safest to assume the largest possible income and calculate the taxes due on what you've already earned based on that figure. If you are wrong you'll get the withheld money back as a refund. If you are right you won't have to take out a loan to pay five or six thousand dollars' worth of taxes on money you've already spent.

Requirements for withholding income tax outside of the United States vary. In the United Kingdom and other European Economic Community (EEC) countries, when you decide to go out on your own you must register as a self-employed person both with the local tax authorities and with the Department of Social Security. You will have to fill in separate forms for each. Your local tax authority can tell you the exact requirements for your country.

Once you are registered, you must periodically send in payments to cover the taxes you estimate you will owe at the end of the year. In the United Kingdom payments are due in January and July, although you do not have to pay these withholding payments the first year that you are in business. In Belgium you pay estimated taxes quarterly. Again, you should contact your own local tax authority to determine your exact tax requirements.

State Income Tax Withholding

If you work in the United States, unless you live in one of the few states that do not levy a state income tax, you will also have to start withholding for state taxes. To determine the particular requirements for withholding in your state, you'll have to call the state department of revenue services or whatever other organization your state maintains to perform this function. Withholding regulations differ in each state, but what they all have in common is that if you don't withhold your taxes correctly you will have to pay a stiff fine.

State Sales Tax and Reseller's Certificates

If you plan to sell hardware and off-the-shelf software to your clients in the United States, you have an additional tax hurdle to negotiate. You will need a *tax identification number* that defines you as a reseller for the purposes of collecting state sales tax. As a reseller, you are exempt from paying sales tax on the hardware and software you purchase for re-sale to your clients. But you must collect state sales taxes when you sell these items to your clients and you must forward the taxes you collect to the state taxation authority at the appropriate time.

The particulars of how this is handled differ from state to state. In California, you get the appropriate forms from the State Board of Equal-ization. Consultant Glenn Casteran reports that he merely had to de-scribe the work he did to a state employee who then filled in the required forms for him. Now he files a quarterly form listing how much he has sold in each state district along with a check for the taxes. The hardest part, he reminds fellow consultants, is to "make sure you don't spend it before the forms get sent in!"

In Illinois you must apply for a Retailer's Occupational Tax License and file reports on an annual, quarterly, or monthly basis depending on the volume of sales you do. A typical computer consultant will proba-bly have to file these reports only once a year.

Some states, among them Connecticut, levy sales taxes not only on the goods you sell clients, but on pure consulting services. Connecticut consultants must get a *sales tax number* and charge clients the state's 6 percent sales tax on the amounts they bill them for programming and consulting services. Failure to do so can invoke stiff penalties. Other states are considering adopting similar policies in their never-ending quest for more revenue, so don't assume that because you aren't selling hardware you won't need to worry about state sales tax.

In Canada, cities and towns may not collect sales taxes, however, de-pending on where you live, you may have to collect a provincial sales tax on the sales of hardgoods or off-the-shelf software. Check with your provincial ministry of revenue for the laws that apply in your province. Some provinces, including Ontario, do not require you to collect sales tax on pure consulting services, others may.

Because regulations governing sales taxes vary from state to state and may even vary from municipality to municipality, it is vital that you *contact your state and city taxation agency to determine the appropri-ate method of proceeding.*

The biggest caveat here is that you must not let yourself be tempted to avoid paying sales tax on purchases you make for yourself and do not intend to resell. States routinely run audits on resellers and on their clients. As one consultant relates, "A couple of my clients were audited for sales tax. If you can't prove where you got your computer and show a receipt for it with the sales tax (or a statement showing you paid a use tax if you got it mail order), you can be in for a large surprise."

Value-Added Taxes

Consultants working in EEC countries are required to collect value-added tax (VAT) on the sales of equipment, software, and services they make to clients if they do more than a certain volume of business annually. For example, in the United Kingdom you must register if you earn more than $40,000 a year. If you do not earn this much you are not required to collect VAT from your clients. However you may still choose to register for VAT even if you do not earn the threshold amount. Doing this may be advantageous to you because registering for VAT allows you to recover the VAT you pay on your own purchases from suppliers. The U.K. VAT is 17.5 percent of the purchase price and applies to all software, both commercial and bespoke (custom). You must pay VAT payments quarterly, with the amount due being the amount of VAT you have collected from clients less the VAT you have paid out on your own business purchases.

In other EEC countries the regulations differ. For example, in Belgium, VAT payments must be made monthly. Again, you will have to contact your local tax authority to learn the exact regulations that apply to you.

The Canadian version of VAT is the 7 percent federal goods and services tax (GST). This tax applies to consulting services you sell if you do more than $30,000 worth of business a year. Because this is a "value-added tax," you can deduct the amount of GST you've paid out while doing your consulting work from what you remit to the government. You can register for a GST license by phoning the Department of National Revenue, GST tax branch. How frequently you must remit the GST you collect depends on how much business you do. For most consultants you'll probably only have to pay it annually.

Although you may be relieved to discover that your consulting business is not big enough that you have to register to pay a value-added tax, you might want to give the matter some further thought. As Canadian consultant Lawrence Fox points out, many consultants who don't qualify register anyway as a marketing move. "They don't want their clients to know that their gross billings are less than $30K, so they'll collect GST anyway."

The Benefit of Being a Reseller

Although the additional paperwork is a pain, getting a reseller's certificate or registering for VAT brings one significant benefit with it. Once you have the paperwork done, you will be able to buy computer equipment and software from large wholesalers such as Merisel and Ingram

Micro who do not sell to retail customers. Although wholesale prices for computer-related products may not be all that much lower than what the retail buyer can get from mail-order houses, many consultants still prefer to buy from wholesalers. Consultant John Brobston is one of these. He says, "Prices are similar to mail order but service is *much* better—typically overnight delivery at no extra charge. There's never a hassle about returns. In general it's a pleasure to do business with them and once they know you, most will give you net 30 as well." (The phrase *net 30* refers to payment terms that allow you to pay within thirty days rather than right away.)

If you live in a state that doesn't levy a sales tax and thus doesn't issue reseller numbers, you must use a different method of certifying yourself as a reseller to wholesalers. In Oregon, for instance, consultants who are resellers must obtain a federal tax ID number and use it when dealing with wholesalers. This is a tax identification number issued by the IRS that is used to identify a business the way a social security number is used to identify an individual. To apply for a federal tax ID number you fill in an SS-4 form, available by calling the IRS at 800-829-1040, and submit it to the IRS.

ACCOUNTING BASICS FOR CONSULTANTS

Now that you're running a business you will need to keep much more detailed records of income and expenses than you have probably been used to keeping. These records are necessary if you are to pay your taxes accurately—and if you are to avoid paying more taxes than are necessary. Accounting for earnings from a business is far more complex than accounting for salary income. Your business income is likely to arrive in dribs and drabs and unless you have good accounting procedures in place it is all too easy to forget that you collected a check until you—and the tax authorities—receive a tax reporting form from your client at year end.

As a business owner, you are allowed to significantly diminish your tax liability on the income you earn by deducting for legitimate business expenses. While it is not necessary to rush out immediately and pay an accountant to handle this aspect of your business—at least, not until you've generated a significant amount of income—you should try to get into the habit of logging in every single check when you receive it. Just as important, you should get used to noting down every possible business-related expense you incur, when you incur it, against the day when you will be looking frantically for ways to reduce your business income on your tax return.

Many consultants use software packages to track income and expenses. Simple packages like Quicken, Intuit, and Managing Your

Money are all suitable for the simple accounting you need to do now. Another easy way to keep your business records is to get a copy of the IRS Schedule C—the form used to reporting self-employed income and expenses for tax purposes—and to use the line items you find on it to set up your own accounting spreadsheet.

The following lists some of the expense items you should keep track of:

- Any purchases you make for business items such as office supplies, diskettes, hardware, software. Be careful to save the receipts.
- Computer books you buy and the computer-related magazines you subscribe to.
- Your on-line connect charges. Save the credit card bills that document these.
- Expenses for every letter or package you send out.
- Your phone bills, with notations that indicate which long-distance phone calls were made for business purposes.
- Your mileage for trips related to business, including trips to the library to research prospects and trips to the Post Office or UPS vendor to mail packages.

Many of these items seem small, but over the course of the year the cost of items as seemingly trivial as postage stamps can mount up to several hundred dollars of expense that you can write off against your profits. Getting into the habit of tracking expenses in a detailed and orderly way when you start your business will pay off greatly later on.

As soon as possible you should open a separate checking and savings account for your business, and avoid mixing personal expenses with business expenses. This is not a legal requirement, but it is recommended by nearly all accountants and lawyers. The maintenance of separate business accounts will be of inestimable value should the IRS or other tax authority choose to audit your business and question your deductions.

Accounting for Software Purchases

If you are a PC programmer in the United States, one of your bigger expenses will be the cost of purchasing software. Although common sense might suggest that you could treat the money spent on software as just another expense to be deducted against income at the end of the year, you'd be wrong. Accountant and computer consultant Irvin Feldman explains that the tax laws governing how software is treated were written back in the days when the only software on the market was packages for mainframes costing many thousands of dollars apiece. As a result, instead of being treated as an expense, *software must be capitalized and then amortized* over a period of five years. Amortization is the term accountants use for the tax treatment of significant intangible assets and is not to be confused with depreciation, which applies only to tangible ones. In practical terms what this means to computer consultants is that if you have significant software expenses, you cannot write them off as expenses nor can you take a Section 179 onetime depreciation writeoff for them as you can for hardware purchases less than the Section 179 limit.

There are exceptions to this rule:

- You can expense the costs of shareware, as what you are paying for, technically, when registering it is a copying fee.
- You can also expense the cost of software that you buy for evaluation purposes rather than for ongoing use.
- You may treat as an expense the cost of software that has a one-year time-limited use, such as income tax software.
- In practice, most consultants also expense the cost of inexpensive software that represents no more than one or two percent of their annual gross income. But if you are buying many thousands of dollars' worth of software for your own ongoing use, though you may spend the money now you will have to write it off over a five-year period.

The Home Office Deduction

If you conduct your consulting practice out of your home in the United States, you may be able to deduct a great number of expenses related to your home office. This is by far the juiciest tax deduction open to many of the self-employed as it allows you to deduct as legitimate business expenses the proportion of your mortgage, home maintenance, and utility bills that correspond to the portion of your home that you have set aside for business use. For example, if you live in a five-room condo and use one bedroom as an office, you can deduct from your taxable income fully one-fifth of all your mortgage and utilities expenses this way. You may even deduct the same proportion of the money you spend on maid service, interior painting, and pest control services for your entire home.

However, because this is a juicy deduction for the average taxpayer, and one that has always been subject to abuse by people whose only reason for having a home office is to claim a tax deduction, the IRS is very strict about whom it allows to take this deduction. To qualify for the home office deduction, your home office must be *a dedicated area that is not used for any other purpose*. A desk in your bedroom that your spouse also uses when paying family bills doesn't count. It is also important that you earn more money from the business that you conduct out of your home office than you deduct for home office expenses. Should you incur home office expenses greater than your home business income in any given year, you can carry these home office expenses over into a future year and deduct them when you have more income, but home business expenses may not be used to claim a business loss.

Finally, remember that your home office must be used for income-generating work. It helps if you can document that you do significant work in your office or that you are visited by clients there. This is particularly important if your consulting is a part-time gig that supplements a day job. The IRS takes a dim view of employees who attempt to use the home office deduction for offices where they do work for an employer or who use it to indulge in a hobby. A home office may also be disallowed if the IRS can show that you also have an office elsewhere. If you intend to take this deduction be sure to keep impeccable records to document that the work you did in the office was essential to the earning of your self-employment income. Also be aware that claiming a home office deduction when filing your taxes makes it more likely that you will be audited.

If you own a home and plan to sell it soon, there is a further consideration to be aware of. By taking the home office deduction you are, in effect, converting the portion of your home used for business away from residential use. That means that when you sell your home, the profit you make on the portion of the home your home office constitutes cannot be rolled over, untaxed, into a new home as can the rest of it. You must pay capital gains taxes on the profit made on the sale of the business portion. You may also be liable for recapture of depreciation you have claimed on previous tax returns. It is possible to get around this problem by converting your home office back to residential use before you sell, but before you claim the home office deduction you should consult with an accountant familiar with the tax laws in your state, particularly if you have built up significant equity in your home and if there is any chance that you may be selling it in the near future.

THE LICENSES YOU'LL NEED

For many consultants setting up an accounting system and keeping track of taxes may be the only official requirement they must attend to when starting their new consulting business. But others may also have to apply for appropriate licenses before they can begin.

Business Licenses and DBAs

In the United States, many states require that the consultant obtain a business license. However, this is by no means true in all states as consultant Esther Schindler discovered when she tried to get one in Maine. As she recounts, "There's no 'business license' here. On the advice of other consultants, when we first incorporated I went to the town office and explained that I wanted to get a license. The only one they could find was a dog license. They asked, did I want that one?" If a business license is required, you usually get it by applying to the state's taxation authority.

Requirements for business licenses vary widely outside of the United States. Contact your local chamber of commerce or similar organization for information about local regulations.

As you prepare to register your new business, keep in mind that in some regions you may qualify for grants made to start-ups. For example, Belgian consultant Jean-Pierre Elsener found that in Belgium businesses that notify the Regional Business Promotion Office before setting up shop can get cash grants that are not available to companies already doing business.

In addition, if you give your consulting business a name other than your given name, you may have to register a DBA with your town or county clerk. DBA stands for "doing business as" and it links your business name with your personal name. For example, if you named your practice CompuFriend, you would have to file a DBA that identified you as "Ellen Smith Doing Business as CompuFriend." The DBA's legal purpose is to make sure that it is possible for someone who wants to sue your company to find out who is behind the company name.

The costs to register a DBA vary although they are generally low. In New York the cost of registering a DBA is only $35, but in Pennsylvania the costs are much higher. Although the actual cost of registering a business name is about $45, in Pennsylvania there is an additional legal requirement that you place advertisements in the local journal of record announcing your new business name, whether your business is incorporated or not. The cost of these ads can run between $100 and $150.

You can usually avoid the requirement of having to register your business name this way by including your personal name in your business name, for example, by calling your business "Ellen Smith & Associates" rather than "CompuFriend." But as local regulations vary on whether you need to include both your first and last name or just the last in your business name and on other points related to registering your business name, be sure to find out the rules that apply in your own state.

Make Sure Your Business Name Is Unique

If you decide to go with a name like CompuFriend, you will also need to determine that no one else has already claimed that name. If someone has, you will have to choose another name. Some consultants are content with doing a local or statewide search, which may involve nothing more than going to your county clerk's office and reading through old ledgers to make sure that no one else has registered a similar name there.

But if there is a chance you might want to incorporate someday under the name you are using now, it is a good idea also to make sure that the name you've chosen isn't already trademarked by another company anywhere else. Consultant Steve Zilora, who discovered that the business name he'd been using was registered by another company when he moved to a new state, warns that if another company already has rights to your name, they may be able to claim that you are infringing on their ability to do business in your area. Even worse, he adds, if another company with your name does lousy work, "you may have to do a lot of explaining."

The actual process of *registering a trademark* for your business name is an expensive process that can cost a thousand dollars or more. Such registration should be done by an attorney and is not something that the fledgling consultant needs to do at the start of his or her practice. But you can search for existing trademarks yourself, using the TradeMarkScan State and TradeMarkScan Federal databases available on DIALOG or through CompuServe's IQUEST gateway. The cost for such a search will range from a dollar or two to over a hundred dollars, depending on how many hits you get and how many names you ask for information about. Such a search will ensure that you don't choose a name that is obviously taken. However, be aware that these trademark databases do not include all enforceable trademarks and that you will still need an attorney's help when you decide to register a trademark of your own.

Even if a trademark has not been registered, you may run into trouble if you use a name that has already been used by another company. Attorney Frederic Wilf, who specializes in intellectual property law relating to computers, points out that "Trademark law does provide protection under the common law to unregistered trademarks, so long as they are still used. State and federal registrations provide rights above the rights a trademark user has without a registration."

Wilf also reminds consultants that they may not use the circle-R registered trademark character for a product or service unless they've been issued a *federal trademark*—an expensive and lengthy process. You may, however, use "SM," which is short for "service mark," with your business name.

If you have thoughts of incorporating your company at some future time, some states, including Connecticut, allow you to reserve your company's name by registering it without a corporate designation.

The requirements for registering a business name outside of the United States are usually similar to those in the United States, although it is more likely that there will be a centralized government bureau that handles business name registrations. For example, to register a business name in Australia, you should first visit your local office of the Department of Consumer Affairs where you can search a computerized Name Index to make sure the name you have chosen is unique. If it is, you file an Application for Registration of a Business Name with the Department of Consumer Affairs, which should process it within the week. However, regulations require that you may not register a business name more than two months before you begin doing business under that name.

FCC CERTIFICATION

If you plan to build computer systems for your clients, you need to be aware of the FCC regulations that govern the amount of radio frequency (RF) interference that a piece of hardware can generate. The FCC certifies systems at two levels:

- Class B certification is more stringent and is required for sales to users who plan to use the computer in their homes. An FCC certified lab must issue the Class B certification and the Class B certification number must appear on the machine.
- Class A standards are less stringent and apply to machinery sold to businesses. Although the manufacturer must be able to provide data to prove that the machine complies with the standard, they can conduct their own testing and no certification label is required on the machine itself.

End users are allowed to build three noncertified machines for their own use. Some consultants use this as a loophole to mean that if they assemble parts provided by a client he is "building" the machine and the consultant is merely an agent providing parts and services, not the machine itself. However, if you take this route you must be very careful how you advertise and perform your services.

In general, it is advisable that when buying motherboards or bare-bones systems for resale you make sure to buy Class B–certified systems. When adding parts to a bare-bones system it is also advisable to get FCC-certified components where possible. The FCC does issue Class B certifications for components. However, not all components, particularly hard drives, are available in Class B–certified form.

This is not something to stay up all night worrying about. Lawyers discussing the topic on CompuServe's LAWSIG in 1991 pointed out that there is no record of prosecution for consultants installing non-Class B components in a certified machine except in situations where the machine generated a complaint. But it is something you should be aware of if you plan to resell hardware or put together custom machinery for clients.

DO YOU NEED TO INCORPORATE?

People often believe that they must decide at the outset of their consulting practice which form of business they should select for it. If they have done some reading on the subject they may worry about whether they should be setting up their practices as a C corporation or S corporation or wonder if they should be taking advantage of even more obscure legal forms of business. It is not unheard of for new consultants to invest heavily in expensive legal and accounting services to help them establish the "correct" form for their business long before they've cashed a single client check.

But worrying about the form of your consulting business before you've built one up is generally a waste of time. It absorbs energy that could be put to better use in lining up your first clients. In the United States there is a very adequate default built into the system that you can use without any effort or expense at all: *sole proprietorship*, Unless you do something legal to indicate that you are not a sole proprietorship, you'll be treated as one. If you list your consulting earnings as self-employment income and file a Schedule C with your income tax return, no other legal steps will be required of you.

SECTION 1706 OF THE TAX REFORM ACT OF 1986 AND INCORPORATION

Unfortunately, in the United States, before you have earned a single penny as a consultant, you may run into clients who refuse to work with you unless you incorporate.

This may be because the client believes that incorporated consultants are more likely to be in business for the long haul and are therefore safer to deal with. But it is much more likely that their concern is founded on a misinterpretation of a piece of legislation known as Section 1706 of the Tax Reform Act of 1986—a few ambiguous lines that pertain to the question of when a computer consultant can be treated as an independent contractor.

History of Section 1706

A little background is needed to clarify what Section 1706 is really about. The IRS recognizes two distinct classes of workers: employees and independent contractors. It treats these two classes of workers in very different ways. For example:

- An employee's taxes are automatically withheld from each paycheck, whereas the independent contractor has no money withheld from his checks but must pay quarterly withholding on his own.
- An employee has her FICA/Medicare tax payment matched by an equivalent payment made by her employer, whereas the contractor pays the whole of the self-employment tax she owes by herself.
- Finally, an employee has very few deductions available to him when filing his tax return, whereas the independent contractor is

treated as a business owner and may deduct all the expenses involved in earning his income—deductions that can reduce his taxable income by many thousands of dollars.

Historically, employers have tried to treat as many workers as possible as independent contractors, because it is much simpler and often cheaper to do so, for the following reasons:

- A company using independent contractors doesn't have to go through the bother of withholding taxes.
- The company doesn't have to pay its share of the worker's FICA.
- The company doesn't have to make payments into unemployment insurance funds for independent consultants or include them in company pension and health insurance plans.
- When using contractors a company doesn't have to worry about conforming to the huge body of antidiscrimination and labor law that has grown up to regulate relations between employers and employees.

From the worker's perspective there are benefits to being an independent contractor too—all those business deductions that the employee cannot take.

Twenty Factors That Determine Independent Contractor Status

To keep employers and employees from abusing independent contractor status, the IRS has developed a set of guidelines it uses to determine whether a worker should be considered an employee or an independent contractor. These guidelines are a set of twenty factors that examine the work that a worker does and test to see whether that worker behaves like an employee or a business owner. The twenty factors pose questions such as:

- Do workers use their own tools or tools supplied by the employer?
- Do workers set their own hours of work, or work at times set by the employer?
- Are workers required to work on the employer's premises, or on their own?
- Do workers have the right to bring in and pay their own assistants?
- Can workers lose money in the course of their work?

These and other questions establish how much *risk* workers assume and how much *control* they have over their work, and in most cases do distinguish fairly between employees and independent business owners.

The complete text of the twenty factors as defined by the IRS can be found in Appendix B. However, because no one expected an independent computer consultant to supply his or her own mainframe, a "safe harbor" Section 530 of the Revenue Act of 1978 exempted certain technical service workers, including programmers and engineers, from having to meet all twenty of these criteria to qualify for independent contractor status. Section 530 stated that a person hiring a worker could treat him or her as a contractor if "treatment of such individual for such period was in reasonable reliance on . . . long standing recognized practice of a significant segment of the industry in which such individual was engaged." As technical people had been working in industry as independent contractors for many years, Section 530 freed contract computer personnel from having to worry about the IRS challenging their tax status.

No More Safe Harbor

Section 1706 of the Tax Reform Act of 1986 removed this safe harbor from some computer consultants, forcing them, again, to meet the criteria set by the twenty factors if they want to claim independent contractor status and making it much more difficult for computer consultants, particularly those who work on mainframes or serve the Fortune 100 companies as contract programmers, to qualify as independent contractors.

The actual wording included in Section 1706 is only that Section 530

> shall not apply in the case of an individual who, pursuant to an arrangement between the taxpayer and another person, provides services for such other person as an engineer, designer, drafter, computer programmer, systems analyst or other similarly skilled worker engaged in a similar line of work.

Given the crystalline clarity of this statement there has never been total agreement as to what it really means.

At first, Section 1706 was generally interpreted as applying only in third-party situations—situations where a broker or job shop placed a worker on a contract and billed the client for his work. But gun-shy corporate lawyers have tended to interpret it to suggest that *all* computer consultants working as independent contractors are at risk of being reclassified as employees by the IRS, and the IRS itself has not made the situation any clearer with its own rulings. As a result many larger firms will no longer allow any computer consultant to work for them as an independent contractor.

Educating Your Clients about Section 1706

What makes Section 1706 so frightening to clients is that the full weight of it falls squarely on the shoulders of the client. If the IRS audits the client and reclassifies its consultants as the client's employees, the client will be assessed huge penalties and interest payments on the payroll and FICA taxes that the IRS will claim the client should have withheld, even though the reclassified consultants may already have paid every cent of tax required on those same earnings.

Many large corporations now deal with this threat either by insisting that all consultants who work for them come in as salaried employees of large consulting firms. A few will allow independents to work for them directly if they are incorporated. By doing this they are hoping to protect themselves from an IRS audit, assuming that if you are an employee of your own corporation they will be safe from having the IRS classify you as their employee.

Unfortunately, they won't be. Incorporation alone doesn't protect your client should the IRS determine that you don't satisfy the twenty-question criteria for being an independent contractor. Only if you can meet those criteria will the client be sure to come out safe on an audit.

Since 1987 there have been several attempts by industry lobbyists to induce legislators to change 1706, but none has been effective, nor are future results likely to be any more successful, given the small size and great lack of organization of the independent computer consulting community. In 1996, a bill was introduced that would have changed the way the IRS established independence for *all* types of contractors. HR 1972, The Independent Contractor's Tax Simplification Act, would have replaced the twenty factors with clearer criteria. However, as of the end of 1996 the bill had still not made it through committee and passing it does not appear to be high on the list of Congress's priorities. If anything does change, you can get an update on the current status of the bill from the Computer and Software Industry Association's (CSIA) Web site.

Protecting Yourself from Section 1706

If you do run into a client who offers you significant amounts of work if you incorporate—and there are many—it may be worth going through the hassle and expense of incorporating for the sake of giving the client the spurious peace of mind he insists on. But if you take this route you must familiarize yourself with the twenty factors (found in Appendix B) and make sure that should the IRS audit your client you can document that you have met the criteria they specify.

Even if your clients are not aware of this regulation, it is still important that you be aware of your standing vis-à-vis the IRS. It may be true that if the client is audited, it is he, not you, who pays the penalties. But before you breathe a sigh of relief, consider what will happen to your consulting career once word gets out in your local business community that you were the consultant who screwed your client with the IRS.

Mainframe contract programmers are those hardest hit by Section

1706. As things stand now, most of them are forced to work as a W-2 employee of some larger firm. If your consulting is a mix of on-site and off-site work for corporate clients, and if one client requires that you consult as the employee of a large TSF, be aware that once you have filed a W-2 for that consulting work, the IRS will make it much harder for you to justify claiming independent status for the other consulting assignments you may take on. For this reason, many consultants who can meet the twenty questions in some of the work that they do make it a policy to turn down all assignments that require that they assume employee status, in order to protect the rest of their clients and their own claims to be running a business.

WHAT ARE THE BENEFITS OF INCORPORATING?

Setting aside issues related to Section 1706, what are the benefits to incorporating for computer consultants? There is no unanimity on this topic within the consultant community. Indeed, any time a large group of computer consultants gets together, when they have stopped arguing about who is a "real" consultant, you are likely to hear a lively debate on the subject of whether computer consultants should incorporate.

The two arguments most commonly cited for incorporating are (1) it can shelter the consultant's income from taxation, and (2) it provides a shield against liability. These are attractive points well worth considering. But there is no one-size-fits-all solution for all business situations, and leaping into do-it-yourself incorporation without understanding what you are getting into may end up being a costly and foolish mistake.

Incorporation turns your business into a legal entity separate from you as an individual. Although regulations vary from state to state, to form a corporation you usually have to file a sheaf of papers with the state, one of which is a *corporate charter*, written in such a way that it permits your corporation to perform all the businesses that you might want to pursue with that corporation.

Corporations are owned by a single owner or by shareholders who receive a share of the corporation's profits when dividends are paid to them. As legal entities, corporations must pay taxes on their earnings, although there are often legal ways of decreasing the corporation's tax liability, including paying out much of its earnings in salaries to the owner and shareholders.

Protection from Liability

Perhaps the single most important benefit of incorporation for a consultant is the protection that it gives the consultant against liability. Think of what could happen if a client sued you claiming that the software you sold her contained a virus that caused her to lose business records pertaining to millions of dollars' worth of orders! As a sole proprietor, your own assets would be available to anyone who could win a legal judgment against you in such a situation. In contrast, when you work through a corporation, your exposure would be limited to the corporation's assets and income.

As important as this is, it is even more significant when a consulting company has more than one principal. If you do not incorporate but instead run a joint business as a partnership, *each* of the owners may be *personally liable* for the actions of the others. What this means in basic English is that you could lose your house and all your savings if your partner turns out to be a jerk. Incorporation will protect you in this situation and limit your exposure to the assets of the corporation.

Consultants sometimes wonder whether incorporation will provide them this kind of protection because they have heard that the professional corporation (PC) used by attorneys and physicians does not limit the liability of the individual practitioner. However, as Attorney Lance Rose, an intellectual property lawyer who specializes in computer-related work, explains, "A regular corporation, even for someone who is skilled and 'professional' in the colloquial (but not technically legal) sense, will shield the individual just fine."

Rose goes on to explain the legal thinking behind incorporation, saying, "If you conduct your corporate affairs properly (keep the accounts separate, sign as a corporation and not as an individual, etc.), your corporation, though only one person, will protect you from liability from corporate acts. This is the primary purpose for which states permit businesses to be conducted in the corporate form—so that business can be conducted which would otherwise be shied away from due to the potentially great or ruinous liability." But it is important that if you do incorporate you do it right. Rose warns consultants that "It is possible to make such a mess of your affairs that you could become personally liable for what should have been purely corporate acts. This makes it important to get solid information on how to run your corporation properly."

C Corporations and S Corporations

In the United States, consultants can choose between two different forms of corporation for their businesses. When you file your corporate application you automatically become a C corporation. However, there is another form, the S corporation, which was designed to meet the needs of the small corporation that is owned by a few owner-participants. Its goal is to avoid the double taxation that occurs when the corporation first must pay corporate tax on its earnings and then, when the owners of the corporation receive what is left of those earnings as salary or dividends, they must pay taxes on that money again. To prevent this, the S corporation allows all corporate profits to be passed through untaxed to the stockholder(s) as a distribution so that the money is taxed only once as stockholders' income.

You get S corporation status by requesting it from the IRS within seventy-five days of the beginning of the fiscal year. Thus if your fiscal year starts on January 1, you must make your request for a change to S corporation status before March 15. You may change back to C corporation status at any time; however, once you have made that change you must wait five years before again requesting S status.

There can be additional tax benefits to forming an S corporation, particularly in a state like Indiana, where ordinary corporate gross income is taxed, rather than net profits, and where the owner of a C corporation might end up having to pay significant taxes on income that was completely eaten up by business expenses. In addition, although in many ways an S corporation resembles a sole proprietorship, the profit of an S corporation appears on IRS Schedule E and is not subject to the 15.3 percent self-employment tax that a sole proprietor must pay on the same income.

But there are disadvantages to S corporations too. In contrast to C corporations, S corporations are limited in the pension and health benefits they can offer their owners and can only offer the same plans that a sole proprietorship can. There are limitations on how many people can participate in an S corporation and on how much business the corporation can do outside of the United States. If an S corporation inadvertently violates the regulations governing its creation and operation, the IRS may find upon audit that the corporation forfeited its S corporation status the year before and assess its owners enormous penalties and interest.

Not all states recognize S corporations for taxation purposes. Consultant Larry Finch, who owns an S corporation, describes the complications that having one introduced into his life before New Jersey recognized them in 1995, explaining, "We keep two sets of books, one for the IRS and the other for the state. Depreciation rules are different, as well as some accounting standards. The state also requires an annual fee ($40) just to be a corporation in the state. It's all a real pain." In Massachusetts the benefits of having an S corporation are also diminished as the state taxes the gross income of S corporations that have suffered a net loss with its minimum corporate excise tax.

Limited Liability Companies

If you are planning to go into business with a partner, another form of business that allows you to avoid incorporation while protecting yourself from liability is available to you. Popular for some time in Europe and now legal in many states in the United States, the limited liability company (LLC) is a relatively new form of business that allows you to pay your taxes as a partnership but still provides individual partners with the protection against liability for a partner's actions that is notoriously lacking in traditional partnerships. You form an LLC by filing a registration document of some sort with the state, although the exact requirements vary widely from state to state. The workings of the LLC are then governed by a separate operating agreement signed by the partners.

An LLC may provide tax advantages to its members. Income and expenses are passed through to the individual partner as they are in an S corporation and are not taxed at the organizational level, and some of the restrictions that apply to S corporations do not apply. However, state laws vary widely in how they treat LLCs, and some states do not recognize them at all, which may pose a problem for consultants who work for clients in such states. In addition, the newness of this form of business means that many tax and legal issues relative to their use have not yet gone through the courts. So from a legal standpoint they are still highly experimental in nature. Because of this, many attorneys advise that an S corporation may be a safer option than an LLC for computer consultants who wish to form businesses with others.

Incorporation Outside of the United States

Although legal details differ in each country, the broad outlines of incorporation are similar. In the United Kingdom, for example, the self-employed consultant who operates as a "sole trader" has simpler tax requirements than does the incorporated limited liability company, a corporation, but his personal assets are at risk should he rack up business debts or be involved in a lawsuit. Yet although the consultant technically has this choice, consultant Chris Bryce reports that most *agencies* (the British term for consulting brokers) insist that consultants they place work through limited liability companies rather than as sole traders. In Canada, you can operate as a sole proprietorship or a corporation, however in contrast to the experience of contractors elsewhere, Canadian consultant Kate Gregory reports that "brokers never insisted on incorporation. In fact they seemed to find it annoying and had to be reminded to make the cheques to Gregory Consulting Limited rather than to the human who they were placing."

As in the United States, the tax authorities in most countries usually demand that those claiming to be self-employed, whether incorporated or not, meet certain criteria for determining that individuals are truly in business for themselves and not simply employees whose employer is trying to avoid following the regulations that apply to employees. These criteria include the same issues covered in the IRS twenty factors, such as whether workers work for more than one company at a time, whether they've made a significant financial investment in their business, and how much control they have over the work they do.

Outside of the United States, clients and brokers may prefer to work with self-employed consultants, incorporated or not, rather than try to force these consultants to work as employees, as is common in the United States. This is because government policies meant to discourage layoffs may make it expensive to employ short-term employees. For example, in Belgium employers must pay hefty termination dues when they fire a worker, making it far cheaper to bring in a self-employed consultant to do a job.

The Costs of Incorporating

In spite of what you might have heard, incorporation is not always the path to great savings. In fact, it may end up costing you more than it saves you, because in some jurisdictions, such as Massachusetts, you may have to pay hefty minimum corporate taxes even when you have not earned a profit. Besides that, dealing with more complex tax and legal requirements that apply to corporations may oblige you to pay for expensive legal and accounting services, both to set up your corporation and to ensure that you run it properly.

In order to save money, many consultants opt to do it themselves, using books that teach them how to incorporate themselves or purchasing the services of one-size-fits-all companies that advertise widely that they can incorporate your business for a mere $50. Although this approach may save you the $750 or more than an attorney would charge to set up your corporation, there are some serious dangers here. The books you buy may not include recent tax or legal changes, which may cause you to make expensive mistakes. Cheapie incorporation companies will mail you a set of forms you can file to incorporate in your state or theirs, but you may not get from them the advice you need in order to conduct your ongoing corporation in a way that conforms to state and federal law. This could become a problem should you run into an IRS audit or a future lawsuit, where it becomes advantageous to your adversary to strip you of the protection that a properly established corporation affords you.

And while you may have heard that there are significant advantages to incorporating in Delaware rather than in your state of residence, this is no longer true. At the present time, registering a corporation in Delaware does not excuse you from having to meet all the tax and legal requirements that apply to corporations doing business in your own state, so out-of-state registration may simply saddle you with more paperwork.

Consult with Professional Advisors before You Incorporate

As you've probably realized by now, incorporation is complex enough that it is worthwhile to confer with professionals to determine what the costs and benefits of incorporation will be in your particular circumstances. The money you spend on a competent accountant or attorney will probably be less than what you might end up paying in penalties and fines—or unsuccessful lawsuits—should you decide to handle the whole thing yourself or with the aid of a book you found in the library that contains outdated advice.

However, this brings up an important point. How do you find the right professional to help you? Consultants who have been this route say that it takes some effort to find an attorney or an accountant who can give you the service you need for your consulting practice. The person who handled your real estate closing or your divorce may be a wonderful attorney for those situations but be out of his or her depth when confronting the issues that you now need to consider. As one experienced consultant relates, "My original attorney was a nice guy and a friend, but knew zip about software and some of its implications. He had a strong reputation, but it turned out to be in areas that didn't help me. Once I got smart I was able to select someone more in tune with my business needs."

The attorney and accountants that you want to work with are those who have extensive experience serving other computer consultants. The best way to find them is through recommendations of others in the business. Get referrals from other consultants, and when you do locate a professional, feel free to interview him or her before you make a commitment to working with them. L. J. Kutten, an expert on computer law, points out, "There is no recognized specialty in intellectual property outside of patent law. Anyone can claim he/she is a computer law expert." To locate an attorney who really is experienced in computer law, Kutten suggests you ask whether he or she belongs to the Computer Law Association and whether he or she subscribes and/or has contributed articles to any of the following journals: *Computer Lawyer, Chicago-Kent Computer Law Journal, Santa Clara Journal of High Technology Law, Rutgers Journal of Computer Law,* or *Jurismetrics.* Kutten also suggests that you scan their bookshelves for multivolume treatises with titles referring to computer law.

If, as your relationship progresses you feel that the advice being given you doesn't ring true or seems to be slanted more toward the needs of a business much larger or more sophisticated than your own, don't hesitate to ignore their advice and look for a new adviser who has more experience dealing with businesses like your own. Only by acting in this way are you likely to get long-lasting benefits out of their service.

4

PREPARING TO DO BUSINESS—INSURING YOUR BUSINESS AND ESTABLISHING YOUR IMAGE

We've covered the formal requirements you must meet to begin your business. Now we look at a few more things you must take care of before you will be ready to go to work for your clients. We start out with the insurance you will need both for yourself and for your clients. Then we examine the rest of the business paraphernalia you'll want to assemble before you begin your consulting practice, putting particular emphasis on the materials you'll use to put across a businesslike image.

INSURANCE FOR CONSULTANTS

One of the most frequently asked questions posted by new consultants visiting CONSULT, one that is almost as common as "where do I find new clients," is "How can I find health insurance for my family now that I'm consulting?" The difficulties of finding insurance for themselves, their families, and their businesses rank high among the headaches faced by beginning consultants. If you are making the transition to consulting from being an employee it is likely that insurance will be the single most expensive new line item on your budget. Insurance for the self-employed is not only expensive, it is increasingly difficult to find—even when you are willing to pay for it. But though finding insurance can be a problem, the problem is not unsolvable; in this chapter, we'll look at how you can deal with it when you start out consulting.

HEALTH INSURANCE

If you've been getting your health insurance as an employee benefit, prepare for sticker shock when you quit your job and have to purchase your own coverage. Health insurance for a family can run anywhere from $2,000 to $8,000 a year. You may say to yourself, "We're generally healthy, I'll pay my health expenses as they come up and do without insurance." But before you make this decision, consider that a hospitalization lasting a few days can easily cost $20,000, while an extended health emergency like pediatric cancer that requires ongoing high-tech intervention can run up bills of a million dollars or more. If you have no insurance, you stand to lose your home and all your assets should such a health emergency arise.

Health Insurance Portability

Another reason why you should not postpone making a decision about buying health insurance when you leave benefited salaried employment is that a 1996 federal law, P.L. 104-191, the Kennedy/Kassebaum Health Insurance Reform Act of 1995, gives you some protection against discrimination by insurance companies that you may lose once you have spent a period being self-employed. The law became effective in July of 1997.

The reason that it is so important is that most health insurance plans open to the self-employed have long refused to offer coverage to people who have any record of having—or of a family member having—a chronic illness. And insurance companies have defined as chronic illnesses conditions as benign as asthma, being on antidepressant therapy, participation in marriage counseling, or PMS. Even when these companies have offered policies to the self-employed, they almost universally excluded coverage of any illnesses related in any way to such preexisting conditions.

Under the terms of the new law, group health insurance plans must now offer membership to anyone who has been covered by another group health insurance plan for the previous eighteen months—at the same rates offered to other plan members. However, once you leave the group plan, you lose this protection. Although the new health insurance reform law does tighten up the extent to which insurers offering individual plans may discriminate against people with preexisting conditions, insurers may still impose waiting periods on them or charge them exorbitant rates. So if you have any questionable family health history, you'll want to find group insurance as soon as you leave a job with health benefits before the expiration of this grace period.

COBRA Benefits

When you leave salaried, benefited employment, another federal law, the Consolidated Omnibus Budget Reconciliation Act of 1986 (COBRA), mandates that your former employer must allow you to continue in its group health plan for eighteen months after you are terminated or quit, as long as you pay your own premiums. You have forty-five days after leaving your job to pick up this coverage. Unfortunately, most ex-employees investigating COBRA coverage find that the premiums are exorbitant. Consultants report rates as high as $350 per month for an individual and $700 per month for a family. Other group plans are usually a better deal than COBRA extensions. So it is worthwhile to investigate other group health plans available to small businesses in your region before you sign the COBRA health benefits extension form your ex-employer mails you.

Finding Health Insurance

There are a number of different approaches open to you when you go shopping for affordable health insurance. If you are pursuing your consulting as an independent contractor, your best bet might be to investigate a small business plan offered by a reputable local organization like the chamber of commerce or by a well-known professional organization such as the Institute of Electrical and Electronic Engineers (IEEE). These organizations can offer you traditional insurance coverage or membership in local managed-care plans.

Read the descriptions of any plan offered by such groups very carefully. Find out if the plan covers prescriptions—many small business plans do not. See if the plan allows you to see a specialist outside of the plan if you come down with something exotic. You'll also want to find out whether the plan covers school-required children's physicals and what you are expected to do (and pay for) if a child has an accident during the weekend.

Another option is to buy an individual policy through an independent insurance agent. These plans can be much less expensive than group coverage and often give you the option of electing to pay a high deductible—$1,000 or more—in return for a lower premium. This sounds appealing. Unfortunately, consultants often report that these plans make it very difficult to collect when they have claims. Consultants report insurers who reject paying for tests or impose arbitrary limits on how much they will pay for a procedure, leaving the consultant to wrangle endlessly for payment. Others have had insurers claim that a new illness is evidence of a preexisting condition that should have been disclosed to them and then refuse to pay for it. This kind of nightmare is the last thing you need to deal with when you or a family member are seriously ill. So it's worth looking for satisfied policy holders who have a significant claims history before signing up.

Before buying an individual health policy, it's a good idea to ask a number of competing independent insurance agents about the insurer's reputation for covering claims. You can also check out a company with the office of your state insurance commissioner. However, in practice, such state regulatory agencies rarely flag problems with any but the sleaziest of insurers.

Sleazy Group Plans

While there are many legitimate groups selling insurance nowadays, the insurance crisis has also spawned a horde of bogus business organizations whose only real function is to sell group insurance plans, some of them of dubious value. Perhaps the most well known of these is NASE (National Association of the Self-Employed), which was described in the January 1992 issue of *Home Office Computing*. The article reported on the difficulty claimants had had collecting on this organization's policies and on the high number of complaints received by regulators about the company ("Are Health Care Costs Killing Your Business?" Linda Stern, *HOC*, Jan. 1992, pp. 30–37). NASE was founded by PFL Life Insurance, the Dallas insurer whose products it sells its members. At the time the article was written, NASE was under investigation by the Department of Insurance in Texas, which was looking into the claim that the sole reason for the organization's existence was to sell insurance. The *Home Office Computing* article reported that people who signed up for NASE insurance ended up with very expensive insurance that offered them exceptionally poor coverage. For example, the deductibles on the policy were written on a per-illness, not a per-year basis, as is customary. It also reported that although NASE signed on new clients by offering attractive low rates, most members reported that soon after they signed up, the company raised their premiums to unacceptable levels.

NASE representatives have a reputation for using extreme hard-sell techniques too. One consultant who frequents the CONSULT forum reports that he had to call the police to get rid of an NASE representative who would not leave his office even after giving him an unwanted two-and-a-half-hour sales pitch.

NASE represents an extreme, but there are other questionable insurance-oriented groups around. So you should *do some serious investigating before you pay a membership fee* to sign up for an unknown organization's insurance. In particular, find out which insurance company underwrites the policy and stay away from ones you've never heard of. One computer consultant who's run into a few of these groups recommends that if a representative of an obscure organization solicits you, holding out insurance as a lure, ask how you can attend a meeting of the association so that you can talk to other members and get involved in their activities before you consider their insurance plan. If there are no local meetings, beware. Most bogus groups provide no activities at all except insurance sales.

DISABILITY INSURANCE

Every consultant should also give some serious thought to buying disability insurance. This is another of the kinds of insurance coverage that you may have taken for granted when you got it as part of a company-paid benefit plan. Many consultants skimp on disability coverage, but to do so is a grave mistake. Should you be the victim of an accident or suffer a serious illness while pursuing your consulting career, disability insurance would provide you with an ongoing income and prevent you and your family from facing financial ruin. When you are disabled for more than a short period of time, disability insurance pays you a percentage of your previous income for as long as you are physically unable to pursue your current line of work.

It is also important to remember that when you are paying for your own health insurance, the loss of income caused by a serious extended illness could make it very hard for you to keep up the premiums on the health insurance that pays for your treatment for that illness. So if you must skimp, skimp elsewhere. Disability insurance is important!

There are several things to watch out for when shopping for this kind of insurance. The most important are overly restrictive definitions of disability. Watch out for policies that specify that the disability must make it impossible for you to pursue "all" the usual tasks involved in your work, or specify that you must be unable to pursue "any" work.

Another important condition to be aware of when selecting a policy is the length of time you must be disabled before the policy begins payment and whether the time you lose from work that is used in determining eligibility must be consecutive days. If you are in and out of the hospital six times during a given year but your stays only last two months each, you will not be able to collect benefits on a policy that stipulates that any covered disability must extend for three consecutive months. Look for policies that look at cumulative days lost rather than consecutive days.

Another important issue for consultants, or any self-employed person, is the way that the insurer calculates your real income. Different ways of treating retainers, money received for ongoing maintenance contracts, and unpaid accounts receivable can make an enormous difference in how much replacement income you may be due under various kinds of policies. The worst policies may treat money owed you as income you are currently earning even when you can't collect it. They may also refuse to consider you disabled if you are receiving money from past royalties, retainers, or other agreements made before you become disabled. Make sure that the policy you buy calculates your current income during a period of disability based only on actual cash you generate and receive in the period.

You will probably have to wait for a year after making the transition to self-employed consulting from being an employee before you can get disability insurance written against your income as a consultant, even if you are not changing professions. However, if Section 1706 forces you to work as a nonbenefited W-2 employee and you have a track record as an employee doing computer work, you may be able to buy disability insurance based on your W-2 income immediately.

Because companies offer disability policies with a dizzying number of restrictions and hidden weasel factors, the cheapest policy may very well not be the best for you. Spend some time talking with several different insurance agents before buying any plan and make sure that you are getting one that has a reasonable likelihood of paying benefits should you be unable to work. Another thing to be aware of is that, like health insurers, disability insurers are likely to exclude any preexisting conditions from disability coverage. They may also reject your application completely if you have a record of any psychological treatments—including marriage counseling—or if you have a history of back problems. So this is another situation in which it is best to buy the insurance before there is any hint in your medical record that you might someday need it.

LIABILITY INSURANCE

When the client presents you with your first contract you may find a clause in it that requires you to provide liability insurance. This can be confusing as there are several different kinds of coverages that cover a consultant's liability, and clients who are more accustomed to dealing with the kind of contractor who install air conditioning equipment or driveways may not understand what liability insurance does and does not cover when working with computer consultants.

General Liability (GL) Insurance

General liability insurance (called *public liability insurance* in the United Kingdom) is a very common form of business insurance. It is intended to protect the business against claims for bodily injury and property damage. In the case of a computer consultant, it would come in useful if you were to drop a client's machine and break it, or if a client were to trip over a cable in your office and break his leg. GL is usually relatively inexpensive with premiums typically running between $400 and $500 per year.

Unfortunately, it can be difficult to find an insurer willing to provide this kind of coverage to computer consultants, because of the fear that the insurer may be called on to defend a policyholder whose computer work is alleged to have caused damage to a client's business. As a result, even when they do manage to sign up for coverage, consultants often report having the insurer cancel their policy a few months later on the grounds that they don't cover people working with computers.

Some consultants have gotten around this by not using the "C" words—"computer consultant"—on their insurance applications and by calling themselves "programmers" instead. Even here, though, there can be problems. For example, most insurers will not cover programmers who work with aerospace firms or defense subcontractors or who do medical programming.

If you run into a problem finding general liability insurance, don't despair. There are commercial insurers who will write a GL policy for computer consultants that specifically excludes coverage for professional liability while retaining coverage for personal injury and property damage. If your agent isn't aware of this, or doesn't have previous experience insuring computer consultants, hunt around for a new agent.

If your clients are disturbed to find that your policy includes an exclusion for professional malpractice, you will have to educate them about the realities of insurance coverage for all computer consultants. If clients are not convinced, give them the name of an agent they can call to confirm that your problem in finding general liability insurance does not stem from anything in your personal record but is an industrywide problem. Many consultants report that after they had done this, clients were willing to strike a boilerplate clause requiring GL insurance out of the contract.

Errors and Omissions (E&O) Insurance

This form of commercial insurance (called *professional indemnity* in the United Kingdom) is intended to cover professional liability and protect you against claims for damages your professional services might have caused. It is meant to cover situations such as when your programming errors cause a client financial loss, or when you inadvertently introduce a virus into a client's system that ends up destroying irreplaceable data. The only situations that E&O insurance is not intended to cover are ones in which a professional knowingly causes the loss, in short, where the loss is a result of deliberate malpractice rather than incompetence. Unlike general liability insurance, errors and omissions insurance stays in effect for years after you complete your work for a client.

Not surprisingly, this kind of coverage is very expensive. Premiums are usually figured as a percentage of the payroll of a multiperson firm or as a percentage of annual gross billings of a one-person operation. Typical annual premiums for E&O insurance for a one-person consultancy can run between $4,000 and $5,000.

Attorney Lance Rose states that this kind of insurance is rarely worth the premium and that "anyone suing you as a consultant could try an 'end run' around it anyway, claiming that you're a 'professional' and that as such your professional liability would likely be disclaimed in the policy." Rose suggests that for the consultant worried about exposure to lawsuits, incorporation is a much better defense, as the incorporated consultant who is sued can lose at worst only the assets of the corporation, which, for most computer consultants, are rarely extensive. However, if you incorporate your practice this way, the protection you buy for yourself increases your client's exposure and may intensify that client's demand that you supply professional malpractice insurance in case the assets of your company aren't capable of reimbursing them for a major loss you might cause.

If a client does insist that you get this kind of coverage, the ICCA offers its member firms E&O coverage tailored to the needs of computer consultants. Given its expense, many consultants who buy this coverage negotiate its price into their contracts with clients who demand it, since such insurance works almost entirely for the benefit of the client.

Performance Bonds

Yet another kind of insurance that clients may ask for is a performance bond. These bonds are issued on a project-by-project basis, often by insurance companies, and guarantee payment to the client from the bonding company should you fail to complete the work you have contracted to do. These arrangements are not usually used for computer work, but clients who are used to dealing with other kinds of general contractors sometimes ask for them.

Consultants who have looked into getting this kind of insurance report that it is impossible to get unless you have collateral to put up of a value equal to the amount of the bond. As few consultancies have significant assets, you are most likely to be asked to use your house equity to back up your promise to complete the job. This is often a kind of coverage you can talk your client out of requiring by explaining that it is not customarily used by computer consultants.

OTHER COVERAGES YOU PROBABLY DON'T NEED

Workers' Compensation

Workers' compensation (also known as "workman's compensation") is a state-mandated insurance program intended to cover the medical and disability expenses of employees who are injured on the job. You usually only need to obtain workers' compensation insurance coverage if you have other people working for you as employees. The details of where you buy this insurance and how much is required vary greatly from state to state. Some states provide state-run insurance programs, while in others workers' compensation insurance is sold through independent insurance brokers.

State law may require that corporations provide such insurance for their employees, so if you are your own corporation's employee, you may wonder if you need this kind of coverage. However, few states allow the principal of a business to collect under their workers' compensation plans. So if you are the sole employee of your own corporation, you may be able to request a waiver that relieves you of the responsibility of buying workers' comp.

Some boilerplate contracts clients may present you with may also require that you carry this kind of coverage. However, if you are working alone, the client should be willing to eliminate this clause for the reasons just cited. When a client won't budge on this issue, consultant Ken Werner suggests purchasing a policy to cover a temporary employee working twenty hours a month and then, at the end of the year, reporting no wages paid to that employee. He says that in his home state, Texas, this strategy results in getting a policy with a cover page stating that your corporation is covered, which is enough to satisfy your client.

Unemployment Compensation

Unemployment compensation is another type of insurance that you only have to worry about buying if you employ others. If you do, you'll usually have to pay a percentage of your employee's wages into a state fund intended to pay the employee a weekly unemployment check should they be laid off. Again the details vary from state to state. However, what does not vary is that the owner of a company or a sole proprietor cannot collect unemployment, so you usually do not have to pay into this fund if you are the sole employee of your own corporation. Check with your state department of labor to find out what laws apply in your jurisdiction.

However, unemployment compensation provides a silver lining for contractors forced to work for a broker as a W-2 employee. If your contract ends and the broker can not find you another one, you may be able to file for unemployment and receive a weekly check to tide you over until you get a new assignment, as long as you have worked enough hours during the previous year to qualify. Because this is a possibility, when a W-2 contract ends and the broker lets you go without offering you a new placement, be sure to request that they issue you a "pink slip"—the layoff notice you must present at the unemployment office to file a claim.

INSURING YOUR EQUIPMENT

Contrary to what you might believe, computer equipment you use for business in your home office is not covered by your homeowner's policy. You will need to insure it separately by purchasing what is known as "Inland Marine" coverage from a commercial insurer. Companies who will insure computer hardware include Hartford Steam Boiler, Computer Insurance Agency, and Safeware. Besides covering your hardware, these policies may also cover expenses associated with the loss of data through a hardware failure. Whenever questions have been posted on CONSULT asking what other consultants' claims experience has been with this kind of insurance, the answers have always been reassuring. Premiums are reasonable, and most people report that when they had claims, their insurer paid promptly. This seems to be the one area of insurance in which consultants don't report encountering nasty surprises.

CREATING A BUSINESS IMAGE THAT WON'T LEAVE YOU BROKE

Before you begin business you will have to invest some thought and money in business paraphernalia that you will use to convey a professional image when dealing with your new clients. Image enhancement is an area where many beginning consultants are tempted to ring up big bills, believing that investing in image will increase their ability to attract new clients. But most working consultants have found that very little of the money they invest in image-builders at the outset of their practice translates into billable work. Let's look now at what you really need to create a workable business image for your new consulting practice.

YOUR OFFICE

It is unlikely that you will need to rent an office for your business when you start out. Many highly successful consultants work out of their homes, and there is no stigma associated with working at home for computer consultants. When you have no clear idea of what kind of income your consulting practice is going to bring in, it is foolish to commit yourself to paying the high fixed expenses that an office entails. And these expenses can be high indeed, as consultant Robert West attests when he explains, "I have found that the overhead [on my office] runs close to $1,000 per month since I end up paying business phone rates rather than home phone rates and since my landlord requires $1 million in liability insurance for the business." This kind of expenditure makes sense for an established consultant who may find that separating home and office is the only way to reclaim his personal life, but it is not advisable for consultants just starting out who have little idea of how viable their practice may be.

Still, many beginning consultants are concerned that operating out of a home office might mark them as unprofessional, or worse, fly-by-nights, who will disappear from the consulting scene as soon as they can scrounge up a new salaried job. As a result, they resort to various strategies to get around this perception. One consultant adds the phrase, "Suite 49" to her address to make it sound less residential. Another consultant uses a box number rather than an address. Another solution is to hire a professional answering service.

Sharing Office Space and Services

If you want to go one step further you can enhance your business image by paying for the services offered by a shared office provider. In these arrangements, you pay a monthly fee, usually between $150 and $200, which provides you with the services of a live receptionist to answer your phone when you are out and allows you to use a mailing address that suggests an office in a prestigious office building. Shared office providers usually also allow you to make occasional use of professional secretarial support services as you need them and to rent conference rooms and other business facilities at the shared site, all at an additional hourly charge. Shared office providers can usually be found listed in the yellow pages under "Office and Desk Space." If you are concerned with establishing a professional image, this can be a cost-effective way of doing it.

But before you get too carried away worrying about image, take to heart the words of network integration specialist Dorothy Creswell. She advises, "Don't buy if you can borrow, buy service, or rent," explaining that it is better to save money on nonessentials and to put that money toward things that contribute to more significant gains in your practice. Creswell took the money she saved by doing business out of a home office furnished with used corporate-quality furniture and invested it in having a custom logo designed for her printed materials, as well as in a separate business telephone line with a high-quality answering machine with a businesslike message, a full-featured word processor, and most importantly, membership dues for professional organizations, in several of which she rose to leadership positions.

CHOOSING AN EFFECTIVE BUSINESS NAME

Your business name will be an important part of your business image, and once you begin to do business under a particular name, changing it can involve a lot of effort, so it is worth putting some effort at the outset of your practice into selecting a good one. In Chapter 3, we looked at the legal issues that surround your business name. Now, we'll look at some things you need to be aware of if your business name is to enhance rather than hobble your new consulting business.

Consultants take several approaches when naming their practices. Many consultants simply use their own names, perhaps tacking on "& Associates" to make themselves sound like a larger operation. This approach has worked just fine for many consultants, including huge multinational consulting groups like Andersen Consulting. But some consultants consider this approach uncreative, or worry that including their name in the firm's name will cause them to be perceived as a small-time operation.

Many consultants prefer to use business names that tell the client something about the kind of work they do, such as Network Affiliates or InvestComp. This too can be a fruitful approach—as long as you are careful not to select a name that is too constricting. Business conditions change and you may want to expand into other areas in the future. If your business name is too limiting, you may have to change it later and lose the benefits of customer recognition of your old name. For example, it would be a bad idea to name your company Insurance Solutions if you are going to be offering services that might also interest retailers.

But the majority of beginning consultants incline to yet another approach to choosing their new business name. Perhaps influenced by the torrent of advertising that inundates us all, they invent snappy designations more appropriate for a new brand of potato chips than for a consulting practice. Such names often embody a computer jargon pun or some other humorous element, like "GUISoft."

But the purveyors of potato chips are able to build name recognition for their new products by subjecting the public to a barrage of millions of dollars of advertising, while you, the beginning consultant, will at best be able to place only a few pieces of paper featuring your new name under a potential client's nose. Therefore, when you introduce yourself to clients at a meeting or in a phone call, the chances of them connecting you with your snappy business name are very low—particularly if you've chosen a snappy computer-related name that sounds, to the uninitiated, exactly like all the other snappy computer-related names that other computer consultants favor.

Remember that the primary function of your business name is to *identify you*. The harder it is for the client to connect you with your business name, the more of a liability it will be. As a worst-case scenario, picture the client muttering to himself, "Hmmm, what was that name? ComputerSoft? CompuTech? ComputerAid? AccuComp? ComputerWorks? Damn, I'll just call Joe Ortega Associates. Joe seemed like a smart guy and I can find him in the phone book."

A related point to remember when using a name other than your personal name for your business is that the client now needs to remember two names, not one. When your given name is part of the company name, clients calling you know who to ask for, saving them some embarrassment. But when you use a name that doesn't include your name, the client who remembers the company name but forgets the name of the principal may find himself embarrassed when calling you. If you pick up the phone and identify yourself as "GlitchSoft, Incorporated," the client may be left murmuring, "May I please speak with . . . uh . . . er . . . ." This doesn't put the client into a frame of mind conducive to building a relaxed and pleasant business relationship.

This is not to say that you shouldn't use a business name that doesn't incorporate your personal name. Thousands of computer consultants do. But it points up the fact that when choosing such a name you should strive for something that is memorable and not easily confused with other consultants' names, and that it is important to make sure that you include your personal name on all business cards, flyers, letterheads, brochures, and other business tools along with the company name.

If you come up with a creative monicker, it is a good idea to test it out with friends to ensure that they pronounce it the way that you intended it to be pronounced. If there is any doubt, use another name. Otherwise, reports a consultant who chose an ambiguous name, you will constantly find yourself faced with the choice of correcting a new client's pronunciation or letting them mispronounce it and suffer embarrassment later when they discover their error, neither of which is conducive to building a relaxed business relationship.

One last thing to be aware of when choosing a business name is that you should be careful about including the word *engineer* anywhere in your company name or using it on your business materials. In some states, including California, you can be fined for using the term when you are not a licensed engineer.

BUSINESS CARDS

Once you've decided on a name, you will need to give attention to developing a set of interface materials—the tangible tools you use to connect with potential clients and remind them of who you are and what you do. First among these, of course, is the business card. Your card will often be all that a potential client has to remind him of your existence, so clearly this should not be an item on which to scrimp. Pay for decent card stock and quality printing. A cheap card signals that you are not serious about staying in business.

However, it is not necessary to come up with a fancy logo and layout. There are standard formats that business card printers provide that should be adequate for your card. Indeed, it is often better to use one of these canned formats than to attempt to design something of your own. Graphic design is as much a specialty as computer programming and an amateur layout or a badly drawn logo does nothing to put across your professionality. If you do decide to diverge from one of these stock designs, it is worth paying for the services of a professional designer.

New consultants frequently wonder what title they should use to refer to themselves on their cards. It is tempting to describe yourself as the "President" or "Chairman" of your new firm. But some consultants warn against doing this, arguing that it may strike potential clients as pretentious when you are clearly a one-person operation. The word "Consultant" or perhaps, "Principal" after your name should be sufficient.

It might also be advisable to include on the card a couple of words that remind the client of what kind of work you do. For example, you might include a phrase like "Custom Accounting Systems," or "Word Processing Training" on your card if that is the kind of work you want clients to call on you for. The primary function of a business card is to help someone remember who you are, so anything that you can include on the card that might help them reconnect the name on the card with your face and a conversation you might have had during a brief personal contact can only benefit you.

One alternative to standard business cards is a specially prepared business card that is prepunched so that it converts into a Rolodex card. Figure 4-1 shows a sample Rolodex business card. These are considerably more expensive than regular business cards but might improve the chances of the client finding your number when they need to contact you. Consultants who have used this kind of card warn that you must buy the expensive kind. Burt Johnson points out that the cheap ones are "a bear to get out and have all sorts of ugly nubs around them when they are removed." Since you are creating a minibillboard every time your client looks at the Rolodex, he suggests that you choose cards that have a high quality feel.

Another common question consultants have is what kind of contact information to put on their cards. Many consultants have several e-mail addresses. To accommodate clients and subtly enhance their image as technical sophisticates, many consultants include all these e-mail addresses on their business cards, along with the more traditional phone numbers and fax numbers. However, this can cause problems. A card that includes five e-mail addresses can look cluttered, and there may be

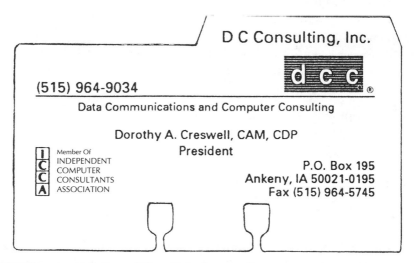

FIGURE 4-1   DC Consulting Rolodex card.

another problem with listing so many e-mail addresses too. As consultant Karl Mormer points out, the point of the address is to let people get hold of you in a timely manner. If you don't check the e-mail boxes listed on your card on a daily basis, he warns, you may end up defeating your purpose when a client contacts you by e-mail and has to wait days or weeks to hear from you. He advises that you not list any e-mail address that you don't intend to check on a daily basis.

STATIONERY

How valuable is high-quality stationery topped by a custom-crafted, professionally produced logo, to your fledgling consulting practice? This is another one of those questions that spawns endless and surprisingly acrimonious debate. Herman Holtz, the author of the consulting classic, *How to Succeed as an Independent Consultant*, frames one side of the argument elegantly when he says, "Nobody murmurs, 'Nice stationery. He's impressive so we'll give him the job.' " But many computer consultants claim that something very akin to that does in fact take place in the client's mind. As Michael Stein explains, "I have been told several times that because we submitted something that 'leapt off my desk' we were immediately in the finalists for the bid." Another consultant, Larry Spencer, reports having similar experiences, remarking "Personally I've spent a fortune getting stationery that not only has two colors, but has a classy logo in silver foil. Let me tell you, I get *lots* of favorable comments on presenting my business card—not a bad way to begin a conversation."

But other computer consultants have found that once they get going, they actually don't have much use for stationery. Much of their contact with clients may be by phone, on-line, or in person, and more than one consultant who invested in a fancy logo and two-color stationery reports that his letterhead is used almost exclusively for invoices and the very few reports he prepares that aren't time sensitive. "I don't regret my expenditures on 'designed' stationery" says one such consultant, "but I can't attribute any business to it. It's more of a psychic pleasure than anything else."

The chances are that you can probably get along just fine with a letterhead you print on regular paper with your laser printer. One consultant who admits rather shamefacedly to using a rubber stamp on the envelopes used for his clients' bills, remarks, "Would you believe, I have more business than ever, and *no one* has mentioned it?"

Indeed, a little thought would suggest that it probably would make a lot more sense in business terms to invest your limited dollars in buying a better quality laser printer that has a host of business uses, rather than blowing it on stationery, much of which is likely to sit in a box in a closet or get thrown out when, as often happens, your office address or business name changes—or the phone company assigns you a new area code.

BROCHURES

The glossy brochure is another item that beginning computer consultants are tempted to spend money on. Many expect these brochures to be a powerful marketing tool and plan to start their businesses off by mass-mailing these brochures to bring in new clients. But while it is true that established consultants do indeed use glossy brochures, they do not consider them to be primary marketing tools. Instead, they use them, like their business cards, as reinforcers—something that the client can look at to help them remember who the consultant is after an initial contact; or else they use their brochures to make a specific point, for example, to stress their area of expertise.

Custom software developer Paul Ferrara says, "I use a professionally prepared brochure that tells them why they should use custom software and why we should be the ones to write it. I usually give one of these out at the first meeting along with a client list on letterhead." Ferrara adds that if a client shows serious interest, he gives him an additional one-page list of five references that includes information about the jobs his firm did for each client.

The problem with brochures for the beginning consultant is that, because of the high cost of having them designed and printed, the consultant has to keep the information on them relatively generic. But often what is needed to clinch the sale—or attract a particular client—is a reinforcer that includes very targeted specific information of a kind that is not appropriate for a brochure.

Clearly then, if your budget for such things is limited, the brochure might be a dispensable item. Contract programmer Burt Johnson says, "I have found no particular benefit to a brochure, myself. Also, none of the successful software consultants that I know in this area have one." Consultant Edward Branley agrees that a brochure is probably not very useful to consultants specializing in contract programming work. Their clients want very specific information about the previous projects that the consultant has completed. He recommends brochures only to consultants providing general small business support.

Pointing up the fact that brochures are not a magic wand you wave to bring in new clients, in 1991 a CONSULT Forum study group ran a special brochure workshop. Members mailed each other their brochures for critiquing and suggested numerous improvements. While the exercise was enjoyed by all, and many useful suggestions emerged, months later most of the workshop members confided that they could not attribute any new business to their improved brochures.

However, the brochures that did result from the workshop are still worth some attention. One of the best is shown in Figure 4-2. It manages to do a good job of mixing generic appeal with specific detail, and of reminding the client of the kind of work the consultants do as well as of their impressive qualifications and experience.

A much cheaper alternative to buying professionally printed brochures that beginning consultants might do well to consider is to buy preprinted blank brochure forms, such as the beautifully designed ones available from the mail-order company, Paper Direct, and to print their text on these forms themselves using their laser printers. Four-color professionally designed preprinted brochure forms are available in a dizzying array of designs, and can be purchased in quantities as small as one hundred, for about twenty cents apiece. Brochures produced this way can be more attractive than far more expensive brochures produced by a mediocre print shop. Best of all you can print this type of brochure on demand and can modify the copy to suit the particular use you have in mind.

RESUMES

An alternative to the brochure that many consultants use, particularly those who do contract programming, is a resume. Some consultants consider the use of a resume to be unprofessional, smacking too much of salaried employment and thus undercutting the image that they'd like to project. But other consultants report that their clients request re-

What Is CSS?

Creative Software Solutions is a small software consulting firm with offices in New York and New Jersey. CSS specializes in custom application development, particularly database management systems for PC and mainframe environments.

- ■
- ■
- ■

THE CSS PHILOSOPHY . . .

Creative Software Solutions approaches every project with the same four point philosophy:

1. *Solve the Right Problem.* Our personnel are highly trained and experienced in problem analysis. This allows them to understand your needs and determine the most cost-effective way to help you.

2. *Consider the Big Picture.* We do not work in a vacuum; we will not propose solutions that are at odds with other projects or your company strategies. Likewise, we will not propose solutions that render your existing technology useless.

3. *Apply Current Technology.* We participate in a number of professional societies and user's groups, and we stay in constant touch with current techniques and trends. We combine this information with your existing technology base to help you evolve smoothly.

4. *Deliver High Quality Work.* Most importantly, we do not consider a job complete unless it meets *your* needs, is fully documented, and can be maintained easily. And CSS does not stop there! We also offer training services and continuing support services.

CSS Services . . .

CONTRACT PROGRAMMING . . .

We can help supplement your staff with our contract programming services. Our personnel are available for custom program development on projects ranging from new systems to simple bug fixing. We have experts in many different programming languages, database packages, and environments.

MANAGEMENT CONSULTING . . .

We can help you define your needs and evaluate your options through our high-level management consulting services. We can assist you in systems analysis, system design, and database design. We also consult on a number of software engineering issues (for example, design and maintenance of systems), and conduct software selection studies. Because CSS does not have any affiliation with hardware or software vendors, we can provide objective recommendations based solely on your needs.

TRAINING . . .

CSS is in the business of consulting. That means we *share* the knowledge that we have. We do this informally whenever we are at your site, and formally through a series of courses designed to increase the productivity of your staff. Ask about our courses ranging from "Introduction to PCs" to "Topics in Software Engineering."

Our Principals . . .

KAREN ZILORA,
President

Karen holds a B.S. in chemical engineering from the University of Rochester, and an M.S. in chemical engineering from Columbia University. Since 1981, she has been designing and developing applications on mainframes and microcomputers. While Karen is experienced in a number of areas, her strongest expertise lies in systems analysis and database design. She enjoys all aspects of application development, particularly functional analysis, database design, and development of user interfaces. Karen also finds teaching very rewarding, and has taught courses at the college level and for various clients.

STEVE ZILORA,
Vice President

Steve holds a B.S. in chemical engineering from the University of Rochester and an M.S. in computer science from the New Jersey Institute of Technology. Steve has over 10 years of experience in process engineering and software development. This combination puts him in an excellent position to analyze the users' needs and deliver a software product that meets those needs. Steve is heavily involved in the issues of software engineering and is an active proponent of these principles in the American Institute of Chemical Engineering (AIChE). Steve's special area of expertise is software maintenance and software integration.

(continued on next page)

Creative Software Solutions

- ■
- ■
- ■

CSS can help you . . .

- ■ learn how to deliver systems on time and on budget
- ■ deliver systems faster without increasing your staff
- ■ get the expertise you need in key skill areas
- ■ incorporate new technology without sacrificing your existing investment in hardware and software
- ■ put new technology in perspective
- ■ integrate several programs into a single, cohesive package
- ■ evaluate commercial software (or your competitors' products) in an objective fashion

Creative Software Solutions, Inc.
P.O. Box 168
Penfield, NY 14526
(716) 377-4235
(800) 433-4408

Examples of Projects . . .

The corporate education and training unit of a client wanted to convert their inefficient paper-based system for tracking facilities and enrollments to an integrated computer application. CSS designed and delivered a multiuser LAN-based application to meet the diverse needs of their users. This integrated business application encompasses all administrative aspects of operating a corporate training center. Highlights of the system include interfaces to their corporate desktop publishing software for the production of corporate course catalogs, and use of bar code and OMR scanning technology for fast and accurate capture of course evaluation scores.

- ■

The cost tracking system of one of our clients stopped working when their parent company installed a new accounting system. CSS analyzed the undocumented tracking system, redefined the interfaces to the accounting system, and streamlined the data collection process from several days to less than an hour.

- ■

CSS conducted an extensive workflow analysis of a client's 200-person engineering department. As a result of the study, CSS proposed more than 30 recommendations for improving the productivity of the department and the quality of its work. Many of the recommendations were zero-cost solutions to problems identified during the study. Other recommendations included specifications for new computing tools to help streamline early design work and specifications for the integration of existing computing tools to minimize manual data entry by engineers.

- ■

An existing database management system, based on dataset storage, was unmaintainable, difficult to use, and unable to cope with changing user needs. CSS developed a prototype which utilized a VM/CMS windows-based front-end to an SQL/DS database, permitting easy access to the data and customizable reports. This new system allows many of the client's other programs to access the data, and its modular structure accommodates the need for frequent technology updates.

FIGURE 4-2 Sample brochure.

sumes from them and that they consider them an important item in their set of marketing tools.

Resumes provide a significant advantage to the consultant. Unlike the brochure, which requires great attention to layout and visual detail if it is not to look cheap and tacky, a respectable resume can be designed and printed by most consultants using only their word processor and a laser printer. This gives consultants the ability to be flexible and to custom tailor their resumes to the demands of a specific contract.

But you cannot just take the old resume you used when job hunting and give it to clients. An effective consultant's resume must be structured very differently from one used to seek employment and must be given a very different slant. As you are undoubtedly aware, there are many different ways to write a resume, each of which highlights a different aspect of the career it portrays. Look at the following example to see how differently the same job can be represented in a brief resume entry. First, here is a description of a project described with a management emphasis:

> Team Leader. Apr. 1995–Aug. 1996. Coordinated development of customer information query system, ABC Corporation. As leader of six-person development team was responsible for on-time delivery of state-of-the-art database system. Awarded "Company Star Performer" bonus.

Here is the same project described with a technology emphasis:

> Internet Development. ABC Corp. Apr. 1995–Aug. 1996. Led team that designed and implemented new intranet-based customer information query system replacing legacy DB2 system. System was written in Visual C++ and also used SQL Server, HTML, and CGI scripting to interface with a Sybase database server. Implementation resulted in a 45 percent decrease in system operation cost.

The first entry gets across the subject's leadership abilities—something that might be of little interest to a client looking for a consultant to develop a database. The second emphasizes technical skills and an employer-independent benefit—technology-linked cost cutting. This has immediate appeal to any client looking to implement a database solution.

Consultants should always rewrite their resumes to emphasize employer-independent skills and the kinds of benefits that the consultant can provide a client. Examine every sentence on your own resume to make sure it does this. Eliminate any irrelevant information. As an example of how he did this, consultant Nigel Dyson-Hudson explains, "I took my job-oriented resume: worked for xxx doing a, b, and c, and changed it to task-oriented: Programming—x, y, and z companies. Technical Writing—m, x, and z companies."

Remember that most people will only scan your resume. It's a good idea to provide clear-cut headings and highlighted keywords that get the gist of your selling points across during a casual inspection. If your strong point is your technical skills, provide a section that contains nothing but a list of acronyms surrounded by white space, so that they immediately leap out to the reader. If you have done work for clients whose names other clients will recognize and find impressive, a separate easy-to-read client list section might be called for, with a few words describing the projects you completed for these clients. Just make sure, of course, that any client you do mention is one that, if contacted, will put in a good word for you.

If you have only recently made the transition to consulting from salaried employment, it is not necessary to distinguish on your resume between work you did as an employee and work you did as a consultant. If you slant your resume properly, it should be possible to mention the name of the employer or client and the nature of the work done for either without giving any clue as to your status on the job. If the client asks, you should, of course, answer truthfully, but chances are that the client will be more interested in the skills you used and the benefits your work provided the people you did it for than in your job title while you did the work.

Finally, to avoid looking too much like an employee, do not mention references on your resume. If you get to a point where a client shows serious interest in bringing you in, it is appropriate to give them a separate detailed reference sheet that mentions specific clients by name and gives contact information. But this detailed information about other clients should never be on your resume. Not the least of the reasons for this is that should your resume fall into the hands of a broker or other competitor, the knowledge that your previous clients use a particular kind of consulting service could be used to woo them away from you.

ACCEPTING CREDIT CARDS

If you intend to sell services or software to the public or to small businesses, you may consider getting merchant status—the ability to process credit card transactions. To find out how to establish merchant status, contact your bank. Some banks will issue you merchant status themselves. Others may refer you to a third-party vendor, particularly if you do not maintain a storefront. When applying for merchant status, you should expect to pay a setup fee in the hundred dollar range, a monthly statement fee, a fee for processing each transaction, and the costs of either renting a card-processing machine or buying card-processing software. Beyond these expenses, you'll also pay the credit card issuer 2–3 percent of the amount charged to the card. Given the expense involved, unless you foresee processing a lot of card transactions, it may be simpler to refuse to accept credit cards, as many computer consultants do.

If you do accept credit cards, you'll need to be careful to deliver any products charged to a credit card in a way that provides you with a proof of delivery. This is because dissatisfied buyers can refuse to pay a credit card charge claiming that they did not receive the goods bought with the credit card. Shipping goods via Federal Express or another carrier who requires a signature is one way of preventing this sort of problem. If you deliver goods yourself, make sure you have the client sign for them at delivery. If too many clients complain to your credit card processor about problems with your company, you may lose the ability to process cards.

DO YOU NEED A COMPANY CAR?

Although it may seem like a good idea to buy or lease a car for your consulting company because of the tax deductions that this strategy might generate, there is a hidden pitfall here. As Bob Upham, a CONSULT sysop, points out, it may be a better strategy to "lease it personally and have the company reimburse you for the expense associated with its business use." Why? Because "business insurance is VERY high. When I looked into it, the cost was more than three times the amount of a personal policy."

HOW USEFUL ARE WEB SITES?

A Web site might seem like the most natural marketing medium for your new consulting business, but there are some hidden pitfalls. It takes time and effort to design a good site, and many consultants who have set them up report that they end up taking a lot more time than they'd originally estimated—five times as much, several consultants report. One solution many busy consultants find to this problem is to pay a professional to design and maintain the site for them. However, this can be expensive, and it is by no means certain that you will earn back the costs of the site from the new business it generates for you. Cheaper generic Web mall sites or listings in consulting directories that take forever to come up and then do nothing more than display your phone number and address are more likely to annoy a prospect rather than impress them with your abilities.

Experienced consultants report that even the best sites rarely bring in totally new clients. Even when a consultant's site gets plenty of hits—

particularly if it offers substantive information rather than just self-puffery—most of these hits are likely to be from random surfers or from people looking for free advice. As one consultant says of the contacts generated by his page, "Too often they are from people expecting me to give them advice or solve their problems by e-mail for nothing. They seem to feel that their problem is too small to charge for."

Consultants do find their Web sites useful as a central repository for the kinds of information that they used to mail out to prospects after making an initial contact. Once you have a site, you can refer potential clients to it to view your brochure, read up on the products or technology you support, or to review your listings of past clients and previous projects. You can also use your site to provide detailed contact information, answers to commonly asked questions, or to provide visitors with pages from a newsletter that enhances your professional image. Ed Yourdon reports that when people ask him, "Do you have an outline and seminar description of your presentation on object-oriented widgets?" he merely replies, "Yes, look on my Web page."

Paul Ferrara has come up with another highly useful function for his Web site. He says that it "saves us hundreds of dollars per month in shipping costs" because clients can download upgrades to his Accounting for Delphi software package directly from his site, rather than having him mail them out.

But if you are just starting out in business and are not already running your own Internet server, the costs—both in time and money—of setting up a serious Web site may be prohibitive. Beyond the costs of renting a site on an Internet Service Provider's (ISP) server and establishing your own domain name, you'll also have to cover the cost of developing a professional looking site and keeping it up-to-date. That's why, when you are just setting up a new practice, unless you already have some experience with Web site design or are planning to concentrate on selling sophisticated Web site design services to your clients, it is probably not worth paying to have a high-end site designed for you.

If you want to test the waters, you might consider setting up a do-it-yourself site on a free homepage that is offered as part of a monthly subscription to a local ISP. You may find that the servers that provide these free sites are not set up to provide sophisticated client-side functions such as CGI script processing and database retrieval. But even with such limitations, after a few hours of fooling around with an HTML editor, you should be able to design a pilot site that provides a lot of information to potential clients and gives them the ability to contact you through e-mail or via a well-designed form that generates e-mail. Setting up a test site this way can give you a much better idea of what you can expect from a more sophisticated site while allowing you to save your money for more effective marketing efforts.

If you decide to set up a site, investigate the reliability and speed of the ISP's server before committing your page to it. One consultant reports, "The biggest mistake we made was in choosing an Internet service provider. We went with what we thought was a large provider. They were, but their services were not. They did not provide us with help when we needed it. Often requests for support would go several weeks before they even acknowledged we had sent them one." If your server has problems responding quickly to requests for your page, visitors who attempt to retrieve it may instead experience timeouts and receive "page not found" messages, or your page may drop off the indexes.

Another mistake to avoid is getting overly enthusiastic when your site is new. As another consultant reports, "The mistake I made was putting it up too fast. I had my site complete to where I thought it looked good, loaded it up to my server, then submitted my URL everywhere. Then as I looked at other sites and mine, I realized it didn't really appear that good. Now everyone was checking out my site because of the URL submissions, and they were greeted with a not-so-pleasing site. So I would say, wait until your site makes you jump out of your seat and yell 'That's it!' before you offer it to the world."

Yet another common mistake is to fill your pages with self-indulgent graphics that load quickly when you test them on your own machine but take many minutes for visitors to load over the Net. Nothing is more annoying than a long wait for a homepage. So keep your graphics loading quickly by keeping them not much bigger than icon size, and ask yourself just how interesting a larger graphic might be to a visitor before you subject them to a long wait. You'll impress everyone with your pages' speed if, unlike 90 percent of page designers on the Web, you remember to include height and width parameters on every image reference so that the text portions of your page can be displayed before slower graphics files are completely downloaded.

Finally, before you get carried away with all the bells and whistles you can put on your page, remember that your visitors will not be using the same kind of monitor or browser as you are. What looks gorgeous on your high-res monitor using the latest Netscape extensions may be unreadable when displayed on your prospect's Packard Bell home computer running an old copy of Mosaic. You'll need to test your pages carefully on a variety of platforms and browsers before publishing them to the world.

5

WHAT SHOULD YOU CHARGE?

Perhaps the most anxiety-provoking question that new consultants face is "How much should I charge for my services?" No matter what rate new consultants settle on, or what billing techniques they employ, there will always be someone who claims to be billing twice as much and whose boasting makes them wonder if they've made a stupid mistake. But the thought of raising rates brings with it another set of anxieties. New consultants worry that too high a rate will repel clients and destroy their new practices before they get off the ground. Indeed, many are tempted to lower their rates, worrying that they are missing out on business opportunities by not offering potential clients free samples and hefty discounts.

Once they've settled on a rate, consultants still face additional dilemmas. For which of the many hours they spend at work should they be billing their clients? Is a phone call to be treated as billable time? What about the time they spend in local travel? Who should pay for the hotel when the consultant goes out of town? And the questions don't end there. What about hardware sales? Many new consultants wonder whether they are missing out on a financial bonanza by not reselling hardware—while consultants who are resellers often wonder whether they'd be better off billing only for their advice and leaving the headaches of hardware sales to others.

Learning how to charge for your work properly will be among the most difficult challenges you will face as a new consultant. The penalty for error can be severe. Many a consultant has learned the difference between income and profit the hard way, working busily for weeks or even months only to see the money he has earned get eaten up by unforeseen expenses.

But rate-setting is not a black art. There are tried and tested methods you can use to arrive at a rate you can live with. This chapter describes how experienced consultants establish their rates. We'll share with you some things they've learned in the process so you can begin to understand what you will have to charge to stay in business and how you can use the rates you charge to attract the kinds of clients you want to serve and to keep them satisfied.

TIME AND MATERIALS: BILLING AN HOURLY RATE

The billing technique used by most computer consultants is to bill for time and materials, often abbreviated T&M. Under this arrangement consultants charge their clients an hourly rate for the time they devote to their projects and pass through to them the costs of any software or hardware they buy on the client's behalf.

Under a T&M arrangement, a consultant who has installed an accounting system for a client would charge for this work by billing the client $1,500 to cover twenty hours of time charged at a rate of $75 per hour, and would then add to his invoice the itemized costs of the equipment installed by the consultant, such as a mail-order computer and printer, as well as the retail cost of the accounting package that the consultant customized for him. Using this method to bill for projects is generally the safest way for a new consultant to start out, but it requires some research to set an appropriate hourly rate that cheats neither yourself nor your client.

WHAT DO OTHER CONSULTANTS CHARGE?

To get some idea of the range of hourly rates computer consultants charge, we'll turn to the results of my 1996 Real Rate Survey. The survey was posted on several CompuServe forums in February of 1996 and then moved to my Computer Consultant's Resource Page Web site, where visitors could contribute their own rates by filling in a form. Respondents were asked to describe the rates charged by actual consultants working on real contracts, including the length of the contract, the language, platform, or niche involved, whether it was brokered, and any relevant information about their experience level.

The following information was extracted from an analysis of the first 201 rates submitted to the Real Rate Survey. As is the case with just about every survey of consulting rates I've seen, this survey revealed a wide range of rates—from $15 to $200 per hour. However, it is significant that more than half of all the rates collected clustered within $15 per hour of the median rate, which was $55 per hour for brokered consultants and subcontractors and $65 per hour for independents working without middlemen.

When the rates were broken down by type of work, significant differences emerged. As you can see in Figures 5-1 and 5-2, the median rates by specialty ranged from a low of $42 per hour for work with the end-user-oriented Microsoft Access database to a high of $104.50 for programming and design in Smalltalk, a complex object-oriented programming language. However, it is worth noting that 57 percent of the rates reported were reported by consultants working in specialties whose median rates fell in the lower, $40 to $59 per hour, range while only 4 percent of the total rates reported applied to specialties whose median rates were about $80 per hour. So the rarity of consultants working in these niches may explain their ability to charge these premium rates.

When rates were broken down by geographical distribution, another important trend emerged. Although rates covered a wide range in almost all regions, median rates by region tracked pretty closely to the costs of living in those regions. As you can see from Figure 5-3, the median rates billed by consultants working in high-cost urban areas such as Southern California, New York, Chicago, and Philadelphia were more than $30 an hour higher than the median rate billed by consultants working in the American South.

The length of the contract is yet another factor that had an impact on rates. As you can see from Figure 5-4, the highest median rate is found in the group of contracts lasting under a week—many of them only lasting a couple of hours. Many of the very highest rates reported were charged for these brief assignments. The rest of the median rates clustered within a narrow $10 per hour range extending from $55 to $65 per hour. The median rates were higher for contracts lasting from three to nine months than for longer contracts. This probably reflects the fact that longer contracts tend to be worked by brokered contract programmers whose rates, as we have seen above, tend to be lower.

There was no indication that either vendor-supplied certifications like the CNE or MCP or advanced university degrees improved the rate the consultant could charge (Figure 5-5). Consultants who cited certifications in their survey replies reported rates from $30 to $130 per hour, but their median rate was only $50 per hour—less than the median rate for the whole group. The median rate of consultants who cited graduate degrees in their survey responses was even lower—$32 per hour, and that group included some of the lowest rates in the survey. This probably reflects the fact that consultants who listed their degrees in the survey "experience" field rather than real-world hardware and software experience were less experienced than the group at large.

There was little correlation between consultants' years of experience and their rates (Figure 5-6). While consultants with the longest careers showed slightly higher median rates than those who had just started out, those with 5 to 10 years of experience had lower median rates than less-experienced consultants. This is probably because it is these consultants

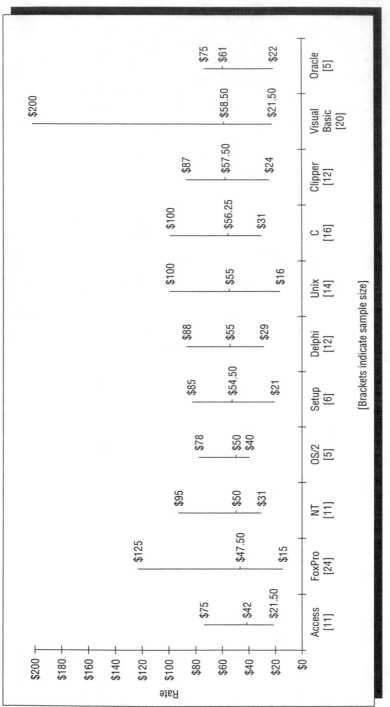

FIGURE 5-1 High, low, and median rates by specialty, part 1.

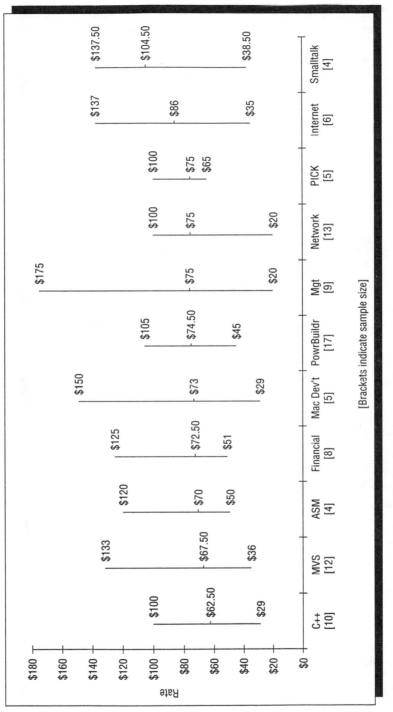

FIGURE 5-2 High, low, and median rates by specialty, part 2.

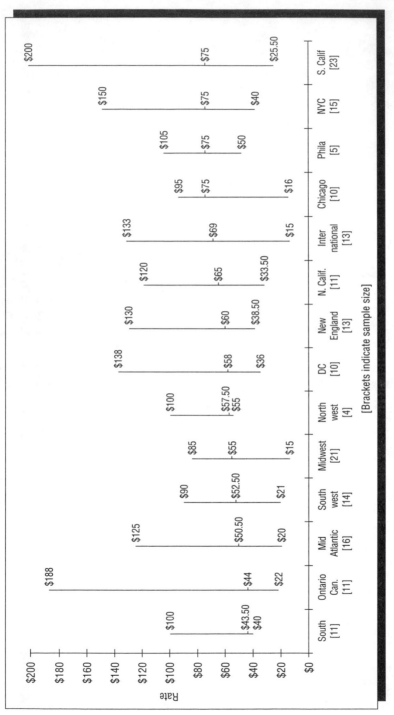

FIGURE 5-3 High, low, and median rates by region.

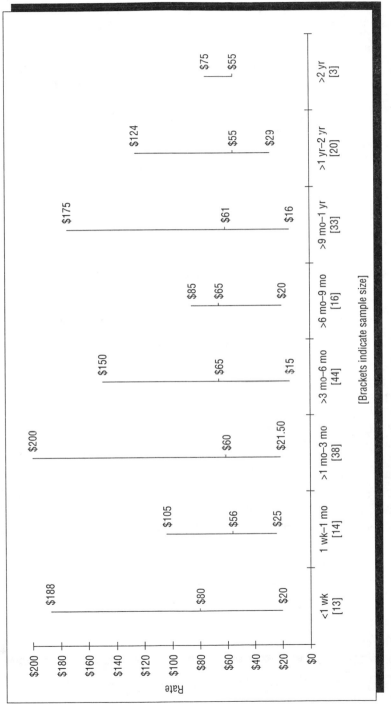

FIGURE 5-4 High, low, and median rates by length of contract.

91

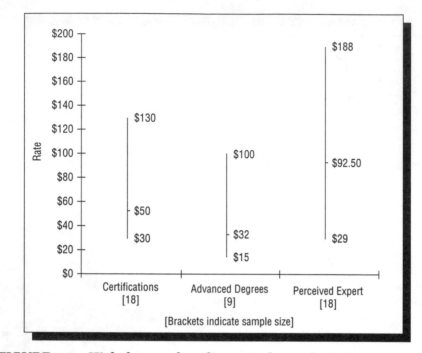

FIGURE 5-5   High, low, and median rates by credential.

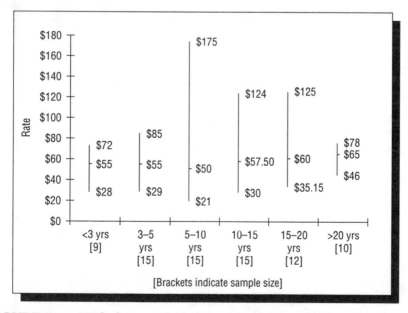

FIGURE 5-6   High, low, and median rates by reported years of experience.

who are likely to have specialized in technologies that were hot 5 years ago and are now becoming obsolete.

The survey did turn up a clear link between the consultants' skill levels and their rates. Consultants billing $100 per hour and more for long-term contracts almost always reported highly specialized skills such as the ability to reverse engineer ASM code or to manage a methodology-intensive MIS project. Higher rates also tracked well against the perceived complexity of the task, with those providing technically sophisticated services such as network planning or financial analysis to large corporate clients earning the highest rates overall.

SETTING A RATE USING THE GOING RATE

So you can see now that to set your own rate you must consider a number of factors. You'll need to determine what rates are usual for consultants working in your own specialty. You'll need to take into account how the local economy where you live will affect your rate. You'll need to consider how long the contracts you plan to work will typically last and how that length will affect your rate, and you need to have a good idea of where you fall, personally, on the spectrum of perceived expertise. The best way to find the answers you need to do all this is to attend local functions where you can meet other local consultants working in niches similar to your own and to ask them what kind of rates they are charging. But doing this requires tact and a certain amount of cunning. If you ask people point-blank what they charge, the answers you will get may be misleading. Consultants tend to inflate their own rates because of a belief that if they admit to charging a lower rate than what they hear others bragging about, they will be perceived as failures. As a result, when you ask consultants directly what their own rates might be they are likely to cite the highest and most impressive rate they've ever been able to bill rather than the much lower rate they bill to most of their clients. The person who tells you he bills $125 per hour frequently leaves out the information that he's only been able to find ten hours of that kind of work in the past year and he has billed out all the rest of his time at $40 per hour.

A better way of eliciting rate information is to ask other consultants what they think you should bill, or what they believe the going rate to be in the region for your specialty, making it clear by your manner of asking that you know that someone as successful as they are can bill much higher amounts. A query phrased in this way is much more likely to bear fruit.

Another way to determine the going rate is to talk with several local consulting brokers and ask them what they could pay you for your services billed on an hourly basis. When they give you a figure, add an additional 40 percent (20 percent outside the United States) to it to account for the broker's hefty commission, and you will have the hourly rate they would be billing their clients for your work. However, remember that brokers usually place only people who do programming work and rarely work with consultants who do systems integration or who offer services to small businesses. To determine the going rates for these other types of nonbrokered work you'll have to rely on your network of consulting acquaintances.

You can also use the resources available on the Internet to learn what other consultants are charging. We update The Computer Consultant's Resource Page Real Rate Survey every few weeks so it makes a good place to stop in to learn what other consultants are charging. Find its current location by searching for "Janet Ruhl" on any of the popular Web indexes. You can also often get information about current rates by posting messages on the Compuserve forum or Internet newsgroup that serves people in your specialty.

If all else fails, another way of determining the going rate is to ask businesspeople who use consultants what they'd expect to pay for your kind of services. But don't stamp yourself as an amateur by asking this of your own potential clients!

ESTABLISHING A RATE BASED ON EXPENSES

Experienced consultants who've been in business for some time often take another approach to rate setting and base their rate on their estimates of what it costs them to do business. These consultants estimate their expenses, set an income target, and then calculate the hourly rate that will cover these expenses and yield the income they want to earn. Consultants who figure their rates this way usually assume that they will be able to bill a thousand hours a year, or roughly half of the hours that a salaried employee is paid for. This thousand-hour figure may turn out to be more hours than the typical consultant can find of premium high-level consulting work, and it is considerably fewer hours than a top-notch contract programmer can expect to bill, but it is the figure that CPAs and other professionals who bill on an hourly basis use when estimating their annual hours, so given the uncertainties of this kind of estimate it serves as a useful standard, and one most likely to yield a usable result.

Briefly stated, this method uses the following formula:

$$\frac{\text{Desired Gross Income} + \text{Total Expenses}}{1000} = \text{Hourly Rate}$$

There are pitfalls to using this system, particularly if you are new to consulting and have little practical experience of what market conditions are like or what your expenses are likely to be. If you decide you'd like to net $100K a year, the formula above may suggest that to meet your goal you will have to charge $140 per hour. But the rate survey we looked at earlier shows that this rate is so much higher than the rates most computer consultants charge anywhere that it is unlikely you'll find any work at that rate at all unless you are extremely well established. While it is very possible to earn an income of $100,000 a year or more from computer consulting, almost all the consultants who do, achieve their goal not by charging extremely high rates but by working a greater numbers of hours per year at normal rates.

Nevertheless, this system of calculating rates is very useful in protecting you from committing one of the most disastrous mistakes new consultants make: charging a rate that is too low to allow you to build up a sustainable consulting practice. Beginning consultants are often tempted to keep their rates low in the hopes of attracting new clients and getting work that they would otherwise miss out on. But in doing this they often neglect to consider the expenses of running their business and in the worst case they may end up charging a rate that doesn't even cover those expenses, so that their work ends up costing them money.

Estimating Your Expenses

To use this method of estimating rates effectively, you need to have a good idea of what the expenses of running a computer consulting practice are likely to be. Here are the most significant overhead items encountered by computer consultants:

- The costs of the hardware and software they need to keep up with a rapidly evolving technology
- The costs of seminars and classes that also help them keep up with that technology
- Phone costs
- Travel costs
- Marketing costs
- The cost of office supplies
- The cost of health insurance and disability insurance

The costs of hardware, education, and insurance alone can easily add up to $15,000 in expenses, eating up a full $15 of the rate billed for every one of those estimated 1,000 hours. Table 5-1 shows a typical consultant's annual expenses.

The expenses incurred by different kinds of consultants vary widely. Contract programmers who perform work on a client's mainframe at the client's site are going to run up far lower expenses than PC consultants

TABLE 5-1   Sample Consultant Annual Expense Sheet

Postage for newsletter mailing (400 copies four times a year)	$ 464
Printing cost of newsletter	480
Other postage	125
Phone (business phone plus long distance)	927
Local seminars	1,800
Professional conference (registration, travel, hotel)	1,750
Hardware	5,276
Software	4,322
Online/Internet/Web Site	1,540
Health insurance	2,825
Disability insurance	1,750
Business insurance	450
Local travel (car expenses, gas, tolls, parking)	1,773
Legal, accounting services	2,275
Miscellaneous	2,482
TOTAL	$28,239

who must be able to duplicate a client's network in a home office. This method of rate setting makes it clear why such contract programmers may be able to charge a lower rate and still end up netting more income than a PC systems integrator. It also makes it clear why consultants who must do a lot of long-distance travel to serve clients, such as trainers, must charge a higher-than-usual rate to cover their necessarily higher expenses.

If you decide to use this system, it is a good idea to resist the temptation to include in your list of expenses items like the costs of normal commuting, lunch, and maintaining a business wardrobe. You will not be paying more for these items than you did as an employee and including them in your estimates might tempt you to artificially inflate your rate.

But when you are just starting out, no matter how conservative you might be, you probably won't be able to come up with an accurate estimate of your expenses. Nor are you likely to estimate correctly how many hours you will be able to bill. So as a new consultant you should be cautious when using this approach, and employ it mostly to sanity check a rate you've come up with using another technique, to make sure that it isn't going to be too low to provide you a living, rather than relying on it as a technique for coming up with a hard-and-fast figure.

Only when you have been in business for a few years and have enough historical data to be able to predict income and expenses accurately will this method become an effective way of setting your rate.

SETTING YOUR RATE USING A SIMPLE RULE OF THUMB

There is yet another way of setting a rate—one that has the advantage of mind-blistering simplicity. As consultant Charles Wangersky explains, to use this technique you simply "take the annual salary that a person of your experience would be receiving and divide by one thousand. As a concrete example: If your current salary is $45,000 per year, charge $45 per hour." Given that most MIS professionals who have worked in industry for seven to ten years are earning annual salaries in the $45,000 to $65,000 range, and that median consulting rates seem to cluster around $50 per hour, it certainly does look like this method may be used by more consultants than might be willing to admit to using such a simplistic technique.

SHOULD YOU CHARGE DIFFERENT RATES FOR DIFFERENT WORK?

No discussion of hourly rates can be complete without mentioning another controversy that rages among computer consultants: whether, once you've set a rate, you should apply it to all your clients all the time, or whether you should adjust it to fit different circumstances.

There is absolutely no unanimity on this question among computer consultants. "If you are programming, you are going to charge a different rate than if you are documenting or training," says consultant Sharon J. Podlin. "You will even charge different rates within a category. For example, I charge more to train Networking or C programming than I do to teach a WordPerfect class. There are two reasons for this: I can teach WordPerfect in my sleep and therefore it requires no prep time, and frankly, I can get more for networking or programming classes." In contrast, consultant Michael Devore states, "You should *never* charge more than your standard work fee simply because the client can afford it. To me that's borderline unethical."

Reasons for Higher-than-Usual Rates

Consultants who believe it's legitimate to charge a higher rate in some situations give many reasons why they do so. Consultant Richard K. Herzog says it's worth considering raising your rate in the situation where "You really don't want to do the job because they really want you to do something you're good at but hate." He says that he'd also consider raising his rate when the client "can afford it and it's what they expect to pay for quality work."

This second point is worth some further attention. Although the point is hotly debated among consultants, a significant number of consultants support the argument that certain kinds of clients may reject your services if they are priced too low. As David S. Reich explains it, "If a client thinks, incorrectly, that a consultant of the quality they are seeking would charge a higher rate than your usual rate, and if your rate is a lot lower, they will assume that you are not a good enough consultant for them." He adds that this kind of client is usually a naive one who does not have the technical ability to evaluate your skills and thus uses the rate as a measuring stick. Consultant Larry Bradshaw agrees. "If you are way below their number, they'll consider you incompetent or stupid. It pays to identify [the client's] numbers by market research prior to opening discussions with them."

Another situation in which some experienced consultants argue it is advisable to charge a higher rate to one client than to another is one in which the client only wants to buy an hour or two of your time. If you must drive to the client's site, spend time recalling all the details of his application, and drive home, the one hour the client is willing to pay for may well eat up two or three hours of your day. A higher billing rate for such short assignments will compensate for the lost time involved in filling them and may also keep clients from demanding a lot of one-hour visits except when they are truly necessary.

Why and When You Should Raise Your Rates

Many new consultants believe that they must keep their rates low or else risk scaring away clients, or they may feel that the only way to get a foot in the door is to compete with other consultants on price and offer clients a lower rate as an incentive to give them a chance to break in. They assume that the higher their rates, the less likely they are to find work. But the experience of some experienced consultants contradicts this assumption. These consultants report that when they have raised their own rates dramatically, rather than losing work, they actually found themselves busier!

John C. Brobston's experience provides a good example of this. "I used to charge what seemed a high rate to me," he relates. "The business I got was generally spotty. They always tried to negotiate me down, and I kept getting bombed with 'my brother-in-law says you should have used Unix, Novell, INET, Lantastic, Concurrent DOS'—pick one. I now charge more than twice that rate. Nobody negotiates. Nobody listens to their brother-in-law, and I get twice the sales volume—which surprised the living daylights out of me. I had heard this below but was surprised to find that it was true."

Brobston explains the phenomenon by saying, "The rate you set affects the way you come across to the client. If your rate is one value then you are equated to a tradesman—a plumber or electrician, for example. If your rate is another value, you are equated to a professional, a doctor or lawyer." Consultant Roger Loeb experienced something similar. "A few years ago I doubled my rates," he says. "This had the consequences of more than doubling my income, [getting] several new clients calling and expecting me to drop everything and take on their assignment, and interfering with my diligent pursuit of fly-fishing, skiing, skeetshooting, eating, wine tasting, hiking, camping, and eating chocolate."

Rather than worrying about scaring off a client with a rate that is too high, these consultants suggest you should *look at the higher rate as a screening mechanism.* "Since keeping a client is easier than finding a new one, it makes sense to invest in your relationships with those clients who can afford your services," says consultant David Welcher. "If the client cannot afford to pay your rates, then find another client. You won't be happy working for less and he won't keep you very long."

Consultant Rud Merriam says that when a client is very resistant to the rate he has quoted, and when he knows that the rate is well within the range for the kind of service he is providing, he often attempts to discourage the client from working with him because he knows that an initial negative reaction to the rate means that "subsequently they were going to drive me crazy trying to reduce costs or be really critical to make sure they got their money's worth." John Brobston agrees, explaining that the clients who insist on hiring the bargain $35-per-hour consultant "are the ones who ask me to come to a meeting which I sit through for eight hours in which about ten minutes' of business gets transacted, then tell me that they aren't going to pay me because I can 'get business' as a result of the meeting. They are also the ones who owe you $15,000 and want to pay $500 per month with no interest." He explains too, that while clients may select a $100-per-hour consultant over one who charges $120 per hour, they won't hire a $25-per-hour consultant to do anything for which they expect to need continuing support.

But it is tough knowing when you are ready to raise your rates, and whether you will be one of the fortunate ones who find this strategy works for them. Gerry Verdone, who has been consulting since 1984, says "no matter what your rate is, someone will scoff at it—usually out of ignorance." He suggests using this simple rule to determine whether your rates are right: "If too many potential clients scoff at your rate, it's probably too high. Whenever a client remarks that your rates are too low, raise them."

Consultant John Hale uses another method to decide when it's time to raise his rates. He explains, "I decided to work no more than fifty hours per week all together—billable and nonbillable work. When I'm consistently seventy to eighty percent sold out, it's time to raise rates, effective immediately with new clients and six months later for existing clients. Rates are high enough when my billable hours slip back down to fifty percent or so, with no loss of income. When I stay at this plateau for too long, I'll know I'm at the top of the market for my particular combination of specialty, technical, and people skills."

Charging Less Than Usual

While it's nice to contemplate being in a position to raise your rates this way, new consultants are more tempted to lower their rates in the hope that by doing so they can attract new clients and build up their practice. The most extreme examples of this are the consultants who work for free, hoping that giving potential clients a free sample of their work will convince them to bring them in for paying assignments. This might sound like an appealing marketing strategy, but selling consulting is not like selling ice cream, and this strategy has a tendency to backfire. Many consultants report that few if any of the people who take advantage of work they do for free ever offer to pay for that same kind of work. As one consultant remarked ruefully, "I still give away far too much, but now it's because I really want to do it, and not with the expectation of landing a client. It does sometimes lead to work, but most of the time it's just fun."

Consultant Bill Fries sounds a similar theme when he explains, "My philosophy about free information goes something like this: If you force someone to pay for advice, then they will see the wisdom and value. My experiences bear out the fact that advice with no strings attached is not used, appreciated, or valued. Learn to charge what you are worth, provide value for that advice, hold your head high, and know that time is money and free advice costs you time."

But many consultants have found that discounting their rates, rather than working for free, can be a useful strategy. As one consultant explains, "We have a 'published' rate schedule that we use. We have often deviated downward from the schedule according to the duration of the project, the type of client, the probability and potential for future business, the value of the reference, and how badly we wanted/needed/were interested in the project. We have never gone above the schedule and I suspect that we never will. We would probably just create a new schedule and continue to discount from the new base."

Consultant Larry Bradshaw adds that if you do discount your rate it is important to be clear about what you are doing and why you are doing it. "My best clients today," he says, "are the ones I approached when I first went into business and said, 'I'm just now going into business and I'd like to offer my services to you. Initially, my rates will be rather low as I've no intention of billing you for experience I cannot yet offer.'" But he still cautions new consultants not to price their services below a certain floor—in his region it is $45 per hour—explaining that "anyone who charges less than that is not regarded as a serious professional with professional expenses."

But even here there is no agreement. Longtime custom software developer Paul Ferrara asserts that "someone relatively new to the business, and even some not so new, should take every job they can get that falls into their area of expertise, and the hell with the rate." Although the consultant might make less money this way, Ferrara argues that in the long run he will end up with "twice as many clients, twice as many references, twice as much experience."

Using Discounts to Influence Client Behavior

Rather than cut their rate, many consultants prefer to negotiate with clients for discounts that encourage clients to behave in ways that benefit the consultant. The *volume discount* is one such arrangement. Many consultants offer a client a hefty discount, often 30 or 40 percent of their usual rate, once some target number of hours has been billed and paid for, anywhere from five hundred or more hours. Consultants who use this approach argue that when working under such long-term arrangements their costs are lower because they don't have to invest as much time and effort into marketing their services. However, not all consultants believe this to be a good idea. Some experienced consultants caution that this kind of arrangement tends to lure consultants into becoming too dependent on a small number of clients and thus prone to failure if their big clients suddenly cease needing their services.

Rather than offering an explicit discount, other consultants report that they sometimes discount their rates by "eating some hours" in order to build goodwill with a good, steady client, either by doing a bit of additional work for no charge, fixing something for free, or doing a fixed-price contract at a lower-than-usual cost. By not explicitly offering a discounted rate they don't raise the client's expectation that they will continue to work for a lower rate, but they still are able to reward a client for continuing patronage.

Another kind of discount that some consultants have experimented with is one that gives a client a small discount for prompt payment. Collecting fees in a timely manner is one of the biggest headaches that independent consultants face, so it is tempting to offer the client a two or three percent discount in exchange for payment terms specifying "payment net 15" or "net 30," rather than having to wait many months for the client to pay. Unfortunately, consultants who have tried this approach report that while clients are happy to sign contracts with such terms, they very rarely have any impact on payment schedules. Most accounting departments pay their bills as long after receiving them as possible. Therefore, as consultant Curtis Russell warns, before you offer clients a prompt payment discount you should "keep in mind that almost all accounts payable managers will take the discount and pay late anyway, knowing that unless they really abuse the situation no one will waste time to follow up on that two percent unless it's a really big bill."

FIXED BIDS

Up until now we've been talking exclusively as if computer consultants only charged for their services using an hourly rate. But this method of billing is not the only method available to consultants. If you've looked through any of the more generic books describing consulting, you've already discovered that there is an alternative, one that many people consider more professional than billing on an hourly basis: the fixed bid.

The idea behind a fixed bid is simple. You estimate the actual time it will take you to do the project, throw in a bit of extra to cover errors in your estimate, and then give the client a set price for the whole operation. This arrangement is appealing to clients because they know at the outset what the entire cost of the project will be and don't have to worry that you will artificially inflate your hours to boost your profits. The appeal to the consultant is that if you are more efficient and more highly skilled than other consultants, or if you know that you can adapt already existing code to the new requirements rather than having to do the work from scratch, you can present the client with a finished product very quickly, and make a much higher sum than you could if you were only charging for the actual hours worked.

The Problem with the Fixed Bid

It's an attractive concept, but one that rarely works out to the consultant's benefit. "Every time I've done one I've regretted it," says one experienced consultant. "I've lost my shirt a few times before I learned to estimate properly," says another, adding, "And I've lost it once or twice since, if the truth be known." Yet another experienced consultant claims, "When I first started, I accepted several fixed fee contracts and I was burned on each and every one." "Don't do work on a fixed price if you can ever avoid it," cautions another, explaining, "Fixed price is bad for you and potentially very bad for the client. It means either you get screwed or your client gets overcharged. In order to bid fixed price you must overbid. This is just a fact. It does not reflect well on you or your practice."

The reasons for this are simple. As consultant John Edwards explains, "You quote the client a $2,000 flat rate fee. You expect the conversion process to take about one week. And then it happens. The inevitable snafu. A series of glitches and other dilemmas occur. The project you once thought was going to take a week now extends into three, four, and yes, possibly a six- to eight-week engagement." In the end, he explains, you end up earning approximately $250 per week before taxes.

You may think this only happens to beginners who don't know what they're doing. But it doesn't. Any number of things can go wrong in a software- or hardware-based project that are beyond the control of the consultant. Manufacturers deliver defective equipment and it takes a week to get the correct replacement parts. The off-the-shelf software you depend on turns out not to work on the client's system and it takes the consultant three days to determine that it is some incompatibility in the client's hardware or an "undocumented feature" of the software causing the problem. Perhaps the client's employees aren't as enthusiastic about the new system as the boss is and show their displeasure by being unavailable for meetings or by "accidentally" giving the consultant incorrect files to work with.

Even if none of these events occurs, most consultants, even extremely competent ones, find it extremely difficult to come up with accurate estimates. As one consultant sums it up, "The job always takes longer and rarely, rarely, shorter than your estimate. You frequently 'forget' to list some work that needs to be done. You rarely estimate work that doesn't need to be done."

There's another major problem with fixed bids when applied to technical projects: often the clients who are the most enthusiastic about this kind of contract are those who do not understand what is involved in developing custom software who are the least likely to be able to provide you with a clearly thought out project description at the outset of the project. As one consultant complains, "They will ask for fixed bids on a piece of software when they have invested zero time and effort in defining what the software will do through requirements and functional specifications." He personally finds this insulting and asks, "Would someone ask a construction firm to fixed bid on a building with no floor plans?"

Computer consultant Steve Zilora explains that many clients, even those with technical backgrounds themselves, simply to not understand the software development cycle. In dealing with the chemical engineers who make up a big part of his client base he's found, "Here's a bunch of people who would never even consider building a reactor without plenty of up-front work. But the thought of applying the same principles to software development is foreign to them."

Because of widespread client ignorance of the realities of software development, the fixed bid has one other major drawback for the consultant who attempts to develop software and hardware solutions for the client under this arrangement. As Burt Johnson explains, "A fixed bid puts us on opposite sides of the table every time we talk. If [the client] wants to add or change something, I am over on the other side of the table as an adversary telling him the cost, instead of being on his team helping him improve the idea still further."

Making Fixed Bids Work

Even so, some consultants report that there are a few situations in which they find working under a fixed-bid arrangement advantageous. Consultant Andy Harmon says that he will consider a fixed bid when he is able to incorporate earlier work into the current project. "The other thing that governs my decision to do fixed price or hourly," he explains, "is how much real control I have over a project; if I am doing hardware, software, design, and full implementation, I will almost always fix price. If I am to be a 'hired gun,' it's almost always hourly with full disclaimer and no guaranteed results." He also adds that one advantage of the fixed-bid contract for him is that "when you are hourly you may find yourself confined to on-site work only and that often monitored with a stopwatch. Being tracked around like a school kid and haggling nickel and dimes is not my cup of tea."

Nicholas Delonas, a Lotus Notes expert, is another consultant who has done well with fixed-bid contracts. "For those specialized jobs that we're really good at, I jump at a fixed-price opportunity," he explains. "We're happy because we're making more and the customer is happy because he's paying less." In these cases, he says, "I can and do bid twice my estimated normal hourly wage feeling quite certain that no one else will be able to match the bid or even come close."

Because of the nature of the competitive bidding situation where you are pitted against other consultants and consulting firms eager to get the client's business, you may find yourself in situations where you are competing with other consultants who are willing to offer the client fixed bids, even though you may have decided that you will never touch one. If you find yourself in this kind of situation, almost all consultants suggest that you make your best estimate of the time the project will take and then *double* it. This is the only way they've found to protect themselves.

There are some other strategies you can use when confronted by a desirable client who wants you to submit a fixed bid. Tom Campbell offers such clients two price quotations, one for doing the project on an hourly basis and one for the fixed bid, which is always higher. "Nobody," he says, "takes the fixed bid." He points out that his jobs almost always involve "lots of new code and frequently new hardware. If we did the same job over and over again, presumably our confidence in estimating would improve."

Michael Stein takes another approach. He likes to suggest to the client that they have "two contracts, one for developing the spec and one for implementation. The proposal will cite a firm price for developing the spec and a ballpark for the implementation." Only after the detailed spec has been developed does he give the client a firm price for implementation. And when he does, he offers the client a high and low estimate, "the high conforming to their complete wish list and the low to the original ballpark but without full functionality." Dick Monahan has also been successful using this approach. He offers to write the specification for a fixed price suggesting that the client can then use the specification to get accurate bids for the implementation. "While I have never made much money on the spec," he says, "I have also never had a client go out to bids." His clients always end up negotiating a price for the rest of the project based on the completed spec he's done for them.

Glenn Jones uses a similar approach that involves a detailed proposal done for a fixed price. He also explains his success with fixed bids as being due to using sophisticated estimating techniques. "We've built several spreadsheet models that we use to estimate. Also, since we have our own time and expense system, we can always query our database for the amount of time it took to accomplish the same tasks in a similar project in the past."

T&M with a Cap

The main reason that many clients are wary of letting you do a project on an hourly basis is the fear that you will drag the job out much longer than necessary so that you can keep on billing for your time. In order to address this reasonable fear, some consultants negotiate a hybrid contract. They give the client a proposal based on time and materials, but they also give them a cap or cost ceiling beyond which the cost of the project will not go. "It's not a lose–lose situation," explains Carl Brown, "because the cap does not have to be competitive." When he uses this kind of quote, Brown gives the client three figures: a total estimate for the project that he is confident he can meet, his hourly or daily rate, and the cap, which is always higher than he would bid on a fixed-price quote. He finds that this strategy can often help sell the project to the client who is afraid of runaway costs.

But attorney Lance Rose cautions the consultant to beware of the customer who wants to straddle the fence between T&M and a fixed fee. With the cap, he points out, you are basically working a fixed-fee contract, without the possibility of reaping any additional benefit from efficient work. If you do the work faster than the client expected, he pays the lower hourly rate, rather than the fixed price. If you run into trouble, you end up working a fixed-price contract. He suggests that if you do work under such an arrangement you insist on a very high cap.

Still, this kind of arrangement may be what it takes to reassure nervous first-time clients that an hourly rate arrangement will not give you carte blanche to drive costs up beyond what they can handle.

COMMON BILLING QUESTIONS

Once you've decided on an hourly rate, you may still have some issues to clarify about how that rate should be applied. What happens when the client needs only a few minutes of phone support or a half-an-hour site visit? Should you bill for the time you spend educating yourself in new technologies for a client?

What Is the Smallest Amount of Time You Should Bill For?

Consultants vary greatly in how precise they get about what fraction of an hour to bill for. Consultant Richard Morochove, who comes to computer consulting from a background in accounting, bills his clients in ten-minute increments. But he cautions newcomers that his rates are on the high side and that he billed in larger increments several years ago when his rates were lower. He adds that he knows many consultants who bill in half-hour increments and others who will not charge for less than one day at a time.

It is probably not as important what the smallest unit of time you decide to bill for is, as that you make sure that your client is aware of how you intend to bill and is comfortable with it. Clients who are unexpectedly billed for an hour as a result of a ten-minute phone call may well feel ripped off, where if they had understood that that was how you operated, they'd have saved their questions until the next time they had an hour's worth of work for you.

How Do You Bill for Phone Support?

How to bill for phone support is a thorny question. While some consultants bill the time spent on the phone the same way they'd bill any other time, others treat it as a special case. Because building a long-term ongoing relationship with a client so often leads to more work, many consultants feel it is worthwhile to offer incentives to the client to use phone support in order to keep the relationship active. Curtis Hertwig explains how he might approach such a situation. He offers clients a contract that "for a flat rate (say $300 per month) assures the client of up to *x* hours per month, say five. After that he pays my regular rate." Not only does this keep the relationship active, but as Hertwig explains, he is assured of getting some money each month and the client is assured of getting service at a discount. Such a deal leaves both consultant and client feeling they've gotten something advantageous from it.

However, this kind of arrangement must be approached with care, as some clients are prone to abuse it and some consultants who make these arrangements find themselves spending far too much time on the phone answering questions that clients could have easily answered themselves with a modicum of research. Richard Morochove charges his full hourly rate, in ten-minute increments, for phone support, precisely to discourage this kind of client laziness. Responding to an even more troublesome client tendency, consultant John Repici reports that "I've chosen to break phone calls to my home into two categories. One for calls received before a certain hour of the night, and one very expensive category for calls received after that hour."

Consultant Doug Johnson has another way of dealing with nuisance calls. As he explains, "One thing I have started to do to keep the five-minute calls from wrecking my life is that I set aside certain callback times and then do all callbacks except for dire emergencies." But he feels that it isn't a good idea to charge for quick calls, explaining, "I want my clients to call. I want to know what their questions are. I want to know what their problems are." So he doesn't charge unless calls extend over fifteen minutes, and he is careful to charge only for support, not for time spent shooting the breeze. That time goes into strengthening his relationship with clients and making sure that the relationship he has with them is one that will keep them calling him with more paying work.

Should You Bill for Local Travel?

As a consultant, you will probably work for several clients at a time and as a result, spend significant amounts of your time on the highway, going from one customer site to another. The time you spend on the road is time you aren't spending on billable work, so many consultants consider it proper to bill their clients for this time. "Time spent commuting is time that I can't get work done or keeps me from being able to do other billable work. Since I wouldn't otherwise be losing that time but for the trip to the client site, it is billed," says Jay R. Giusti. Guy Scharf explains "I have always charged for local travel on a straight time basis. I record time to a five-minute interval. Long trips of over three quarters of an hour are usually rounded down to the nearest fifteen-minute interval." Martin Schiff says he charges for travel in half-hour increments, and reports that he has not had any complaints about this practice.

But billing clients for travel has led to problems for other consultants. "In my first year I tried to get my client to pay for travel, too," reports one consultant who specializes in data security. "The answer, with a dirty look, was 'what are you, a plumber?' " Because of this kind of client reaction, consultant Annie Furrer explains, "you do better, psychologically, to raise your rates than to charge travel time." H. J. Schmidt agrees, "I will structure my bills so that travel time is not a line item. That will keep the client happy. To keep things reasonable for me, I will negotiate a minimum consulting period, so that I don't spend one hour in the car for a fifteen-minute billable event."

Many consultants adopt a compromise attitude toward travel, not charging for local travel but billing for any travel outside of some predefined radius. Data Security expert Mich Kabay charges a per diem fee for any travel outside of the Island of Montreal, where he is located. Bill Sturdivant charges for travel to a client location more than 75 miles from his office. Some busy contract programmers who work out of their own offices report using their method of billing to actively discourage clients from asking them to travel to their sites. John J. Genzano tells his clients up front that he will charge a 10 percent premium for any work done on site and insists, further, that the client pay for a minimum of four hours any time he comes to their site. Burt Johnson also uses a four-hour minimum to deter requests that he make the trip to the client's premises.

However, if you are going to pursue such a policy, you must be able to assure your clients that their needs can be taken care of without your physical presence in the office. Most consultants do this by using remote software like Carbon Copy or PCAnywhere to allow them to access the client's computer from their own offices, so that pressing client problems can indeed be solved without the necessity of a personal visit.

Other consultants use a more flexible gauge in deciding when to charge for travel. Advises one, "If it's a regular customer who brings you a lot of revenue, you might not want to bill travel time. If it's an occasional customer, or one who's a pain in the wazoo and expects you to come on site every time their system sneezes, then charge 'em."

Should You Bill for Long-Distance Travel?

Although computer consultants take many approaches to the question of how to bill for local travel, they are pretty much unanimous in billing for out-of-town trips. But here, too, there are different ways of doing this. While almost all consultants bill the client for the air fare, many consultants cover the rest of their out-of-town travel expenses by charging a flat per diem rate. Some advise using the IRS's daily travel allowance figures or ones available from the General Accounting Office to set reasonable per diem figures. These will provide you with a daily rate that varies from city to city because of differences in local costs of living. For example, one such table gives per diem rates of $151 per day for New York City, $94 per day for New Orleans, and $67 per day for Bay City, Michigan. Other consultants just charge a flat per diem rate, sometimes as high as $300 a day.

Some consultants charge the client for all actual expenses incurred. However, one consultant warns that clients may not be comfortable with this method of charging because they fear having you pass through to them the costs of outrageously priced meals or luxury car rentals. If you do choose to bill for actual travel expenses, it is a good idea to ask the client to recommend a local hotel and car rental company. Many companies have negotiated special corporate rates with local hotels and car rental companies and will appreciate your letting them use those discounts to pay your bills.

Can You Earn Money from Selling Hardware?

There are other ways of earning money as a computer consultant besides selling your services. You can also earn money from the markup on hardware you purchase at wholesale prices and sell the client, and by offering the client service contracts on that hardware. Although many computer consultants do earn money this way, there are some perils involved in this kind of business that the beginning consultant should be aware of.

Value-added reseller Andy Harmon explains, "There are three risks associated with selling hardware. One: Broken or poor-quality hardware and the possibility of a vendor that will not make good on it. Two: Getting the wrong thing or installing a piece of equipment not really suited to the job. It is not always possible to fully evaluate before making a purchase, especially if time is tight. And three: The customer will pull out the August issue of *Computer Shopper* and say, 'Hey, what I just paid you $X for, I can get for $Y at MicroMuck!' "

The first problem is the one that consultants find the most disturbing. One consultant says, "I have been spending more time recently resolving problems from my hardware suppliers than doing revenue-generating work." Woes most frequently reported by consultants who resell hardware include suppliers who ship defective equipment and then file Chapter 11 bankruptcy, suppliers who send incorrectly configured equipment and give them hassles about returns, and hardware that turns out to be incompatible with the client's existing systems but cannot be returned for credit. These situations can end up costing serious money, and almost every consultant who does sell hardware has at least one rueful anecdote to tell about the hardware he had to "eat."

Many consultants report also running into another problem Harmon mentions—price competition from mail-order vendors. Some say that the competition from mail-order sources and cut-rate superstores is too tough to let them earn any significant profit from hardware sales, and that if they sell hardware at all, they do it as a convenience to clients who are buying significant amounts of other kinds of service from them. To avoid what they see as an unwinnable battle, many consultants now merely advise clients on an hourly basis on how to best purchase hardware from discount sources, but won't take responsibility for the ultimate purchase.

Once the hardware is sold, there remains the even trickier problem of what kind of warranty should go along with it and how much ongoing responsibility you, the consultant, must take for that hardware. Consultant Robert Cashman says, "I make it one hundred percent clear that all sales are backed *only* by the manufacturer's warranty and that any service I do is for time and materials." Even so he finds most of his clients are willing to pay him to do repairs, rather than rely on the vagaries of the manufacturer's toll-free service. There are consultants who take full responsibility for service and use service contracts as an additional source of revenue. But experienced consultants warn that doing it right involves a commitment to keeping a significant inventory of spare parts on hand, and may require offering clients twenty-four-hour support because there is no predicting when their hardware may fail.

Consultant Vick Walton points out that consultants who make their money primarily from hardware and support need to have a greater number of clients than those who specialize in custom software projects. "Software guys are in the enviable position of getting one customer and having to support their software for life," he says. "Whereas hardware guys typically are in and out quickly and aren't back in again for quite a while."

Jeff Freeman, who specializes in selling hardware, explains, "Hardware is very different than software development/consulting. Margins are tight and volume has to be high. Though he maintains, "It's possible to do very well in hardware," Freedman suggests that the consultant who specializes in hardware find software developers to work with as an effective strategy for finding new clients. He explains, "Their customers likely need new hardware from time to time. Many times developers have little if any interest in handling the hardware end of things and instead call on you to get the hardware and maintain it. There is typically a referral fee paid—either flat fee or percentage of the sale. It's also common to sell equipment to the developer at cost when it's for their own use. You'll want to talk to some local developers and see if they are interested. We've discovered many of them haven't been getting any referral fee or discounts from the hardware folks. So you could have a wide-open market."

A final factor in how successful you may be with hardware sales is the type of client you typically support. As Michael Sikillian points out, "It is easier selling a hundred modems than spending a hundred hours consulting. If you can sell a hundred you can sell a thousand, and expanding the business is easy." The trick, of course, is to find the kinds of clients who are likely to order one hundred modems.

CONCLUSION

We've completed our survey of how consultants charge for their work. By now you should be aware that what you can charge for your own services has a lot to do with your skill level, the demand for the kind of services you can provide, the kinds of clients that your services attract, the amount of competition there is in your niche, the strength of your preexisting network of business contacts, and your own self-confidence and sales skills.

You've been given some advice in this chapter about how to charge for your work, and you will get a lot more of it any time you get together with a group of consultants. But in the final analysis, there is really only one absolute criteria that you should apply in any rate-setting situation: *Make sure that whatever rate you settle on, both you and the client feel comfortable with it.* As consultant Steve Estvanik puts it, "As long as both of you are satisfied that it's a fair rate, the relationship gets off to a good start. If you were knocked down to a rate that you thought was too cheap, you'd probably have an attitude to go along with it, to no one's benefit." By the same token, if the clients feel they are paying too much, no matter how good a job you do for them, the chances of building a long-term, productive relationship with them are very low.

By now too, you should have started to realize that while when we are talking about billing we are talking about money, we are also talking about *communication*, and that money is a big part of the language you use to communicate with clients. What you bill and how you bill it not only determines your profit, but it signals the client in subtle and not-so-subtle ways not only who you think you are and what you are worth, but how considerate you are of their needs, and how aware you are of their fears. You can use your billing techniques to encourage clients, to reassure them, to motivate them, to discourage unwanted client behaviors, and even to get rid of the problem client. If you keep this in mind when setting your rates and billing policies, you will already be taking a giant step in making the transition from thinking like an employee to thinking like a consultant, and you will be well prepared when you turn to the rest of the issues you must face if you are to attract and keep satisfied clients.

6

MARKETING YOUR
SERVICES

When experienced consultants are asked the secret of their success, most of them will tell you that it is because *even when they are at their busiest, they never stop marketing their services.* If you intend to stay in business, you too will have to master marketing and practice it consistently. But as important as marketing is, new consultants, once they have found a client or two, tend to avoid it. If they are honest they'll tell you why: Marketing professional services is time consuming, annoying, and frustrating—the business equivalent of flossing your teeth.

There's a simple reason for this. When most computer consultants attempt to market their services they go about it the wrong way. They use techniques they find in one-size-fits-all marketing books and seminars—techniques that take into account neither the nature of the complex services they are selling nor the characteristics of their sophisticated client base. As one now-successful consultant remembers, "In my first three months as an independent my phone wasn't exactly ringing off the hook with prospective clients interested in engaging my services. I had to go to the office every day and get on the telephone, meet people, and write letters. Ninety-five percent of this activity was wasted, with no measurable results. The problem is, I couldn't tell beforehand which was a waste and which was not!"

Marketing is no fun when you don't understand what you're doing, so it's no surprise new consultants avoid it. Only when you feel in control of your marketing strategies and are seeing them pay off again and again are you likely to enjoy the process and give it the attention it deserves. So we'll take a look now at how you can avoid the time- and money-wasting techniques that have given marketing such a bad reputation among computer consultants and see how experienced consultants market their services effectively.

MARKETING STRATEGIES THAT DON'T WORK

While most experienced consultants agree that there is no sure-fire marketing technique that will always work for the beginning consultant, almost all will admit to have started off their own practices by indulging in a few obvious techniques that always fail. Prime among these is the "Hello World" mass mailing.

Mass Mailings

Mass Mailings Don't Work

I'll say it again. Mass mailings, no matter how nice your stationery, how aesthetic your logo, and how professional your copy, don't work. They cost a fortune and they don't bring in new clients.

But don't just take my word for it. Listen to what this consultant has to say: "I tried a mailing with a return postcard and got *no* response. The size of the mailing was around five hundred." Or this one: "This year alone I have spent in excess of $12,000 on a variety of mass mailings. They included 'personalized' letters addressed via mail-merge to an executive of the company and tailored, again via mail-merge, to mention their industry and company mission. They also included professionally printed brochures, laser-printed brochures, and an eight-page glossy newsletter. So far, all my business has come from doing something else. Not one cent of my revenue has come from mailings."

Mass mailings don't bring in new clients.

There is a place for a mailing campaign in the marketing grab bag of the experienced consultant. You may find it useful to mail out letters to keep in touch with clients that you've already done work for, or to keep alive a relationship with a prospect you've met face-to-face at a business function. But the mass mailings most new consultants resort to almost always consist of nicely formatted promises and boasts directed at complete strangers—people who are no more likely to call you in on a consulting assignment as a result of reading your brochure than you would be to sign up for brain surgery after getting a brochure from an unknown neurosurgeon.

If You Feel You Have to Mail

Yet there is something almost ritualistic about the need that drives new consultants to inaugurate their practices with such a mailing. I've yet to meet a consultant who hasn't done one. I've done one myself. Perhaps it serves as a symbolic gesture, a ritual that in some arcane way invokes the gods of business success—something concrete you can do that no matter what its effect might be on your potential clients, makes you feel that your brand-new consulting practice is, at last, real.

So if in spite of what you read here you still feel the urge to send out new baby announcements for your practice, go ahead. But keep it small and save the rest of your money for less emotionally satisfying but more effective marketing techniques.

If you do feel driven to do a mass mailing, here are a few pointers that might help you raise your response rate from the usual zero to .05 percent most computer consultants report to a princely 1 or even 2 percent— which is about all any mass marketeer ever achieves from such a mailing:

- Confine your mailing to people with whom you have already established some sort of relationship. Best are people with whom you have worked in the past, to whom it is legitimate to send a letter announcing that you have begun offering your services as a consultant.
- If mailing to people who may not have met you personally, target your mailings to those who would have reason to be impressed by your background or credentials.
- Target a specialty market and precisely address the needs of clients in that market. The biggest mistake that many consultants make is to describe themselves in vague, overly general terms. Fearing that if they describe what they do in more precise terms they might inadvertently turn away a customer with other needs, they end up claiming they can do everything for anyone. It doesn't work.
- Avoid giving a mass-mailed look to your correspondence. Several consultants report getting better results when using regular stamps and envelopes that look like personal mail. If nothing else, the client will at least open them before tossing them, in the hopes that they contain a job offer or a love letter from a long-vanished flame. But don't be surprised if your expensive mailing is flung into the trash with even greater irritation once the client determines that far from containing a love letter that personal-looking envelope holds only another mass-mailed pitch.
- Follow up any mailing with a carefully planned, well-scripted follow-up phone call a few days later. Phone follow-up can significantly increase the response you get from a mailing. Indeed, some consultants claim that it helps to mention in the letter itself that you will be calling in a few days, arguing that without that promise (or, to be more honest, that threat), the potential client knows she can toss your letter without the risk of embarrassment at some future time.

Yellow Pages Ads

Another marketing device almost as popular with fledgling consultants as the "Hello World" mass mailing is the yellow pages display ad.

Unfortunately, it is just about as useful. *Yellow pages advertising is among the most expensive you can buy.* It requires that you pay a hefty monthly charge for each month of the year that your ad appears in the phone book—even though you may quickly discover it to be worthless.

Don't get me wrong. If you buy the yellow pages listing you will get plenty of calls. Unfortunately, they are not going to be from potential clients. "I have a single-line listing in the yellow pages," reports one consultant. "I must get at least one call each business day asking if we need copier supplies, fax paper, temporary help, coffee machine service, stock brokers, panty hose, etc. It's almost not worth having a listing because of the interruptions."

Another consultant reports, "I ran a double quarter-column ad in the San Francisco and Marin yellow pages for two years. With the artwork and charges I spent probably $8,000. All I received in return were hundreds of calls from people trying to sell things to me or people looking for a job." Another consultant who sells nothing but custom software services reports that his yellow pages ad proved annoying because "my phone has been ringing off the hook from people wanting packaged, off-the-shelf software—word processors and such."

The closest to a yellow pages success story I've managed to unearth comes from a very successful, long-established consultant who reports, "I took the default listing when I had my business line installed. Every so often one or two real good leads come in." But even he qualifies this by adding, "Mostly I've been too busy or not comfortable working with whatever was requested to follow through on any of these leads."

You'll get that one-line default listing as soon as you sign up for a business phone, but spending any additional money on yellow pages advertising unless you run a retail store is a waste of your money.

Newspaper Advertising

Can any display advertising bring in new consulting clients? The answer is a qualified "maybe."

Cliff Schaffer, a computer consultant with a background in marketing explains that print advertising does work if it is done right, but that doing it right means the ad must be repeated. "Magazine ads often pull five or ten times as many responses in the twelfth month as they did in the first," he explains. But he's found that for consultants, "The biggest problem is that if your ad is successful, most consulting firms can't keep up with the business and have to stop the ad."

If you are thinking of using a newspaper advertising campaign, you should *be prepared to spend significant amounts of money over an extended period.* Major newspapers may charge anywhere from $50 to $200 per inch for a single ad, so an effective long-term advertising campaign may easily end up costing anywhere from $2,500 to $10,000. Before you commit to this kind of expense, it might be a good idea to look through the paper, locate ads placed by other consultants, and call them to ask what kind of response their ads have pulled. If consultants tell you they have found their ads worthwhile, ask them what kinds of clients they work with and what types of services they sell and compare their client base with the clients you're trying to attract to make sure that an ad would be effective for you.

This is because *a good response rate is only useful if the responses come from people in your target client group.* Those who have tried print ads and abandoned them have usually found that, like the yellow pages ads, they attracted too many bad leads that took too much time to deal with. Someone just starting out, who may have little idea of what to expect from clients and how to sort out the good prospect from the time-wasters, may not find a newspaper advertisement a cost-effective way of building up a client list.

MARKETING STRATEGIES THAT DO WORK

At this point you may be wondering if any marketing strategies will work for you. If ads and mailings don't work, what's left? The answer, in a nutshell, is *intelligent networking.*

The truth is that almost all experienced consultants who have managed to stay in business for any significant time find their clients through *word-of-mouth referrals*, primarily from other satisfied clients.

This is not what you as a newcomer want to hear. It sounds suspiciously like a catch-22. If you have no satisfied clients, where are you going to find referrals? But like it or not, it is how things work in computer consulting. It is essential that you absorb this fact, that you recognize how crucial referrals must be to you, and give this truth the respect it deserves. Otherwise you will run the risk of giving up the sustained effort it takes to develop these referrals in favor of indulging in expensive, ultimately worthless alternatives. Or even worse, you may make the cardinal error that sinks more consultants than any other—considering your marketing done when you've found one or two clients to fill up your calendar, relaxing your efforts, and setting yourself up for a fatal client drought further down the line.

So take a deep breath and contemplate this truth yet again: If you are to stay in business, the majority of your clients will come from word-of-mouth referrals. All the most effective techniques that you can use to market your services—*all* of them—involve activities and behaviors that increase the likelihood of your getting such word-of-mouth referrals.

UNDERSTANDING THE CONSULTING MARKETING CYCLE

Before we look into how you can generate the word-of-mouth referrals that work for computer consultants, we need to give some thought to something that is all too often misunderstood by consultants who attempt to use any of these techniques—the nature of the consulting marketing cycle.

Selling consultant services is by its very nature a slow, start–stop kind of process. You will rarely see results from even your most effective efforts for anywhere from six months to a year. Michael Stein says, "It is not uncommon for [a client] to spend a full year between seeing our stuff demo'd for the first time and awarding us the contract." Disaster security expert Michael Miora concurs: "The typical time lag between 'first contact' and contract start is six to nine months." Consultant Hillary Rettig reports that she found it took "six to eight months before the leads started coming in in force."

Unless you understand that this glacial pace is normal you will quickly burn out in frustration. As long-term consultant Howard Eichenwald explains, "Potential clients are always saying, 'Can you call back next month?' or 'Wait until next quarter,' or 'Call back again in a few weeks,' or 'After the first of the year.' " These clients are not trying to brush you off. They are telling you the truth, and you will succeed only if you do call back in a month or two, and if you structure your marketing approach so that these kinds of delays are not fatal to your business but become part of the natural rhythm of your marketing efforts.

By now it's probably clear that the time to start marketing your consulting services is months or even years before you intend to begin consulting. But this is not an ideal world, so many of us don't have the luxury of approaching consulting this way. If you must begin your marketing efforts at the same time as you begin your consulting practice, take comfort in the fact that though your first few months may be tough, if you can stick with it, the efforts you put out now will ultimately bear fruit in the form of paying clients six months to a year from now. And don't forget when that work does come flooding in, that you must still *continue your marketing efforts* if you are to have new clients to serve when the current batch's needs are satisfied.

Eichenwald suggests a good way to approach sustaining a continuous marketing strategy: "One of the items I tried and was successful using was to take a day off each month from work to attempt to line up the next project. Maybe one-half day two times a month." Contract programmer Burt Johnson follows a similar course, explaining, "I found out years ago that if I only sent out letters when I was looking for work it gave the impression that I was always hungry. Even though they only heard from me every six months or so clients had the impression that I was never working." Now Johnson says he keeps his contacts open and talking. "I try to always arrange to have two active clients at any given time so that if one decides not to follow through after a milestone, I am not caught flat-footed." He adds, "I'm constantly amazed by how many consultants never do learn [the need to market continuously] and finally end up taking 'regular' employee jobs because 'the market has dried up.' "

A successful marketing strategy must be continuous. The successful consultant must depend on no client, no matter how loyal or how promising, but work continuously on building up an ever-widening network of contacts so that there are always new clients waiting in the wings to take the place of those who may drop out.

ASKING FOR REFERRALS

The marketing truth that comes as news to most beginning consultants is that word-of-mouth referrals are not lucky breaks or acts of God, but predictable events whose frequency can be increased by their own assiduous efforts.

To start with, let everyone you've ever established a positive relationship with know that you are now going into business as a consultant. Call your old bosses and let them know that you are looking for contracts. But don't just call old business contacts. Established consultant Michael Stein explains, "My first commercial clients were small businesses belonging to my roommate, a neighbor, and my sister. One of my roommate's customers became my fourth." He urges you not only to tell everyone you might know who runs a business what you are doing but to go further. "Ask them not only if they have any work for you, but if they know anyone who might."

"Tell everyone" means exactly that. Don't overlook your kid's day care teacher or the guy who comes to mow your lawn. The day care teacher may be, as mine was, married to the vice president of IS at a local corporation that uses a lot of consultants. The guy who mows your lawn may be fed up with his inefficient billing system and be thrilled to learn that you can supply him with a better one.

There's another important point to keep in mind about generating referrals. Strategic planner Roger Loeb explains it well when he says, "The 'secret' part, if there is one, is to remember to *ask* people for referrals—not for work, just referrals." He urges consultants not to be shy about saying, "If you happen to know of anyone who could use my services, please be kind enough to mention me."

Consultant Chris Anton is even more proactive with his clients. "What you want to do," he explains, "is get the client to give you the names of people who might be able to use your services and, if possible, to be able to say that the client referred you to them. Active solicitation of contacts is needed. Most of us can't afford to sit around and wait for them to come to us." Another aggressive consultant says, "I frequently ask clients to give me names of people they know from trade shows, business groups, etc." Yet another reveals that he asks satisfied clients for a written testimonial and for permission to show it to other prospects.

Such an aggressive policy may strike some of us, particularly those of us whose skills lie more toward the technical end of the continuum, as bordering on obnoxiousness. But it isn't. It's what it takes to begin the long, slow process of building a stream of referrals sufficient to keep you in business. If you can't bear to ask for work, you are going to have a difficult time staying in business.

EXPANDING YOUR NETWORK

It should be obvious by now that the key to getting referrals is to establish a healthy network of friends and business acquaintances who can serve as a source of referrals. However, if your current network is anemic, or if like many beginning consultants your network consists of a few old employers, don't despair. There are ways to strengthen and expand your existing network.

One very good way of strengthening your network and significantly improving your likelihood of receiving referrals is to *participate in organized groups* whose membership includes influential members of your primary client group. Fully 47 percent of the consultants who answered the ICCA survey reported that networking in professional groups was their most frequent source of work, and the consultants in that survey reported using this kind of networking as a marketing tool far more often than any other sort of formal sales campaign.

If you are trying to sell contract programming to IS managers, it makes sense to join a local chapter of groups such as the Association of Systems Managers (ASM), the Data Processing Managers Association (DPMA), the Software Maintenance Association (SMA), or the Microcomputer Managers Association (MMA). The people you will meet participating in these organizations are likely to be corporate movers and shakers who have good solid networks within their own organizations and know what is going on in others.

Another fruitful approach is to *get active in local civic groups*. As consultant Steve Zilora points out, "it is often personality and friendships that gets you the first job with a client. Selling yourself as a person is easy to do in a civic group."

Many consultants have found *specialized computer users groups* to be a fertile source of contacts. One consultant who is very active in FUSE (the FOCUS users group) says, "Even if I count the value of the hours I put in attending meetings at my normal billing rate, I have gotten twice that back in contract work that is directly attributable to my being involved." A Paradox developer claims he's found over $150,000 worth of work through attending the meetings of a very active local Paradox users group. He attributes his success to two factors: The group attracts many potential clients who already use the product and the group maintains a referral service that gives out names of Paradox developers and trainers. As a result, clients often come to meetings and ask outright if anyone is interested in working for them on a contract basis.

General purpose computer users groups and meetings of technical societies like the Institute of Electrical and Electronic Engineers (IEEE) or the Association for Computing Machinery (ACM) may also be good places to build up your network. Besides offering monthly meetings, these groups often put on special seminars, trade fairs, and other functions that attract a wider audience and may be great places to meet potential clients. At technical group meetings you may meet both potential clients and other consultants, who, if they are favorably impressed with the expertise you show and the help they see you giving people at meetings, may refer overflow customers to you, or send you clients who want work done in a specialty they don't provide.

Indeed, almost any organization can provide you with opportunities to develop new clients. Computer consultant Wayne Orth was asked to address a local meeting of PLOW (Plower's League of Wisconsin). After the meeting two attendees gave him their cards and asked him to call them about potential projects. Another consultant got a significant contract from a contact he made at a group of Ultimate Frisbee enthusiasts.

Some consultants have found that they can improve their network by attending events that attract other businesspeople looking for clients. One consultant reports making valuable contacts at Small Business Administration business fairs, where he explains "I've met many business owners who need my technical writing and training services over the refreshment stands or at the lunch table."

Perils of Networking

But there is an art to making contacts in these kinds of organizational situations. Just as it is possible to make important contacts through organizational networking, it is also possible to use it to destroy any chance of finding clients. We have all run into the network jerk, the guy who fastens onto you at a gathering, cross-examines you about what you do, and then forces his card into your hand with a canned sales spiel or abandons you to chase after someone else more likely to make him rich. Behave like that and you're likely to join the throng of those who say, "Networking doesn't work."

If you are going to network in an organization effectively, you have to show up looking like you've come to give, not to take. If you are to establish relationships with people, you have to give them some reason to want to know you. You can do this by helping people with your skills or by volunteering to do things other people don't want to do. That evening you spend licking stamps may well begin a professional relationship with another professional who knows dozens of people who could use your services, but you'll never find that out until she decides you're someone she likes and truly would like to help out—not just another opportunist.

Speaking to professional groups is another technique that can backfire. The speaker who tells ethnic or sexist jokes or otherwise insults portions of his audience or the expert who drones on until most members of the audience would gladly shoot him are not likely to find new clients. Only by showing consideration for your audience and giving them information that they can really use are you likely to impress them and generate requests to know you further.

If you know that your interpersonal skills are weak, if you are a compulsive talker or prone to try to dominate people in social situations, before you head out to network, it might be a good idea to invest some time and money in training to *improve your interpersonal skills*. Group therapy or more mainstream approaches like Dale Carnegie training can help you get a better idea of how you strike others and provide you with a workshop environment in which to work on improving your ability to connect with other people in a positive, encouraging way.

Making the Most of Network Opportunities

Here are a few other pointers that consultants claim help them make the most of opportunities they encounter in organizational networking situations.

- Always keep a supply of business cards with you so that you can give one to someone you meet. If possible, when you give the person a card, jot down a few words on the back that relate to your discussion.
- When you meet someone who gives you their card, take a moment to jot a few phrases on the back of the card to help you remember who the person was so that you don't confuse her with others you may have met at the same function.
- Mail a pleasant, noncanned-sounding "glad to have met you" letter to anyone you spent any amount of time talking with at a convention or business function.
- Use phone call follow-ups to keep in contact with anyone with whom you've established a relationship. Keep the conversation focused on them and their activities, not yours. Don't brag or mention accomplishments unless the topic flows naturally from the discussion.
- Offer to send follow-up material to people that relates to discussions you have. Saying "If you'll give me your card I'd be happy to send you a copy of that article" is a great way to create an opportunity for an ongoing relationship that doesn't make you look overeager or exploitative.

- Network when you are busy enough that you don't need to find additional work or contacts. One consultant points out that networking reminds him of what used to happen when he was dating in college: "Whenever I happened to be going steady with a girl, it always seemed much easier to strike up conversations and relationships with other girls. But when I wasn't going steady, such encounters were few and awkward." It's the same with potential clients. You are much more likely to find them when you don't need them, just as you are more likely to impress others with your expertise when you are busy and work is making you feel confident and successful. If you put effort into building your network at these times, you're much more likely to find it useful when work runs out.

TREATING OTHER CONSULTANTS AS A RESOURCE

If you hear a consultant referring to another consultant as "the competition," the chances are good that the consultant is new to the business. Experienced consultants know that far from being rivals, most other consultants are a resource for them that, used properly, can help them significantly expand their own practices. Hillary Rettig is one consultant who has found this to be true. She says, "I come down strong on the 'network with other consultants' tactic. That's a lot of what I do, and it's more successful than marketing to prospective clients, at least for me."

There are several reasons for this. One main reason derives from the nature of consulting. Consulting work typically flows in an uneven "feast-or-famine" pattern. Since the majority of independent consultants are one-person practices, there is a limit to how much work any of them can take on. This means that the busy, successful independent consultant can be a prime source of referrals to other consultants, who he or she expects will, at some future time when they are too busy, refer their own overflow clients back to them.

You can expand your contacts with other consultants by participating in the civic and professional groups we've already discussed, or you can join any of a number of formal consultants' organizations. The ICCA has monthly meetings in a number of cities and holds two major conferences a year. The IEEE also sponsors several active consultants' SIGs (special interest groups) in different parts of the country. There are large regional consulting groups too. Where you don't find these you may find consultants' SIGs sponsored by active PC users groups.

Because each of these groups is stronger in certain parts of the country than in others, you'll have to do some research to determine which organization in your area attracts the most participation from consultants. Once you've identified it, participate; remember that the key to making fruitful business relationships in these organizations is to show up ready to give and help, and to do your best not to look hungry.

Internet Networking Strategies

One excellent way to expand your network is to participate in the many technically oriented discussion groups on the Internet. You'll find Usenet newsgroups dedicated to just about any computer language or platform you might want to discuss. CompuServe's technical forums are another rich resource for computer consultants. Browse those newsgroups and forums dedicated to subjects in which you are an expert, and answer questions you find already posted there. Once you've gotten a feeling for what the newsgroup or forum is about, you can also start new discussions on topics that fit into the newsgroup or forum's charter.

Software developer Terry Richards reports that he has pursued this strategy with great success. He routinely spends a lot of time answering questions on Compuserve forums that attract professionals working with the languages he has mastered. He has also written and posted a free Windows editor that breaks the 64K barrier. He says that this free editor has brought him more than its share of paying clients because when people want his editor "it is usually because they have just discovered the size limitation of the standard Windows edit control. Nine times out of ten, the problem doesn't show up until the end of system test when they start throwing some volume at it. A manager with a project that's going down the tubes at the last moment is not a happy manager. If I can walk in and save the day, billing rate is not a serious issue."

Before you participate in any on-line venue, take the time to familiarize yourself with the group's purpose and guidelines. You can often find these described in a FAQ (frequently asked questions) file or message. Take the guidelines seriously. If you violate them, you will irritate the very people you are trying to add to your network. In particular, avoid posting messages that appear to be plugs for your consulting services on public bulletin boards and never explicitly offer your services in any message. Shameless plugs irritate other professionals reading your messages and won't bring you work.

Also, although newsgroups usually allow you to include a canned signature that mentions your business in the messages you post, exercise this right with care. Keep any canned sign-off brief and avoid the temptation to put in an advertising slogan. Reading your slogan over and over again—no matter how cute it might seem initially—will only annoy people who download your messages. In a similar vein, if you maintain an information-rich Web site, you should include your URL in your signature so that visitors reading your posting using a Web browser can click on the live link. But it is enough to give the URL and perhaps a line describing what can be found on your site. Don't annoy readers with lengthy plugs.

You'll find a lot of Help Wanted postings on-line, both in language and platform-oriented venues and more generalized consultants' boards. These are posted by brokers and consulting firms, usually those looking for W-2 contractors. Treat these postings with the same caution you'd give any classified ad. Consultants do find work through responding to them, but because these ads are free and easy to place, you'll find many of them are posted by marginal brokers. Before getting involved with a broker (or client) you find on-line, check out their reputation. If you can't find anyone who has heard of them, ask for local and business references.

Paying Finder's Fees for Referrals

When another consultant sends work your way, it is often a very good idea to do something tangible to demonstrate your gratitude. In many cases it is customary to pay the referring consultant a finder's fee, and you should not be taken aback if a consultant who has referred you a juicy piece of work suggests that you do this. Typical finder's fees range from 5 to 10 percent of your billings for some limited time. If you are selling hardware, it is a good idea to figure the finder's fee on your profit, rather than on your gross sales to the client.

The rationale behind paying these fees is simple—it encourages the referral source to give you further referrals. Consultant Rich Cohen explains, "I've both paid and received finder's fees. The amount of the finder's fee depends on the amount of selling I have to do. If the client calls up, asks me in for a quick interview, and then brings me on board, I'm happy to pay a fee. If I have to have a dozen meetings with the client to get the job, the finder's fee will probably drop to zero. What I'm doing is rewarding someone else for saving me marketing effort." Cohen also makes the important point that it is a good idea to let the client know that a fee is being paid, because in some situations, like certain government contracts, this kind of arrangement is illegal.

If you do pay a finder's fee to another consultant or another referral source, such as a hardware vendor, it is important to get it clear up front what the basis for the fee will be and when such payments will end. Steve Zilora says he limits his to the initial contract, figuring that any additional work he gets from the client stems from his abilities, not those of the person who got him the job.

When deciding how to determine an appropriate finder's fee, most people suggest using common sense. It makes sense to better reward someone who is likely to send you further business. It also makes sense to be generous to someone who has turned you on to what turns into a huge profit-making situation. A finder's fee is supposed to be a way of generating goodwill, so if you do choose to pay one, make sure that the net result is to make the referrer feel good about you and to contribute to the growth of your relationship in a way that will encourage more referrals.

FORMAL REFERRAL SERVICES

As the number of people doing all kinds of consulting grows in society, an increasing number of organizations and businesses are offering services meant to cater to the consultants' need for clients. Some of these services can be quite expensive. Let's look now and see if they are worth it.

Be Wary of Referral Lines

Referral lines are offered both by nonprofit groups like some local chapter of the ICCA and by for-profit companies, many of which are now on the World Wide Web. These services permit you to *upload your resume into a database* where people looking for consultants can scan the entries and, when a match is found to their needs, locate the information they need to contact you.

The problem with these services, both for-profit and nonprofit, is that they rarely do any sort of screening of their participants. A client using such a service has no guarantee of anything except, perhaps, that the people in the database are looking for work—and even this is not certain as many such databases keep old listings on-line even when the consultants listed are booked up for months in advance. As a result the quality of the services that clients get from consultants found through these referral services varies greatly and a significant percentage of clients have experiences bad enough that they are never again likely to use any sort of referral line again.

Even a referral service run by a professional group may not escape this problem, unless the organization screens applicants or insists that members meet some stringent set of professional qualifications—which few do.

If you get access to such a referral service as part of your membership in such a group, it can't hurt to participate. But don't join any group just to get into a database and don't count on such a service to provide you with a steady stream of work. And it is rarely worth paying an entrepreneur to get into a for-profit database. These outfits spring up regularly, advertise in the national trade press or in employment magazines for a few months, and with similar regularity go out of business. Those who have tried to earn money running services report that clients rarely will pay to use them because they can find consultants elsewhere for free and most good consultants won't pay to be in them either.

Watch Out for Directory Scams

Another enticement that organizations may dangle in front of you as an incentive to join is the privilege of being listed in their organizational directory. But do such listings really generate work?

Rarely. One consultant who signed up for the National Association of the Self-Employed (NASE) under a business name he doesn't otherwise use reports that his membership brought him nothing—except for an average of ten pieces of junk mail a week, most of them containing get-rich-quick schemes.

Consultant Harold Melnick, who has received many such solicitations to have his name put in for-pay "professional directories," counsels consultants to consign these to the circular file. "There are a lot of directory scams," he warns. "If you ask them how often they publish, or ask them to sell you a copy and they don't respond, that's about all the indication you need to stay away. At best, they'll publish something once a year and mail copies to a bunch of government agencies."

Don't Depend on Consultant Relations Programs

Many hardware and software vendors encourage you to sign up for special vendor relations programs that they market to consultants as being a way of increasing their business. Some programs are free, or cost only a small registration fee, while others may cost several hundreds of dollars for full membership. In addition, you may have to fill out lengthy applications to join one of these groups. How useful are these programs as a marketing aid?

Again, the answer is "not very." Vendor relations programs do indeed provide many benefits to consultants. They may give you access to valuable technical information about the company's products, lead to invitations to new product roll-outs, and entitle you to hefty discounts on the company's products. They may also give you the right to use the company's logo on your advertising. But few, if any, consultants find that participation in these programs does much to bring them new clients.

A consultant who participated in a program run by the SAS Institute reports that her directory listing resulted only in calls from brokers looking for contract programmers, even though her company's listing made it clear she does not do contract programming. The experiences of others in different niches with different vendor programs are similar. A programmer who designs Macintosh software reports never having gotten a single client through the Apple Developers program, although he did receive several phone calls that led nowhere.

Only occasionally does work result from such listings. After two fruitless years of paying $75 to be listed in the FoxPro Developer directory, Martin Schiff reports that he recently received two good calls as a result of the listing. One of these resulted in a contract with a large corporate client that was worth several thousand dollars and may lead to more work in the future. But many more consultants echo Michael Miora when he reports "I have placed my company name in a number of directories. All I got for my trouble was job seekers and salespeople."

Among the most heavily promoted consultant-oriented programs—and the most controversial—are those provided by Microsoft. Consultants who joined the Microsoft Solutions Provider (SP) program at its start found that the costs of maintaining membership rose quickly. One consultant reported on the CONSULT Forum that the $495 he paid for his initial membership escalated within two years to $1,995. Because the program's contract included wording specifying that if he did not renew his membership he would lose his right to use all the internal use licenses to the software previously obtained through the SP program, the consultant was faced with the choice of coughing up the unexpected $1,995 immediately or replacing most of the software on his systems.

At the same time, many consultants who have paid the escalating fees for the Solutions Provider program report that they rarely if ever got useful referrals from Microsoft. Either the referrals were, as one consultant reports, "more trouble than they are worth" or the promised referrals never materialized. The training director of a San Francisco software and training firm says he got a grand total of three faxed leads from the program. Another VAR tells of getting "about one lead a month—most with incorrect contact information." Another consultant reports that although a Microsoft Reseller Action Pack including six months of sales leads from Microsoft was offered to him at a seminar, "the two Microsoft people I approached both acted as if they were a tad embarrassed to talk about the Microsoft sales lead program." The principal of a large, multiconsultant company explains that in his experience Microsoft sales reps seem to save the worthwhile leads for consultants who are members of the much more expensive Solution Partners program—which requires a hefty $15,000 sign-up fee. He says that the consultants he knows who have bought into that program have received prequalified leads leading to long-term assignments where they were able to bill $125 or more per hour.

Dorothy Creswell participates in several vendor relations programs and suggests that their main marketing value to you is not in the direct referrals they may produce but in the way they may help you present yourself to clients as a professional who maintains a good information flow with the vendors whose products clients plan to use.

GETTING OTHER PEOPLE TO DO YOUR MARKETING

Many consultants wonder if instead of having to do all the hard, unending grunt work of selling their services, they might not do better to hire someone to do the selling for them, particularly if they know themselves to be stronger in technical rather than business skills. After all, lots of people enjoy selling and do it well. So why not bring one of them in to sell your services?

You can, and many consultants do, but almost all who do are consultants working for huge firms or those who sell not only their own services, but also those of a significant number of other employees as well as the company's software products.

Using Professional Sales Reps

For the one-person consulting firm, finding a salesperson who can actually do the job may be very difficult. The problem is that, as Paul Ferrara explains, "a one- or two-man firm can't support a really good salesman, who is typically paid fifteen to twenty percent of the gross billings" because they are in competition with large consulting firms that can offer good salespeople the opportunity of earning commissions approaching $200K a year.

As a result, the professional salespeople you may find who are willing to represent the independent consultant who works alone or with a few other consultants is quite likely to be a loser. "I had a terrible experience with my first sales rep," says one long-term consultant. "It took me about a year to recover both fiscally and emotionally from the trauma."

To give you some idea of what that trauma might involve, another consultant reports that her sales rep "managed to negotiate me into working a month free for one client." Others have had ignorant salespeople commit them to achieving technically impossible feats or promise that they would meet impossible delivery schedules.

Jeff Sachs is one consultant who has worked out a fruitful relationship with a sales rep. He attributes his success to having set up clear-cut guidelines with the rep that prevent her from bundling services or discounting services and products too deeply. He also reports working closely with the salesperson on every proposal and making sure that nothing ever goes out the door without his approval. In addition, he pays the rep strictly on a commission basis when payment is received from the client.

Like other consultants who have worked out satisfactory arrangements with salespeople, Sachs is convinced that the key to finding a good salesperson is looking for one who will work on a straight commission basis, not a salary. However, Sachs is running a multiperson operation that has been in business for many years, not a one-person consultancy. Almost always, the one-person consultancy that wants to avail itself of the services of a sales professional will have to turn to the brokers whose services are discussed in Chapter 7.

Consultant Consortia

Many beginning consultants come up with the idea of pooling their resources with those of other consultants and hiring a salesperson to sell for the consortium thus formed, or, as many law firms do, of having a partner in the group who specializes in being the group's "rainmaker" and bringing in new business. These seem like great ideas, but for some reason, they rarely, if ever, work out. I don't know what the explanation is for the lack of such consortia, but the fact is that they don't exist and that successful consultants do not depend on formal arrangements of this kind for work. Consultants do use informal contacts with other consultants to get and give referrals, but you do not find large computer consulting practices made up of independent consultants operating on the model of CPA firms or law firms.

Perhaps people attracted to computer consulting are just too independent to flourish in a more structured group setting, or perhaps easy access to the placement services of broker firms drains away potential consortium members. Or it may just be that really good consultants are able to find work through informal, referral-based methods and they don't need to join in consortia to get business, leaving such group ventures to consultants whose skills are less than adequate and whose failures to satisfy clients quickly doom any group action.

Alliances with Other Salespeople

Some consultants have found it useful to forge business relationships with the people whose selling activities bring them into contact with their own clients, who do not sell the same services as they do. Perhaps one of the real "secrets" of successful computer consultants may be that when they do invest time and money in marketing efforts they *focus their energy on people and institutions who can provide a steady stream of clients* rather than hunting for clients one by one. As custom developer Paul Ferrara explains, it is best to "concentrate marketing efforts on a handful of referral sources like accountants and resellers rather than directly to end users. Aside from being less work and less expensive, it also puts the prospect in the position of coming to you instead of you going to them."

Ferrara has had a steady stream of clients interested in his customized accounting software referred to him as a result of cultivating relationships with retail salespeople at local computer stores. He explains that when a retailer doesn't provide software services, being able to refer customers to consultants who do offer those services gives the retailer one more way of serving his customers' needs. Ferrara has also found office equipment salespeople to be another good source of referrals.

Consultant Bob Palmer explains that building relationships with salespeople provides excellent referrals because "a computer reseller or dealer is in contact with motivated prospects already. The reseller or dealer has qualified the prospect, determined their willingness to buy, has usually made the sale, and now brings us in as an expert to 'bring the software together' for the client." Palmer says he has found far more qualified prospects through dealers and resellers than he has through referrals from clients, though he gets those too.

Michael Stein reports that he's gotten significant business doing custom software development by forming relationships with systems integrators who sell network hardware. "One of our most effective tools is to do a joint seminar with an integrator," he explains. "It is very time-efficient to see ten prospects instead of one at a meeting, and doing it with a partner with fancier facilities than most consultants have provides you with extra marketing bang: We use their projection monitors, PCs, seminar rooms, etc."

But not everyone finds this approach works. It requires more than a single visit to a retail store to convince the salespeople that you are worthy of a recommendation, and in today's retail environment, the salespeople you encounter on your second visit to the store may not be the ones who worked there the month before. Some consultants report that the referrals they get from salespeople are worthless because the salespeople don't understand the clients' needs and the referrals they send turn out to be people unable to afford consultant services. Also, with the increasing dominance of the low-service superstore and mail-order vendors in the hardware arena, this channel may not be as productive for the new consultant as it was for people like Paul Ferrara, who started out consulting in the early or middle 1980s when the retailers held a more dominating position.

If you do hook up with retailers or integrators, you need to do some research to make sure that they have good reputations with their clients, so that you don't inadvertently damage your reputation by becoming associated with outfits whose clients feel they have been ripped off.

NEWSLETTERS AS A MARKETING TOOL

It has become extremely fashionable nowadays in business circles to recommend the use of a newsletter as a marketing tool to almost everyone, and many beginning consultants wonder whether publishing a newsletter of their own would be an effective marketing strategy.

It may be, and many consultants make a desktop-published newsletter part of their overall marketing campaign. But many more who have tried this strategy have reported mixed results, or are still, a year or more into publishing their newsletter, waiting for it to show demonstrable results.

The problem may well be that clients have numbed out to newsletters now that they get them from their dentist, their health insurer, their electric company, and even the people who run the local vegetable stand. The desktop publishing revolution may have well made what used to be a powerful marketing tool less effective by making it too common.

A newsletter is likely to be effective only when it reaches people who know you well enough not to automatically consign your efforts to the wastebasket along with the rest of their junk mail. A newsletter that is going to avoid that fate will also have to be well written and filled with the kind of eye-opening information that makes people cut out your articles and tack them on bulletin boards. This means that you will need to *focus on problem solving* or *provide resource information* that is relevant to your target reader.

Writing Your Own Newsletter

Clearly, to produce an effective newsletter you must be able to write on a professional level. This is hard work and many consultants decide against doing it because they don't have the time needed to turn out a professional product. Many of the consultants who use this strategy effectively are those who pursue freelance writing on subjects related to their area of specialization as a sideline business that they use to reinforce their consultancy and generate additional income.

One of these, accountant and computer consultant Richard Morochove, distributes 1,500 copies of the eight-page newsletter he writes quarterly. About half the material he publishes comes from recycled columns he's published elsewhere though the rest is written specifically for the newsletter. Consultant Dheeraj Khera sends a newsletter to the small systems developers and systems integrators who make up his client base, reusing material he publishes in his ICCA chapter monthly newsletters.

These consultants' journalistic activities have already trained them to write on deadline and their journalistic success has given them a good feeling for what their target audiences are interested in reading.

Buying Canned Newsletters

It is not necessary to write a newsletter yourself to have one to send to clients. Indeed, several of the consultants who have been the happiest with their newsletters' ability to bring in new business are those who have purchased customized, ready-to-mail newsletters from organizations that sell them to consultants. *Executive Computing*, published by the InterCom Group in Berkeley, California, is one of these. It contains articles aimed at executives who use or are responsible for PCs. You'll find several other providers of generic newsletters listed in Appendix A, Resources for Consultants.

Providers usually put your business name and some business-specific copy on one page of the newsletter. They may also customize the newsletter's title page for you. The rest of the newsletter contains the standard copy that all their customers get. The cost to you is usually around two or three dollars per copy. The newsletter company may ship the newsletter to you so you can mail them out or, for an additional fee, may mail them to a list you supply.

Such canned newsletters are not without problems. One consult regular raved at first about how much his clients enjoyed the Mac-oriented newsletter he purchased. He claimed it helped him earn more than $30,000 in contracts the first year he used it. But he later was left in the lurch when the newsletter's publisher went out of business with only a few weeks' notice. Another obvious problem with a canned newsletter is that other consultants might also send copies neatly personalized with their business names to one of your clients. Although newsletter providers usually agree only to sell their newsletters to a single consultant in a region, if your clientele is not strictly local, you might still run into problems.

Other problems that users of canned newsletters have run into include editorial content that recommends solutions they don't approve of and the inclusion in newsletter articles of plugs for the products or services of competitors.

How Can You Tell If Your Newsletter Is Successful?

Newsletters, whether self-produced or canned, are relatively expensive to mail, so if you do use one it is important to mail them selectively. Common wisdom says that you can't judge the effectiveness of a newsletter campaign until you've been mailing for at least a year. But evidence from consultants who have experimented with newsletters suggests that if you don't start seeing some results sooner than that, by the end of your year you will almost certainly conclude that your newsletter has failed as a marketing tool.

If your newsletter is working you should start hearing from at least one or two of the people you have been mailing it to within a few months—calling with work they want you to do. This is exactly what happens to the consultants who praise their newsletters as useful marketing tools. If it isn't happening, your newsletter, though it may be generating some fuzzy goodwill, may well be a waste of marketing dollars.

One consultant whose clients kept telling her they loved her newsletter had to admit after a year that she could not attribute a single new contract or sale to it. When she suggested that clients who enjoyed the newsletter and wanted to continue receiving it pay a modest subscription fee to cover its costs all of them dropped out. Liking your newsletter isn't enough. The newsletter should be reminding clients of work they need you to do.

Who Should Get Your Newsletter?

Because of the expense of mailing a newsletter it is important not to waste copies on people unlikely to contact you with work, but it is difficult to know in advance who these will be. Computer consultant and accountant Richard Morochove has analyzed the response he has received over several years of mailing out thousands of copies of his newsletter. He found very good results came from mailing his newsletter to current clients and former clients that he'd worked with in his days as an accountant. He also got good results from mailing to people he used to work with at his former employers. He discovered that dormant prospects who received his newsletter occasionally responded with new contracts, as did professionals whose names he got from a small association that permitted him to mail to its mailing list. But mailings he made to people who had attended speeches he'd given were less productive, as was a classified ad that offered to mail the newsletter to subscribers as a special report.

One last group Morochove has found it worth sending his newsletter to is vendors of products reviewed or discussed in its pages. Although he has not received any contracts from vendors, he has been put on their lists of beta testers and has received free review copies of their software.

Because of the expense of mailing a newsletter, there is the question of how long to allow names to remain on your list without some sort of positive feedback. Software developer Michael Nunamaker suggests that if you have any questions about whether it is worthwhile to keep certain prospects on your mailing list rather than dropping them completely, you instead put them on a special list that gets mailed to only once a year. If they don't become active clients after five years of these once-a-year mailings, he suggests you drop them. He follows this strategy because he has found that he has gotten lots of business from people who got his mailings for a few years before buying anything from him.

USING PUBLIC RELATIONS AS A MARKETING TOOL

Pursued properly, a well-crafted public relations campaign can be an effective, though slow-acting, component of your overall marketing strategy.

Public relations is the art of getting information about yourself included in newspaper articles, journals, and other media outlets as part of their editorial content. Like advertising, it must be done in a consistent, long-term manner and your audience must be exposed to your name dozens of times before they will begin to recognize it. But unlike advertising, public relations exposure is free, and readers are much more likely to be impressed by articles written by objective journalists than they are by advertising copy written by yourself.

Though you often hear about expensive public relations campaigns run by politicians or huge corporations, *it is not necessary to spend a lot of money* on crafting an effective campaign for yourself. All you have to do is learn a little about how the media work and to keep in mind that your public relations activities are most likely to succeed if you understand the needs of the media and provide your information in a way that fills those needs.

Editors and the people who put together TV and radio news work in a highly pressured, deadline-driven environment. They must come up with material that will capture the interest of their target audience day after day and week after week. If they lose the interest of that audience their circulation and advertising revenue plummet and they are out of a job. As a result these editors and the journalists that report to them are driven by a single dominating need: the need to come up with good stories that their audience will enjoy. If you provide such a story you're likely to get coverage. If not, you won't.

The Double-Edged Sword of "Story"

This simple fact hides a world of potential agony, because editors and journalists in pursuit of a good story have little or no interest in what that story makes you look like. As a case in point, in an article that accompanied the 1990 *Computerworld* Annual Salary Survey, a journalist quoted a programmer as saying that he disliked his job and wished he could quit it to play rock and roll instead. The article included the programmer's full name. When I asked the author of the article whether it had occurred to him that publishing the programmer's name along with a statement about hating his job might have led to the man's being fired, he expressed surprise and said it had never occurred to him. He'd just loved the quote.

Similar thinking no doubt influences the writers who cover computer consulting in many newspapers' weekly business magazines. When writing about local computer consultants they dwell at length on other businesses that consultants have started that have gone bankrupt, their current lack of clients, and occasionally, on lawsuits that have been brought by unhappy clients. Wonderful anecdotes about water pouring through consultants' ceilings and tales of hilarious bugs that destroyed weeks' worth of data accompany discussions about how the consultants have been turned down for financing by local banks. Such articles may be high in human interest, but they are the last thing on earth that you want to see in print about your own business.

When dealing with a journalist, even in casual contacts, you must remember never to say anything that you don't want to see in a headline. At the same time you must come up with stories of your own that both reflect credibly on yourself and have a strong dose of human interest.

Don't send journalists releases that announce "Joe Shmoe Opens Consulting Practice." They'll end up in the trash or at best end up in one of those fillers full of such announcements that no one reads. Instead send out a release that announces "Joe Shmoe Cuts Local Firm's Payroll Processing Costs in Half," or "Shmoe's Software Helps Investor Pick Winning Stocks." These kinds of items increase your chances of getting noticed in a way that will do your business some good.

If possible, come up with a story hook that has human interest appeal. If you've started out with a $25-dollar investment and now do over a million dollars of business a year, emphasize that rags-to-riches angle. People like success stories. But even here you have to exercise caution when the journalist shows up for the interview. You want her concentrating on the riches, not the rags. You don't want the story to focus on how being fired drove you into consulting or on the obstacles you encountered because of your age, sex, or a physical disability.

Make sure that the punch line of any story you suggest to a writer centers around a business achievement. Don't give the journalist a chance to write an article like "Lightning Strikes Consultant's Equipment Three Times." Give him instead the material he needs to write a headline like "Consultant's Software Enables the Disabled to be Valued Workers." The human interest you dangle beneath the editor's nose should always lead into a major point that stresses the quality of your work.

Consultant Esther Schindler was able to use a human interest hook to get coverage for her consultant practice based in rural Maine by pointing out to an editor that although she was located almost a hundred miles from a city of any size, her role as a sysop, or forum leader, on CompuServe put her in daily contact with business movers and shakers all over the world. In her press release she included a few anecdotes about other rural Maine businesspeople who pursued similar telecommuting strategies. The writer ended up making her the centerpiece of a feature article whose point was that Schindler's professionalism and technical savvy had helped her overcome the number one business challenge faced by professionals in rural Maine.

Consultant Dorothy Creswell, who has also used press releases to good effect, lists a few other human interest slants that have worked for her. Regional pride is one. If you are the first local business owner to achieve some sort of national recognition or award, highlighting the regional aspect may increase your chances of coverage. She says that another useful tactic is to mention it when your company is doing something for community betterment, like aiding the homeless or helping with computer systems that coordinate disaster relief.

Creswell also suggests that when a journalist contacts you for an interview, it's a good idea to provide them with a one-page handout that includes the correct spelling of names, phone numbers, and other pertinent pieces of information about you and your business that they can refer to when they go back to the office to do their write up.

Writing Press Releases

Your tool for pursuing media coverage is the press release you mail to an editor or TV newsperson. A release should be typed on a single sheet of 8½" by 11" paper with wide margins and it should be double-spaced to allow the editor to make changes to it.

At the top of the release put the release date or the phrase, "For Immediate Release." This should be followed by full contact information including the name, title, business name, and day and night phone number of the contact person. Follow this with a headline that emphasizes the story's hook. Like in a good newspaper article, the first paragraph should summarize the main points of the story—answering those five questions you must have encountered in high school English: who, what, where, why, and how. Use active rather than passive verbs. If you must use more than one page, put "More" at the bottom of the page before continuing and end the article with either "-end-" or "###." It helps while preparing the release if you think of yourself as writing a brief article for the overworked, harried editor who will receive it. In many cases this is exactly what you are doing.

PC Week editor and columnist Peter Coffee reminds consultants looking for coverage that before you send out a release, you should make sure you've taken the time to look through the publication you're targeting and that you have a good grasp of who their target audience is and what the editors consider the hot buttons for their readers. The more your release is crafted to push those buttons, the more likely it is to be picked up. Then, he says, "write a press release that tells us why we should care, in other words, one that recognizes our target audience. Don't frame the release in terms of what you've done: frame it in terms of why they should care."

Building a Relationship with the Media

Your chances of having a press release turn into an article will grow exponentially if you take the time to build relationships with editors. A release that arrives in the mail from someone the editor has never heard of will almost certainly go into the "if we get desperate for copy" pile. But if the editor can attach a face and a personality to your name, it may get more consideration. Creswell has found trade shows and conferences good places to make contact with editors and trade journalists. She suggests that you drop into publisher's booths at trade shows and chat with the people there, some of whom may be editorial staff, about your area of specialization and how it might fit in with their needs. If you hit it off, she suggests, "get their card, memorize their face and follow up." If you are invited to speak at conferences, your speaker designation may also be a passport to meeting the press. Some of the larger conferences will have a special reception area where speakers and press may mix.

Software developer Tim Mullen points out that even if you can't make face-to-face contact, you can still do a lot over the phone. Before mailing a release, he calls the editor responsible for the part of the magazine where notice about his software product would appear, introduces himself, explains who he is and makes it clear that he's the author of the software, not a paid flack. Then he asks the editor what he can do to keep his notice out of the slush pile. He's found that listening closely to the reply can indeed lead to success.

Some publications have a reader's guide that they'll send you on request. It lists key sections along with the editor, title, and phone number, and a description of the kind and length of material needed for the section. When you call, you can ask if the publication has such a guide and request a copy of it.

Once you've opened up a relationship with media personnel, it is vital to follow up and keep it going. If you can give the editor an interesting lead, or share a piece of inside information with her, do it. Such friendly, giving contacts are likely to establish you as someone worth chatting with, rather than another consultant wanna-be looking for free coverage.

EVERYONE HATES COLD CALLING BUT IT WORKS

Until now, we've been looking at the long-term strategies that successful computer consultants rely on to stay in business. But what do you do when there's nothing in the hopper and you have to find some business fast? The answer, I'm afraid, is cold calling. Cold calling refers to the process of calling up people who don't know you and attempting to interest them in your services. Doing it means putting yourself in the same category with the folks who interrupt you at dinnertime to sell you frozen meat plans, magazine subscriptions, and cut-rate cemetery plots. I've never yet met anyone who claimed to enjoy it, but I've heard from plenty of consultants who've used cold calling to rejuvenate anemic client lists. You may find the idea repellent, particularly if you tend to be a shy techie, but when you've got no alternatives and aren't quite ready to hire back in as a nine-to-fiver at MegaCorp, cold calling may be what keeps your business alive.

The Point of Cold Calling

The most important thing to realize about cold calling is that its purpose is not to talk people into hiring you or to pressure strangers into giving you work. When you cold call, your only goal is to locate the people who already need your services and who will be glad to hear from you.

If your services are of any value, these people are already out there. Unfortunately, thousands of other people are also out there who are likely to slam down the phone the minute they figure out that you are a telemarketer. Therefore, for a cold calling campaign to succeed you must be able to tolerate rejection. You must treat everyone you call politely, forget the people who aren't interested in what you have to offer, and keep calling others until you find that one person in a hundred who does want to know more about what you have to sell.

Know What You Are Selling

Before you can use any cold calling technique effectively you must be able to convey a clear idea of what you are selling. You will only have a few seconds to get across your message to a potential client and if you are too vague it is unlikely you will be able to spur any interest. Therefore your cold call is most likely to succeed if you *design your message to sell a single clear-cut, easily described service*, rather than a vague smorgasbord of offerings.

Consultant Michael Miora makes this point clearly and dramatically:

> I began as a generalist. I said in my materials, which included top-quality brochures, middle-quality brochures, and homemade laser printed stuff reproduced with color on color copiers, that I performed "Business Systems Analysis" to help growing companies make their business systems do what they need them to do.... These brochures were hard hitting, professional, expensive, and totally ineffective.
>
> One day I had lunch with Ernest Loen, a rather well-known management consultant. He told me the secret to success is to advertise yourself as a specialist, "even if you can do everything." But choose a specialty that will bring you in touch with general fields of interest for your customers.
>
> So, I did. Now I present myself and my prospectus, "Business Systems Analysis for Security and Disaster Recovery," and my advertising materials (the cheaper ones) say, "Protect Yourself."
>
> Suddenly I found myself with all sorts of consulting contracts. I had to subcontract pieces out because I was too busy. I have to find organizations in which to meet people so we can cross-refer, because I am getting contracts I don't want. *But of all my contracts, only a few are*

specifically aimed at security. In all the others, security was the beginning of the discussion and we quickly went on to systems engineering.

So before you can cold call successfully, you need to determine which of your many capabilities you are going to highlight, doing your best to *choose a specialty with broad appeal* that will help you connect with potential clients.

Whom Do You Call?

Next you need to come up with a list of people to call. Telemarketers selling consumer products can survive by calling everyone they find on a page of the telephone directory, but to sell consulting services you will need to use a much more targeted list. Consultants who have had success with cold calling are most often those who *target specialized groups of clients* like attorneys or managers of VAX installations, rather than those who attempt to call everyone who might own a computer. Michael Miora has had the most success calling corporate CFOs at companies with revenues over $100 million. He finds that these executives are much less likely to slam the phone down on him than are lower-level personnel or principals of smaller businesses because these experienced business professionals consider cold calls such as his one of their windows on the world.

Consultant Ed Tignor, who faced the problem of starting a practice in a new community after moving for personal reasons, took a different approach to selecting a target for his cold calling campaign. He got a list of area companies from the chamber of commerce in his new community and after studying it and analyzing the businesses on it decided to target law firms. He was able to parlay a combination of letters to these firms followed up by carefully scripted phone calls into one definite assignment and several other potential jobs. Consultant Jack Poynter has also had success using chamber of commerce lists. He contacted two hundred companies he located using such a list and has ended up with four solid contacts that are still keeping him fed.

Other sources of lists are *industry directories*, which list the names of IS executives and what kinds of hardware their shops employ, and lists you can buy from limited circulation trade magazines like *Computerworld* or *Datamation*, which are compiled from their subscriber lists. The public library is another fertile hunting ground. Ask the reference librarian to show you the section that contains business directories. You will find shelves full of hefty national directories listing companies sorted by their lines of business, as well as locally produced directories that offer varying amounts of information about local businesses and contact information.

Professional groups may also be willing to sell you lists of their mem-

bers, as may civic groups, and if none of these does the job, you may
want to inspect the offerings available from list brokers who advertise
in the yellow pages.

Cold Calling and Mass Mailings

Many consultants who have used cold calling effectively start their
campaign with a carefully crafted letter, in short, with some version of
the mass mailing discussed earlier in this chapter and dismissed as ineffective. But comparing the experiences of consultants who have
mailed letters and then called and those who have started calling without any preliminaries, it doesn't look as if this kind of letter really does
much to improve the success of a cold calling strategy.

Most interesting is the experience of one consultant who found that
he was most successful when doing a "follow-up call" *first*, without
ever mailing a letter. As he explains it, "Most people throw out so much
junk mail, they don't think twice about getting a 'follow-up call' to a
mailing they don't remember. During the phone call they give you a
sympathetic listening because they appreciate you 'following up' as op-
posed to just sending junk mail or cold calling. Sometimes you can tell
that they are a bit embarrassed that they must have discarded your
'mailing' without any notice." Once he's made this initial "follow-up"
call, he then sends a mailing, which he finds gets much more attention.

Although it probably isn't necessary to pretend to have already done
a mailing, this experience does point out how ineffective mailings are
in general and emphasizes the advisability of investing in paper and
postage only when you've established that the prospect has some interest in your services.

Use a Script

Perhaps the most important thing you can do to make your cold calls effective is to prepare a script and practice it before beginning your cold
calling campaign. A script is not the same as a spiel, which is a canned,
memorized line of patter of the sort used by encyclopedia and vacuum
cleaner salespeople. The calling script a consultant uses should be *a
brief list of points* that he or she uses to keep on track and to help avoid
stage fright.

Consultant Chaim Caron points out that people can easily tell when
you are reading from an actual script and suggests that you practice
long enough with whatever script you come up with so the topics you
want to discuss flow naturally in a real conversation. If you are new
to this kind of calling, you should try practicing with a friend a few
times before calling potential clients. Even if you've done this,
though, you should be prepared to experience a bit of stage fright

when you first start out. Consultant Larry Dysert suggests that you come up with a few different scripts and try them all out, keeping track of which ones work the best for you and which ones you feel the most comfortable giving.

What should your cold calling script contain? Paul Ferrara describes his by saying "the gist of my call is I tell them who I am and ask if I can have a meeting of fifteen minutes to a half hour to tell them who we are and what we do. I never try to sell anything on the phone and if I can't get the meeting I rarely follow up." He adds that most calls are successful because he is selective in whom he calls, and the meetings he arranges often result in work, though not necessarily immediately.

Michael Miora's script consists of telling potential clients his name, his specialty—disaster recovery planning—and stating that his reason for calling is to offer his services to the CFO, whom he mentions by name. If he reaches a secretary or assistant, he politely explains that he wants to offer his services to the principal and asks to be connected to him or her. He also emphasizes that the point of a cold call should not be to try to sell services, but only to close a face-to-face appointment.

Consultant Bill Long agrees that the initial cold call should have one and only one purpose: *to secure an initial, face-to-face meeting.* He adds, "Questions are the tools to be used here. Find out if the client has any real problems in the general field of your expertise. If so arrange a meeting. If not, either put him on your calling list for later follow-up, or if there is no chance of him needing your products or services in the future, forget him and move on to the next call."

If you've done a good job of defining what you have to sell and coming up with a carefully selected list of people to call, what you're really doing is not so much cold calling as lukewarm calling. Ed Tignor found this to be the case when he tried this approach. He sent out a preliminary letter he spent several weeks perfecting, that he says stressed "benefits, benefits, benefits for my client if they used my services." He then roughed out a script for his phone calls, "so that I would not sound like an incoherent fool on the phone." The payoff was that his first phone call led to an appointment for an interview.

Tignor was pleasantly surprised to discover that, "I didn't have to sell anything in that first interview. My client knew he needed services like mine. He was just ensuring that I could deliver what I said I could. I didn't have to create a need."

Certainly there was some good luck operating here and most consultants should not expect to get a hit on their first call. But Tignor's success was not entirely due to luck, but happened because he took the time to do his calling the right way. If, like him, you make your calls to people whom you have some reason to expect might need your services, and if you explain briefly and clearly *in a low-pressure way* what those services are, you too are likely to be successful.

SALES TRAINING FOR PEOPLE WHO HATE SALES TRAINING

If you have the kind of technical ability it takes to be a successful computer consultant, the chances are very good that as your career has progressed you've concentrated on learning what you consider to be "real things" rather than on the soft, people skills that more business-oriented, nontechnical people pursue. As an employee you may have dismissed all business talk as buzzwords, and you may have secretly felt a kind of contempt for salespeople who seem so often to have nothing but their mastery of buzzwords to recommend them.

But as comfortable as these attitudes might have made you feel, they are not conducive to success in computer consulting. As Tim Mullen says, "Many programmers are turned off when the subject of sales comes up. Since this is an area foreign to their nature, they should probably be making an extra effort to understand it. There is a technical side to both sales and marketing and it's not some 'black art' practiced by strange men in plaid jackets." Ed Tignor suggests that the most productive way for a technically oriented person to approach marketing is to "treat marketing as an interesting problem to solve."

And solving it may mean, as with solving any technical problem, getting outside help. Many consultants have found that they've learned a lot from reading books they've found at the public library. Among the titles established consultants recommend are Bill Good's landmark book about telemarketing, *Prospecting Your Way to Sales Success*, Jeffrey Lant's guide to successful mailing, *Cash Copy*, and Jay Conrad Levinson's *Guerrilla Marketing*.

Other consultants have felt that they needed the experience of live training to improve their marketing skills. Among the courses they recommend is the Dale Carnegie course in selling techniques, and the course provided by the Sandler Sales Institute.

Whichever approach you take, consultants who feel they've benefited from sales training advise that you stay away from the feel-good school of sales techniques—the simplistic books most often found in retail bookstore business sections, and that you go instead to a college bookstore and look at the books sold to business majors on these topics. They also advise that when looking for seminars you stay away from the motivational speakers and try to find courses that focus on techniques, methods, and behaviors, rather than glib one-size-fits-all buzzwords and simplistic suggestions as to how to adjust your attitude. Investing some time in learning the principles of effective marketing and sales from the experts may well be the critical factor that keeps your computer consulting practice growing.

7

WORKING WITH BROKERS

We've looked at the many marketing techniques independent computer consultants use to find their clients. But a significant number of people who call themselves computer consultants find their clients through a radically different marketing alternative: a single telephone call to a *contract consulting broker*. Analysis of the rates reported to the Real Rate Survey in 1996 suggest that 35 percent of the consultants polled used brokers to find work. Other surveys suggest that those who use brokers find almost 80 percent of their work this way.

Brokered work is a controversial topic within the consulting community. Many consultants reject it outright and refuse to consider those who take it true consultants, but many others accept it as a necessary evil and use it when they have no better prospects. This chapter examines the realities of brokered consulting and shows you how to make it work for you.

WHAT IS BROKERED CONSULTING?

Many beginning consultants wonder whom the term *consultant broker* refers to, as few, if any, of the firms consultants call "brokers" use that term to describe themselves. Briefly, brokers are the companies you see advertising for consultants in the Sunday employment classifieds data processing/computer section and on job search Web sites. These companies usually call themselves "Consulting Firms," though firms that specialize in placing engineers may call themselves technical service firms (TSFs) or job shops. These companies sell their clients the hourly services of both their own regular salaried employee consultants and of independent consultants whom they pay on a hourly rate basis—that rate being some percentage of the rate they bill the end client. The tipoff that a company is in the business of brokering consultants is that their ads include a code phrase like "High Hourly Rates," "Contracts Available," or "Independents Welcome."

In brief, these firms function very much like temporary employment agencies. If you have the proper skills, they will speedily place you on a consulting contract lasting anywhere from a few weeks to many months or even years. In return for their services they receive a hefty chunk of money for every hour you work. But you will also do well. The Real Rate Survey showed that the median brokered consultant earns $55 an hour.

WHAT KIND OF WORK DO BROKERED CONSULTANTS DO?

Consultants who do not use brokers often accuse those who do of being "no better than employees." And indeed, because of the requirement of Section 1706 of the Tax Reform Act of 1986, consultants who work through such brokers are frequently forced to work as W-2 employees rather than independent contractors, although they may be getting consultant-like hourly rates and working on many projects for many different clients over the course of a year. Even so, some 19 percent—almost one-fifth—of the successful consultants who attended an ICCA convention and filled in the ICCA's survey questionnaire reported getting frequent work from brokers. Indeed the percentage of consultants using brokers to find work was only two percentage points less than the number of those who got work by running their own sales and marketing campaigns.

"Real" or not, brokered consultants tend to stay in business for the long term, and anyone who plans to build a career out of consulting cannot afford to utterly write off a marketing avenue that has brought in so much business for other consultants.

Much of the confusion and acrimony that surrounds the topic originates because the term *computer consultant* is a blanket term that covers people who pursue a wide range of business activities and serve a broad spectrum of clients: value-added resellers, custom software developers, contract programmers, systems integrators, and people who help small businesses. Consultant brokers, on the other hand, only place a small subset of the consulting community: contract programmers who serve a strictly limited group of clients—usually Fortune 500 companies.

Because brokers don't place resellers, systems integrators, or consultants who serve smaller businesses, the consultants who fall into these other, nonbrokered, niches often have little exposure to, or knowledge of, the environment in which brokered consultants work, and hence little respect for the work they do. This is probably why they assume that such consultants do nothing more than drudge work, and tend to refer to them in debate using insulting names like "warm bodies" or "mirror foggers."

There are indeed outfits that place armies of contract coders on low-skill assignments that live up to the image that these detractors invoke. But there are also plenty of brokered consultants doing creative, high-level work.

Consultant Charles Miller, who has worked with brokers for several years, explains, "I have the chance to work on projects that a one-man shop would never have the opportunity to get near. For example, I'm acting [now] as assistant project manager on a four-year, ten-million-dollar project." He describes the contract as "an incredible learning experience" and explains that he got it "only because I was working with this broker." Miller adds that the other people the same broker has placed on his project all have excellent skills and that all of them have anywhere from twelve to twenty years of experience in industry, many of them having previously held senior positions.

Another experienced consultant, Joe Scordato, explains that in his more than fifteen years of consulting he's frequently worked through brokers for specific engagements, particularly when working for large Fortune 500 clients in the New York area whose corporate policies require that consultants they bring in be on the corporation's limited-access preferred vendor list. The work Scordato does for these clients can hardly be described as "dead-end coding," but includes a broad range of business systems consulting, including feasibility studies, systems design, hardware and software evaluation, and disaster recovery.

WHY CLIENT COMPANIES PREFER HIRING BROKERED CONSULTANTS

Many beginning consultants wonder why so many corporate clients prefer to use brokered consultants rather than find computer consultants directly, particularly when the brokered consultant is almost always more expensive than the independent because of the hefty markup needed to cover the broker's commission. Others wonder why a competent consultant would work for brokers who take so much of their billing dollar. But there are good reasons for using brokers both from the client's and the consultant's perspective. We'll examine them now.

Convenience

When a corporate manager needs to find a consultant, the chances are that he or she needs that consultant yesterday. Consultants are usually brought into the corporate environment to help out in crisis situations;

by the time the required paperwork and approvals are taken care of, managers rarely have time to spare. One factor that contributes to the success of brokers is that most managers find it impossible to find a consultant with the exact skills they need on this sort of short notice.

Even if the manager has a drawer full of brochures and business cards stashed away for just such an emergency, it is difficult to remember which consultant has the skills necessary to do a particular job. And even after a match is found, the hiring company will have to take time to check references and conduct a rigorous interview with each consultant before hiring one. Worse, when the manager does call competent independent consultants, inevitably they find them busy, their schedules booked up weeks or months into the future, and unable to help the manager deal with his current need.

That's the key to the broker's appeal. Once applied to, a broker can often provide a carefully screened and qualified consultant able to interview that afternoon and willing to start work the next week. The convenience and ease of the process far outweighs the additional cost for almost all corporate managers.

Fear of Section 1706 Audits

But there is another, more compelling reason why corporate managers use brokered consultants: Section 1706 of the Tax Reform Act of 1986. As you'll recall from the discussion in Chapter 3, Section 1706 is that vague portion of the tax code currently interpreted as exposing employers to severe IRS penalties for misclassifying employees as contractors. Although it in fact only applies to three-party, brokered situations, audit-shy corporations have increasingly interpreted it to apply to all contracting situations involving computer consultants. As a result, many such companies now refuse to bring in any independent consultants for fear of having them reclassified as employees by the IRS.

Many companies jumped on the no-independents bandwagon in the early 1990s after learning of widely publicized IRS audits in which large numbers of contractors were reclassified as employees. The reclassification as employees of thousands of contractors working at Microsoft in 1996 intensified client concern. Indeed, it has become common for corporate managers to call consultants who have worked for them in the past to offer them contracts, and then to inform them that if they want the work, they will have to contact one of the few large consulting firms on the company's limited preferred vendor list. The consultant must then call and request that one of these firms hire them in as hourly employees for the length of the contract.

It stinks, but if you intend to do consulting within the larger corporate environment, you will have to deal with it.

Political Realities

The last reason that corporate managers prefer to hire brokered contract programmers rather than bring in independent consultants is a simple one: it is far easier to get upper management approval for bringing in the brokered contract programmer than it is for bringing in the other kind of consultant.

Corporate manager Paul DeBeasi describes the constraints that he faced when he needed help on a project: "I've hired two software contractors over the last five months. In order for me to get my manager—it actually went to the VP level—to sign the purchase order, I had to clearly state that 'I need X to be done. I have a person to do the job for Y dollars. If you don't give me the money, the impact to the schedule will be Z.' " DeBeasi called the people he hired contract programmers when describing them to his VP, but is quick to explain that he got much more than contract programming from them. "The people I hired were sharp. They did a great job. They also, lo and behold, had a lot of technical advice on areas of the project that I did not specifically hire them to work on. If I had gone to my management to ask for money 'in order to get technical advice,' I would never have gotten it."

Savvy managers know that people who ask their bosses for money to pay for consultants to participate in high-level decision making, strategic planning, or any of the other tasks that management considers to fall under a manager's own job description are not only setting themselves up for the request to be rejected, but may even be raising questions in their bosses' minds about whether the request for such high-level aid suggests the managers aren't capable of doing their jobs on their own. This, as much as any other reason, explains why most of the highly experienced consultants who are brought in to contribute their high-level skills to troubled projects come into such projects labeled as contract programmers.

BROKERING ARRANGEMENTS OUTSIDE OF THE UNITED STATES

Outside of the United States it is much less common for brokers to attempt to force contractors into working as salaried employees. The only places where this might not be true may be in countries such as France, that have strong social laws in place. There a contractor who works for a single client full-time for six months may be reclassified as an employee and the client fined for attempting to evade payment of the employee's social security payments. In such countries, brokered consulting is not likely to be as common as it is in other countries such as the United Kingdom, where the status of temporary personnel working as independent contractors is not as likely to come up for review.

You'll also find regional variations in whether brokers insist that you incorporate. You'll need to talk to other consultants in your country to find out what is customary.

ADVANTAGES OF BROKERED WORK FOR THE CONSULTANT

From the previous discussion it should be clear that the consultants who use brokers are not just those with borderline skills or those just breaking in. Consultants with many years in the business draw on the services of brokers. What do they get out of it?

Immediate Work

Obviously the main benefit a broker can offer the consultant is immediate access to clients willing to pay for their services, canceling out the necessity to do all that miserable, ongoing marketing we discussed in Chapter 6.

Whether this access to clients—and freedom from having to market—is a blessing or a curse is up for debate. The very ease with which a skilled consultant can get a broker to place him may lead to laziness in approaching the marketing task. It may also tempt the consultant to take any job a broker shows up with, rather than holding out for the kind of assignment that will increase the consultant's skill level and maintain his long-term viability as a consultant.

But the consultant who has spent several weeks at home, cold calling for all he or she is worth, and who is still looking at an empty work schedule should have no trouble seeing the appeal in the service the broker can offer. Even after paying the broker's hefty commission, 65 percent of something is a whole lot better than 100 percent of nothing.

Guaranteed Payment

But brokers offer the consultant other benefits besides immediate work. The most important is freedom from collection worries. When you work directly for a client you handle your own billings and you get paid when the client feels good and ready to pay you. This may be weeks or even months after you've completed the work—or it may be never. As one consultant says ruefully about her small business clients, "I have no problem at all finding clients. My problem is finding clients who'll pay their bills!" Indeed, collecting money already owned is the number-one headache reported by almost all independent consultants.

A good, reputable broker eliminates this problem for the consultant entirely. A major reason consultants are willing to fork over 40 percent of every dollar billed for their services is that good brokers pay the consultant on a set schedule, usually biweekly, assuming all the risk and hassle of getting the client to pay. Consultant Charles Miller finds this service valuable. As he explains, his client routinely pays 90 to 120 days in arrears, but his broker pays him regularly. In addition, he points out, "If the client doesn't pay, I still get paid. This is sort of like insurance. When you need it, you need it."

WILL A BROKER WORK WITH YOU?

There's no question that brokers can and do get work for computer consultants. But no matter how eager you might be to work with one, you will gain little from canvassing brokers unless your skills fall into the relatively narrow range that brokers traditionally represent. Let's look at those now.

Contract Programming Experience

Although brokers place people who do much more than just code, there's no question that most brokers are looking only for people who can be described as contract programmers. If you can't code at a professional level in an in-demand business computer language, then no matter what your other computer skills or how well you've satisfied the clients you've found on your own, brokers are likely to ignore you.

You can see this by looking at the ads that brokers place. Universally these ads list a series of acronyms citing popular software and operating systems. When one of these ads indicates that the broker is looking for people experienced in Windows they are not looking for someone who has installed Windows software for a client, nor are they looking for someone who is comfortable using Windows applications. They are looking only for someone who can develop software that runs under Windows. Unless you can claim at least three years of experience as a paid programmer with a year or more experience using the software mentioned in a broker ad, few brokers you contact will even bother to call you back.

Experience with Fortune 500 Corporations

Another thing to be aware of is that brokers are interested almost exclusively in people who have been employees of the same kinds of Fortune 500 corporations that make up the bulk of their clients. If you've worked only for small businesses rather than large corporations, then no matter how good your technical skills, you are likely to be at the bottom of the list of people they call about a contract.

Application Experience in Specific Areas

After your technical skills, a broker will look most closely at your application experience. Experience in specialties like investment banking or retail inventory control will make you even more attractive to a broker—if she serves a corporate clientele in those industries. If your experience lies strictly in coding up routines for your own use at home and you've never done paid coding work, you're unlikely to get called at all.

This is important: While it is possible to take "home grown" skills and parlay them into a consulting career, you are not going to be able to enlist the help of a broker in building that career. Legitimate brokers complain that one of the real downers of their jobs is being pestered daily by phone calls from people whose sole experience with computers is home-based hacking. They call up demanding to be sent out on lucrative assignments and often become verbally abusive when it is explained to them that brokers only place people who have significant amounts of experience as paid programmers.

This isn't discrimination, it's just a reflection of the truth that no broker's client is going to pay the broker to turn up the same inexperienced people that deluge the client's human resources department with applications.

No matter how good your code is or how valuable you may imagine your services could be to these clients, if you want to pursue them you'll have to market yourself to them on your own. No reputable broker will place people who can't show significant amounts of paid experience in the workplace on their resume. Indeed, if your experience is entirely home-based, anyone who does promise to place you is probably some kind of scamster who makes his money off of wanna-be consultants rather than a legitimate broker who makes his money from satisfying clients.

HOW DO YOU LOCATE A REPUTABLE BROKER?

Assuming you've made it this far and have some of the skills that brokers are looking for, you now face the problem of finding one you can work with. This is no easy task. Any time consultants discuss brokers, it quickly becomes apparent that brokers range in quality from sleazy scamsters, ripoff artists, and deadbeats to reliable professionals who have earned the gratitude and respect of the consultants who work with them.

It would be nice if there were some handy rules of thumb for determining at once which category an unknown broker falls into, but alas, this is not the case. Some reliable professionals dress in tasteful suits and operate out of sleek corporate offices. But so do some of the scamsters—and some of the most reliable professionals dress in loud plaid sports jackets and sound surprisingly like guys you'd encounter selling jalopies on a used car lot—as do some of the scamsters.

Large frequent ads in the newspapers tell you only that a consulting firm has so far managed to pay their advertising bill. They give you no clue as to whether the firm is advertising real contracts or not. The acronyms you see in a broker ad may represent individual contracts waiting to be filled, or they may merely be bait the broker is using to fish for consultants, hoping that if he attracts a few people with hot skills, he can then find clients to hire them.

Even the fact that a consulting firm is a huge national outfit with a well-known name and offices in twenty-four cities is no guarantee of quality. There are several huge, well-known firms that subject armies of poorly paid consultants to sweatshop conditions and are therefore constantly having to recruit new people to fill the places of victims who quit.

In short, when it comes to brokers, *caveat contractor.*

Using Word-of-Mouth Recommendations

Because there are so many brokers in the marketplace who indulge in questionable business practices, your best bet is to deal only with brokers you've heard recommended by other consultants, or, alternately, to contact broker firms you've encountered during your days as an employee—firms whose consultants impressed you as competent and satisfied with their broker relationship.

If you don't know of any such firms or don't know any brokered consultants who can recommend good brokers to you, then take the time to do some research before you contact any unknown broker firms to make sure you don't end up dealing with someone who could turn you off to brokered work for good.

The best way to check out the reputation of local brokers is to ask consultants you run into at networking affairs which firms they'd recommend—and which ones they would avoid. If you get a recommendation, stash it away for future reference. If you hear a firm mentioned a few times, perhaps it might be worth a call.

However, even here you must be wary. If the recommendation for a consulting firm comes from someone who works for that firm, you might want to inquire delicately if the consultant gets a referral fee for recommending their broker to you. Many firms pay cash bonuses to

their consultants for bringing in new talent. So although the firm may
be reputable, if the person suggesting them is getting paid for recruiting
you, their advice must be somewhat suspect.

Another way of flushing out the good brokers is to ask managers you
know which firms they hire from and what their personal impression
might be of the various broker firms in town. But do this tactfully. If put
on the spot and asked "Is CompuHerd Consulting any good?" many
managers may answer equivocally, unwilling to have word get around
that they are badmouthing local firms. But if you approach managers indirectly and ask instead, "Do any firms around here have the reputation
for being real bozos?" or "What kind of problems have the contractors
you've hired run into with their brokers?" you are much more likely to
flush out the anecdotes that tell you all you need to know about CompuHerd, as well as other local companies, good and bad, you might not
have heard about.

Avoid Long-Distance Brokers

Talking with people who have worked with brokers in your area or
who hire the consultants they place will eventually give you enough information to make an informed choice about which brokers to contact.
Once you contact them, you can use the guidelines we'll discuss in the
rest of this chapter to make sure the broker is someone you'll want to
deal with. But the situation gets much more complex once you expand
the scope of your search beyond the local marketplace.

It is almost impossible to research the quality of out-of-town brokers
whose ads you may encounter on-line or in national publications like
Computerworld or in job finder publications like *CE Weekly* and *PD
News* that cater to professional job shoppers. The positions they advertise may sound tempting, and they may be completely legitimate. Many
are. But many are not, and as someone just starting out in consulting,
you probably don't have the resources to weed out the ones that are
going to mess up your life. As a result it is almost always a mistake to
respond to out-of-town ads unless you are really desperate and willing
to gamble with your career.

And it is a gamble. Out-of-town companies usually offer contracts
that necessitate your relocating to a distant part of the country, to work
for firms you know nothing about, and which are almost impossible to
research by word-of-mouth methods at home. Those out-of-town firms
without a local sales force that claim to be able to offer you local contracts should raise your suspicions, too, as it's unlikely that they can attract any but the most desperate—and impossible to work with—local
clients when in competition with local firms with knowledgeable local
salespeople.

It is difficult enough to find a good broker locally. It seems like stacking the deck against yourself to introduce the additional problems that long-distance contracting entails. If a local contract falls through—as many do—or if you run into broker dirty tricks early in the relationship, the price of quitting is usually nothing more than aggravation and lost time. But consultants who have taken out-of-town contracts offered by broker firms have found themselves stranded in distant cities, without work, losing hefty security deposits on apartments they'd rented expecting to be working for six months or more and being stuck with now-worthless airline tickets. And although there are several forms of recourse you can turn to when faced with bad-guy brokers who refuse to pay, almost all of them are prohibitively expensive to pursue if the broker operates outside of the state where you reside.

There may be a time when you turn to an out-of-town broker for help, but it would be wiser to postpone this until you've had enough experience in the world of brokered work that you're not likely to stumble into an abusive situation.

DEVELOPING A RELATIONSHIP WITH A BROKER

Once you've gotten the name of a reputable local broker, you are still not out of the woods. You will need to evaluate the broker carefully in your initial contacts with them. As consultant Burt Johnson points out, no matter what a firm's reputation might be, the success of your relationship with a given broker will have a lot to do with how well your personalities match and other individual factors. He explains, "I have dealt very successfully with some brokers that other consultants say they would never touch, and personally won't deal with some that others say they like. It is individuals within the company that can make a big difference. Within any particular office, you want to link up with the person that will serve your needs best. Since that person will vary based upon the types of contracting you do—platforms, languages, applications, etc.—the answer you get from someone else [about which broker is best] may *not* be the best for you."

Your relationship with a broker will usually proceed in three stages. During your first contact, when you phone the broker or mail in a resume, your goal will be to impress the broker with the quality of your skills. During the second phase, you'll have a face-to-face meeting with broker representatives and be expected to answer their questions about your credentials and experience. This meeting, before you have made any commitments to the broker, is your best chance to satisfy yourself about the way that the broker does business and to double-check that this is a firm you want to deal with. Finally, once this mutual screening is completed satisfactorily, the broker will call you when he has a specific contract he'd like you to interview for. If you are interested, the broker will arrange an interview with the actual client. If the interview goes well, the broker will contact you again and all subsequent negotiations about your rates and the conditions you will work under for the client will take place between you and the broker. If an agreement can be reached you will sign a contract binding you to the broker, and only then will you begin working for the client.

Your Resume: Making a Positive First Contact

Clearly, before you can get to a position to evaluate a broker and decide whether you want to work with him, you'll have to put some effort into impressing the broker with your skills and convincing him that you are worth his time and effort.

Brokers will almost always request that you send them a resume. But before you stick an old resume in an envelope, it's important to realize that the most effective kind of resume you can send a broker is very different from one you'd submit to a potential employer.

Employers may like to see resumes showing steady promotion, and evidence of management skills, but *brokers care mainly about your technical skills*. Indeed, brokers often seem to work on a "byte by byte compare" basis, matching word-for-word the requirements clients list with what they find on consultant resumes. If a requisition says "Sybase" and your resume says "Sybase" you'll get the call. If your resume says instead "SQL server" the chances are good that even though you used SQL on both jobs, the nontechnical broker salesperson will not realize this and will move on to someone else.

So the best kind of resume to send a broker is one that highlights the *specific hardware and software* you've worked with. Remember that most broker salespeople are just that, salespeople, and their technical knowledge is pretty weak. There are occasional stellar exceptions to this rule, and they are probably the salespeople you want to work with. But it's best to keep your descriptions of your career simple, until you can meet with the salesperson in person and can establish where he or she is coming from.

And your best hope of getting to that face-to-face meeting is to *put on your resume every possible acronym* you can include without lying. Flesh this out with information highlighting the application areas you've specialized in, and be sure to highlight the name of any well-known companies you've worked for. Clients love to know you've come from a name brand background. Figure 7-1 shows an employee resume that was rewritten to make it an effective broker contact tool, emphasizing software skills, application expertise, and Fortune 100 employ-

Joyce Chu   Phone: 203-555-3172
35 Redondo Square
Hartford, CT 06012

EMPLOYMENT HISTORY
MegaCorp.
Benefits Access/Managed Care Service Center. Sept. 1993–Present. Lead Systems Designer. Implemented first DB2-to-Object-Oriented data conversion in the history of MegaCorp using Windows and OS/2 Smalltalk V systems with Sybase database to interface to corporate DB2 database.

Health Plan Benefit System Rewrite. Jan. 1991–Sept. 1993. Technical leader of programming team using DB2 and CICS. Supporting users in Financial, Admin, and Underwriting areas.

QMF Support. Mar. 1990–Dec. 1990. Lead Systems Designer responsible for tech support of health plan personnel in their efforts to write SQL queries in the QMF environment against National DB2 database. Customers also include actuarial and financial personnel. Wrote dialogues utilizing CLIST, ISPEXEC, and REXX languages.

Employee Marketing. Jan. 1988–Mar. 1990. Supported Cybertek COBOL and Assembly language Group Universal Life system. Designed and coded ROSCOE-based user-oriented interactive system to accelerate large-scale administrative functions in support of Group Universal Life product.

CompuHerd Consulting.
Endurance Life Insurance Company. 1986–1987. Provided expert programming services to clients including MVS/XA dump interpretation, OS/JCL, CLISTS, and run time improvements and systems analysis and coding for enhancements to a Mutual Life Insurance Daily Cycle System.

Fiduciary Trust Insurance Company.
Applications Programmer/Analyst. 1983–1984. Maintained and enhanced Agency System applications in CMS, COBOL, VSAM, BAL, TSO, and CICS environment.

SOFTWARE EXPERIENCE

Languages:	COBOL II	IBM 370 Assembly Language	
	Smalltalk V		
Database:	Sybase	DB2/SQL	QMF
On-Line:	CICS		
Operating			
Systems:	MVS/XA (JCL, VSAM, TSO)	OS/2 PM	Windows NT
	VM/CMS (REXX)	PC/DOC	
Other:	Object-oriented design, coding, production implementation.		

EDUCATION
B.S. Computer Science: U. of Connecticut, 1983.
MegaCorp Institute: DB2 SQL. Intro to Sybase. REXX. XEDIT Macros.
Hartford Graduate Center: Command Level CICS.
KSC Knowledge Systems Corp. Smalltalk V, Coding, Analysis and Design.

FIGURE 7-1   Employee resume slanted for consulting.

ment. (Actual names have been fictionalized.) Note in particular the Software Experience section. This easy-to-read table of alphabet soup makes it easy for even the laziest broker salesperson to locate the consultant's skills and match them with open orders.

And don't forget when you mail your resume to any broker to include a friendly cover letter that specifies that your resume is not to be circulated to any clients without your express permission and approval. This is important for reasons we'll discuss later.

The Interview with the Broker

Your initial interview with the broker will be mostly taken up with the broker's attempts to determine your skill level, verify the items on your resume, and ensure that you are someone he would be comfortable sending out for interviews. But this interview is also your opportunity to find out how the broker does business and to make sure that you will be comfortable working for him.

Early in the interview, try to learn a little bit about the background of the person who is interviewing you. Is this the actual salesperson who will place you, or a recruiter whose job is to see if you are technically qualified before passing you on to a technically naive salesperson? If it is a recruiter, make sure you are given a chance to meet the actual salesperson who will represent you before you commit to working with the broker.

During the interview be alert for signs that may tip you off that the interviewer has other goals than getting you contracts. Are you being pumped for contact information? Does the interviewer seem obsessed with trying to talk you into becoming a salaried employee at a low salary when you have made it clear you are only interested in working for a high hourly rate?

Trust your gut feelings. If you don't feel right about the broker personnel, no matter how good the company may sound, don't work with them. Such feelings are almost always a sign that you've picked up on something subliminal.

Watch Out for Pumping

In particular, during the interview, watch out for signs that the interviewer is pumping you for contact information. A good broker will ask you for a few relevant references but he will not pump you for the name of your ex-clients or for contact information for every manager you've ever worked with. Broker personnel who do this may be more interested in building up their lists of clients to cold call than in placing you. If you have supplied a reasonable number of personal references and the interviewer continues to pry for names of old employers and consulting clients, it is legitimate to state that your client list is competitive information and that you do not see any reason for sharing such information with the broker at this point in your relationship.

A good broker should also be willing to give you the names of clients and of other contractors who have worked for them so that you can check them out.

Finally, it is important that you tell the broker's staff during the interview that you don't want them to ever submit your resume anywhere without first contacting you and getting your explicit permission. All reputable brokers will agree to this and it is important that you bring the topic up to prevent misunderstandings. You may end up deciding to work with another broker or working with several at the same time, and you don't want to have to worry about having your resume submitted for the same job from several sources. You also don't want your resume used as part of a bait-and-switch tactic in a situation in which the broker uses your supposed unavailability to throw a job to his own less qualified employee.

How Well Does the Broker Know the Market?

During the interview you should be listening for evidence of how well informed the broker's staff are about local IS shops. Salespeople should show that they are aware of the technologies each is using and about new projects and major reorganizations. A salesperson who doesn't seem aware of what is going on at companies you've worked in locally should be treated with suspicion. You're paying that hefty commission in order to buy sales skills. If the salesperson doesn't know the local market, he or she isn't likely to be able to do a good job representing you.

Likewise, if a broker salesperson's questions indicate that he isn't familiar with common software environments found in the business world and has little experience selling programming services, avoid him. He is unlikely to be able to do a good job. Salespeople don't have to be ex-programmers, but they do have to know enough to be able to match up your skills with appropriate placements.

Negotiating Rates

During the interview the broker's staff will ask you what rate you want for the work you do. Be careful what you say here. When you work with a broker, all rate negotiations take place between you and the broker, not with the client, and you'll have to live with the rate that you demand during this initial interview. You should have a good idea of what your services are worth before you begin this conversation and should never take the first rate a broker offers. It is almost always too low.

But to be able to ask for a better rate that the broker will agree to, you must do research before the interview to *establish what the actual going rate is for brokered contractors* with skills like yours in your region. Once you've determined it, tell the broker the rate you really want to get, and stick with it. Don't let yourself get talked into working for a lower rate—at least not until you determine that no other broker in the area can get you the rate you want.

Salaried versus Hourly Rate Consulting

If brokers find your resume attractive, they will often spend considerable time and energy during the initial interview trying to convince you that it is a much better idea to work for them as a regular salaried broker employee than as a consultant charging a high hourly rate. And indeed, it is—for the broker, who will end up earning a lot more per hour from your work when you work as a salaried employee. The broker will argue that salaried consultants get benefits, paid vacation, sick time, and job security while hourly consultants get only that high hourly rate—if they work. But the energy with which this argument is made should make you suspicious. Indeed, computer consultants with decent skills almost always come out ahead when they opt to work for a high hourly rate even though they have to buy their own benefits.

There are several reasons for this. One is that working for a salary means you'll have no opportunity to earn the much larger amount that could be yours if you can keep busy most of the year. The salaries paid consulting firm employees tend to range from about $32,000 to $50,000 per year. However, a consultant earning a typical brokered rate of $45 per hour for 1,715 hours—the median number of annual hours one 1992 rate survey found computer consultants billing—would earn $77,175. This amount is some $27,000 more than a typical consulting firm salary, even when you deduct the cost of self-paid health and disability insurance. And the hourly consultant would also have four more weeks off than the salaried employee!

If you are worrying about whether you can find those 1,715 hours of contract work, remember that a consulting firm is not likely to offer you a salary in the first place unless your skills are the sort that make it likely that they can keep you busy almost year-round in your local market. And remember something else: If the consulting firm does miscalculate your appeal to clients, they won't keep on paying you that salary. After three or four weeks of unemployment, salaried consultants almost always find themselves laid off, no matter what promises of job security the broker held out to them at the beginning of the relationship.

And when salaried consultants are laid off, they have much less to show for the contracts they did fill than the consultant who filled them for a much higher hourly rate.

That's not all. There's one last, really troubling problem with salaried consulting that few new consultants are aware of. The salaried consultant loses the ability to pick and choose assignments. While the hourly consultant can decide to take only contracts he or she finds attractive and to work for a variety of brokers and rates, the salaried consultant must work every contract the employer-broker presents or face termination. As a result, salaried consultants can rarely steer their careers in a direction that will lead to long-term viability, but are much more likely to end up filling the dead-end, skills-dulling jobs alluded to by those who decry all brokered consulting.

Buying into Benefit Plans

If benefits are an issue, and if you have had trouble qualifying for insurance, some of the better-run broker firms will let you pay your own costs to participate in the broker's benefit plans, deducting the cost of the plan from your earnings. In 1996, participation in such plans cost somewhere around $550 a month and included family medical, dental insurance, and disability coverage. If the broker's benefit plan offers membership in an HMO and does not require you to provide evidence of insurability, it may be a good deal. Remember too, that because of vagaries of the tax code, you will be able to buy these benefits with your pretax dollars—with 100 percent of each earned dollar, rather than with the 60 percent left after taxes have been deducted. So the actual cost to you in real dollars is somewhat lower than it might appear. When you leave the broker's employment you can extend this insurance according to COBRA regulations.

The Marketing Stage

After the initial interview you will hear from the broker's staff when they call to ask for permission to submit your resume to a client for a particular contract. At this point it is often a good idea to ask if you can inspect the resume they have put together for use in selling your services. Reputable brokers will allow you to check their sales materials for accuracy. When a particular contract is mentioned to you, you will want to find out as much as you can about the job, including what company it is in, what kind of work is involved, and what the rate for the work will be. However, at this stage, the broker may not know much more about the position than the name of the company and the department looking for a contractor.

After your resume has been presented to the client if the client expresses interest, the broker will call back to set up an interview. This is when you must probe for information before committing yourself to going through the interview with the client.

You must determine what hourly rate the broker will pay and how long the contract is expected to last. Make it a practice to refuse to interview for jobs where the broker is evasive about the rate or where the rate is much lower than the bottom of the range you originally gave the broker. Don't interview for contracts that are substantially longer or shorter than what you really want, either. It's a waste of your time and the client's to interview for work that isn't what you want, especially since if you do impress the client favorably, you will then have to fight off the salesperson's energetic efforts to convince you to take the job.

It is also a good idea to ask for a clear description of the technology involved in the contract so that you can verify that the broker's salespeople did understand your resume. There is nothing more annoying than wasting an afternoon on an interview for a job that you are unqualified for or find totally unacceptable.

If you do go to the interview and find that the contract was not appropriate for your skills, be a bit wary. If the broker sends you out on a second interview that isn't a good match for your skills, find another broker. Likewise, if a broker salesperson calls you with a contract you know you don't have the skills to fill, and tells you to "fake it" or offers to lend you a book so you can learn a few buzzwords for the interview—as all too many do—it's time to find a more ethical broker.

Finally, if a broker keeps telling you that he is sending out your resume but doesn't call back to schedule a client interview after two or three submissions, beware. There is a good chance that he is not serious about placing you and may be playing games with your resume.

Wrapping Up the Deal

If the broker has done a good job placing you, you should be a good fit for the client's needs and the interview should go smoothly. At the end the client may ask you whether you are interested in taking the contract and inquire when you can begin. But all real negotiations about the job should be conducted with the broker's representative because it is with the broker, not the client, that you will be signing the contract.

If you choose to work for that client, it is vital that you sign a written contract with the broker. If the broker doesn't present you with a written contract within a few days of the offer, warning lights should begin to flash. Consultants who have made the mistake of starting work for brokers without a written contract almost always regret it.

The contract the broker presents you with should state the rate you

- Does not pump for contact information
- Is willing to give you references
- Is knowledgeable about local shops and technology
- Lets you inspect any resume they put together for you
- Never submits your resume without explicit permission
- Does not submit you inappropriately or suggest unethical behavior
- Gets you interviews when your resume is sent out
- Presents you with a reasonable contract in time for your inspection
- Quotes you a rate before the interview that matches the rate that appears on the subsequent contract
- Is willing to negotiate some contract points
- Pays on a regular schedule

FIGURE 7-2   The hallmarks of a good broker.

discussed when accepting the interview. You should expect to find a few objectionable clauses in the contract because broker contracts are written by the broker's lawyers to protect the broker's interests. But a reputable broker will cheerfully offer to modify most offending clauses when you explain why they aren't acceptable. If the broker tries to talk you into signing a contract containing a lower rate than what was originally discussed, or claims that he's sure you can get the rate raised at some future time, or if the broker is not willing to change or strike out unacceptable clauses, as hard as it might be to do, this is the time to bail out. Ethical brokers don't play games with rates or contract clauses.

It is important to check that payment terms are spelled out clearly in your contract and that you will be getting paid on a regular basis that doesn't depend on when the broker receives payment from the client. The broker will be earning a hefty hourly cut for every hour you work. Make sure he does something to earn it.

In summary, Figure 7-2 lists characteristics of a good broker.

THE TYPICAL BROKER CONTRACT

We'll look now at some of the features of a broker contract that you are likely to run into, and show you which kinds of clauses are standard, which are dangerous, and which ones should be renegotiated if at all possible. In the following discussion we'll look at clauses from an actual broker contract [modified slightly to preserve confidentiality]. However, the contract your broker presents to you may be very differently worded and may include clauses not mentioned here. In legal contracts it is not uncommon for the insertion of a single word to alter radically the effect of a contract clause. Therefore, if you have any question about the meaning of a contract presented to you, don't rely on this discussion alone, or on the broker's explanation of what the clauses are supposed to mean, but ask a legal professional to look the contract over and make sure that you aren't signing something you may later regret.

Definition of Parties

Your contract will start with a section listing the parties to the contract and defining their legal relationship. Figure 7-3 shows a sample of such a section. These initial clauses are extremely important because as you can see, they define the consultant as an employee of the broker, thus avoiding the issues raised by Section 1706 (discussed in Chapter 3). As an employee the consultant will receive a W-2 form for the income earned on this contract and must report it as salary, not business income, and thus may not take the business deductions that would be available to an independent contractor.

Many brokers will refuse to let you work on their contracts on any other terms but these, especially if the contracts last more than a week or two and require that you be on-site at a client's offices forty hours a week working at the client's direction. They are correct in doing this as Section 1706 does apply to these situations.

Agreement for Services between
CompuHerd Consulting
123 Elm Street
Anytown, USA
hereinafter known as "Company"
and
Joanna Consultant
24 Happy Acres Drive
Suburb, USA
hereinafter known as "Hourly Associate"

For all purposes connected with the service rendered by Hourly Associate under this contract, Hourly Associate will be paid as an hourly associate and paid for hours actually worked.

In consideration of services performed, Hourly Associate will be paid at an hourly rate of $40.00. For services provided under this agreement, the hourly rate shall remain the same for the period outlined in Section 8 of this agreement.

Company will deduct the appropriate taxes (FIT, SIT) from the Hourly Associate's wages and the Company will match FICA taxes.

FIGURE 7-3   Sample definition of parties to a contract.

The only time that a broker may allow you to work for him as a subcontractor, rather than as an employee of one sort or another, will be in situations where you can clearly demonstrate that you can pass the test of the twenty factors used by the IRS to establish independent contractor status. (Appendix B lists these.) At a minimum, to meet IRS's criteria for being an independent contractor you should be doing the bulk of the work involved in the contract on your own equipment, at your own workplace, structuring your own work and working for more than one client in a given time period. If you can meet these criteria it is worth negotiating with the broker to write the contract to define you as a subcontractor paid on a 1099 basis rather than an hourly associate. If you can't meet them, you'll have no choice but to be classified as an employee.

Time of Payment

Your contract should specify how and when payment must be made. If you are working as a W-2 consultant, you should be paid on a schedule like any other employee, receiving payment every week or two. If you are working as a 1099 contractor or through your own corporation, you may also be able to stipulate that the broker pay you on a regular schedule, but don't be surprised if the broker insists that you wait for payment until the client pays him. Doing that will help justify your claim to independent status because by waiting for payment you are assuming more risk. However, if you plan to wait for payment until the client pays, remember that it often takes many months for larger corporations to pay brokers (or anyone else!). Because of this time lag, some consultants only accept a pass-through arrangement if the broker agrees to take a smaller cut of their billing rate than is usual. It is precisely because many brokers offer their contractors prompt and assured payment that most contractors are willing to give them a larger share of their billings.

The Client Escape Clause

This is a standard clause and one you will be unlikely to alter. Figure 7-4 provides sample wording. Most clients require that the broker include the wording allowing them to terminate a consultant at will.

Hourly Associate agrees to abide by all terms of Company's contracts with clients and is expected to perform in a satisfactory manner as evaluated by client on whose premises Hourly Associate will be performing services. Unsatisfactory performance would be grounds for immediate dismissal.

FIGURE 7-4   Sample client escape clause.

"Unsatisfactory performance" is anything that the client decides it might be. Clients frequently terminate contracts rather than keeping the consultant for the original term written, even when the consultant's work is satisfactory, because their business needs change. There's not much you can do about it except build a good relationship with the client and keep your network of contacts functioning.

In any case, no matter what the wording of your contract, you should never assume that if a conflict comes up with the client the broker will stand up for you, no matter what the facts of the dispute. The broker will invariably protect his long-term relationship with the client, with its promise of work for dozens more contractors, and will happily sacrifice his relationship with you if that is what is required to keep the client happy.

Ownership of Fruits of the Contract

This type of clause is also standard; Figure 7-5 provides sample wording. This clause is particularly important if you are working as an independent contractor rather than an employee: Without such a clause the software developed during the contract by the independent contractor is owned by the contractor rather than by the client for whom the work was done.

Clients hiring contractors to work on mainframe code usually insist on having some form of this wording in brokered contracts. However, if you are developing code that you would like to be able to resell in other situations, you may be able to negotiate this clause. It is also important that you renegotiate it if you will be using libraries of routines you have developed on your own in the development work you plan to do for the client as you must retain the rights to this code to use it elsewhere.

Confidentiality

Another standard clause covers confidentiality of information; Figure 7-6 provides an example. In addition to agreeing to maintain confidentiality, you may have to sign a nondisclosure form supplied by the client.

Hourly Associate agrees that any software, hardware, or other products developed during the performance of any task shall be the property of the Company's clients and Hourly Associate shall not have any rights to such software, hardware, or other products. Any products or software developed outside of or separate from any projects undertaken by the Hourly Associate on the behalf of the Company or its clients shall be solely owned by the Hourly Associate.

FIGURE 7-5   Sample ownership clause.

Hourly Associate agrees to maintain the confidentiality of all information obtained from the Company's clients and to maintain the confidentiality of information obtained from the Company, including, but not limited to, client documentation, software, pricing information, and hardware modifications.

FIGURE 7-6   Sample confidentiality clause.

Scope of Work

This section of a contract defines the work that the contract applies to. Figure 7-7 provides an example of this clause. The important thing to notice about this particular example is that in paragraph b the broker has slipped in a clause that commits the consultant to work an additional contract period, called an extension, at the same rate at which the original contract was negotiated. Make sure you are comfortable agreeing to the extension, and that there is a clear-cut ending date to the extension period. Look out for open-ended extension provisions that may end up committing you to months or even years of working at the original rate. Contracts are often extended, so make sure that if a client loves your work, you can renegotiate a higher rate at the end of a fair period, for example, six months.

The Noncompetition Clause

This noncompetition clause is the most potentially damaging clause in the contract for a consultant. Figure 7-8 provides an example. This clause means that you can't work for the client the broker has found for you for a period of one year after the termination of your brokered work for this client unless you do this work as an employee of this broker. This means you cannot work for that client using another, perhaps better, broker and that you can't do work directly for the client without calling on this broker as an intermediary. You are also prohibited from placing other people at this client shop or working independently in as-

The nature, extent, and timetable of tasks to be performed by Hourly Associate are indicated below and the Hourly Associate agrees to work the entire Schedule of Services as requested.
a. Scope of Effort: Provide systems analysis and programming support to MegaCorp Corporation Customer Support Information Systems.
b. Schedule of Services: From May 1, 1997 to July 31, 1997. Hourly Associate agrees to provide services for an additional three-month period ending October 31, 1997 if approved and requested by the client.

FIGURE 7-7   Sample clause defining scope of work.

Hourly Associate agrees that during the period of services of this Agreement and for a period of twelve (12) months thereafter, Hourly Associate or his/her company, if any, will not, without the written permission of the Company, directly or indirectly compete or attempt to compete with the Company, including but not limited to: (a) by soliciting or accepting employment and/or contracts (including with a third party) to work at clients of the Company with whom the Hourly Associate had worked on behalf of the Company; (b) by soliciting any project work or leading other individuals or companies to solicit contracts or work at clients of the Company for whom the Hourly Associate had worked under this Agreement or any past Agreement with the Company; (c) by inducing any personnel of the Company to leave the service of the Company to engage in activities prohibited to the Hourly Associate under this paragraph.

FIGURE 7-8   Sample noncompetition clause.

sociation with other contractors or salespeople who have worked for this broker.

The noncompetition exclusion period only begins at the end of the current contract *and all extensions.* This makes it very hard to escape these clauses, particularly when the client likes you and keeps asking you to come back to other work on new contracts before that intervening year has passed.

All brokers will insist on a noncompetition clause of some sort, many of them extending five or more years after the end of your contract with them. Although you will have to accept some such clause, you can demand that it only extend for six months to a year after the end of the contract.

Even more important, you should be able to limit the scope of the noncompetition clause to include only the specific departments or division you worked for within a client company, not to the entire company. This is particularly important when you take a contract within a huge corporation that has many different divisions. You may run into a situation where your original broker cannot find you work and another broker can place you in a different division of that company where the original broker doesn't have contacts.

If you have built up your own network of contacts with managers in a company where a broker would like to place you, you should also write into the contract wording that states that the noncompetition clause does not apply to the divisions of the client company where you have your own contacts, and list them by name, or you should exclude by name particular managers with whom you have preexisting relationships.

Be alert for broker-supplied noncompetition clauses that include within the scope of the clause not only the clients for whom you will be working during this contract, but all clients where you may have been "marketed." As the broker's marketing could consist merely of mailing a hundred potential clients your resume, this clause could stymie your ability to work anywhere.

Your best strategy of coping with noncompetition clauses is to keep them as short as possible and to work for a variety of brokers and a variety of clients, so that you can outlast them.

Brokers will try to get you working long, ongoing contracts at a single client site where your reputation does the selling for them. However, it is to your benefit in building up your long-term referral network to work for as many clients as you can and to keep your contracts under six months so that you don't become captive to a single broker. This strategy also will keep you from concentrating on a single, easily obsoleted skill.

Once the competition clause has expired you can contact the managers you have worked for before and work for them as an independent subcontractor without the services of a broker and for a full billing rate, as long as their company policies don't forbid direct hiring of consultants.

When confronted by an abusive noncompetition clause, don't hesitate to whip out your pen and cross it out. A broker who insists on too restrictive a noncompetition clause is not one you want to deal with. In addition, courts have generally upheld the rights of the employee in the case of overly restrictive noncompetition clauses. However, this cuts two ways. Attorneys familiar with the subject explain that, in general, the more explicit and reasonable a clause is, the more enforceable it is.

Attorney Fred Wilf says that he's found that courts will enforce noncompetition clauses only when there is a real basis for the limitation, other than keeping the employee from working, and when the geographic and time limitation of the clause is reasonable. However, the laws governing this vary on a state-by-state basis. In Pennsylvania, where Wilf practices, a judge has the right to change an unreasonable noncompetition clause to a reasonable one, while in other states the judge may just throw an unreasonable one out. Knowing this can help you negotiate a more reasonable clause as it is to the broker's benefit as well as your own.

But enforceable or not, you should always negotiate this clause with the assumption in mind that you will have to live up to it. One consultant reports that he found that it would cost him between $3,000 and $30,000 to fight an unjust clause, even though he was likely to win.

Resolving Disputes

Another common type of clause covers the resolution of disputes; Figure 7-9 offers an example. Beware of versions of this clause that state that the consultant will pay the costs of any legal activity. A better alternative is a clause that says the parties will use a specified arbitrator

---

In the event either party breaches any clause of this Agreement, such party shall pay all reasonable and applicable losses, costs, and attorney's fees incurred by the nonbreaching party in enforcing this Agreement against the breaching party.

FIGURE 7-9   Sample clause for resolving disputes.

before going to court over a dispute. Consultants who have tried arbitration seem to be pleased with it as an alternative to expensive litigation.

BROKER DIRTY TRICKS

Brokers can provide a reliable source of work when your network of contacts does not come through for you, or when you need money fast. But sadly, almost every brokered consultant—and I include myself in this number—seems to have one broker horror story to recount.

Nonpayment

Not surprisingly, companies that don't pay contractors are at the head of the list when consultants swap such ideas.

"I have had unscrupulous brokers skip town without paying me and leaving the client in the lurch," says one consultant who specializes in doing complex mainframe systems programming work.

Another recounts a typical scenario that unfolded with an out-of-town firm: "They said they had three weeks' worth of work that urgently needed doing, so why not come to Atlanta for the period. We [the company] will pay all your expenses and you can see if it works out." He goes on to say, "The bottom line is that at the end of the three weeks I said, 'Thanks, but no thanks.' After a couple weeks more I began to wonder where the expense money was and where a chunk of the pay was. Finally it comes down that since I decided not to stay on, they decided not to pay. Idiot that I am, all this was done by phone. I don't see how I can afford to sue for three or four thousand dollars, even if I could figure out what state to file it in."

Sleazy Sales Tactics

Another common problem consultants encounter is brokers who submit their resumes without permission so that a client gets two copies of the same resume with two different rates being asked for the same consultant's services.

Even worse is the bait-and-switch tactic described here by a consultant who has worked with brokers for five years. He says, "Brokers will submit the resume of an extremely qualified individual, such as myself, for an assignment with absolutely no intentions of ever using that individual. When the client asks to speak with that individual, the broker informs the client that they are no longer available, but that there is another individual who is almost as qualified who IS available."

It gets even worse. The following description of unsavory sales practices was given to me by a broker salesperson in return for a promise not to reveal his identity. He says, "It is standard policy of any and all brokers to lock out all possible candidates on a job for as long as possible. Let me explain: Scenario: I have a DB2 with IMS DB/DC programming requirement and ten possible candidates. I will, at the request of the client, only submit what I (emphasis on the word *I*) consider my best three. The other seven will be told that they may be submitted, or are being submitted by the less scrupulous population, to avoid them going in through a competitor. The manager will never see those seven."

Contract Abuses

Another set of broker dirty tricks revolve around the contract, or rather around the *lack* of a contract. The sleazy broker often conducts all negotiations orally and assures the consultant that the contract will be there "tomorrow." Or he may promise to meet the consultant at the job site on the first day of the contract and bring the paperwork along then. The consultant begins work without signing that vital piece of paper, and lo and behold, when the contract does finally appear it does not match the original agreement. Rates may be lower, the noncompetition clause may be brutally inclusive, and the consultant may discover that she is agreeing to work at a discounted rate for months or even years. But by then the broker has the consultant over a barrel, as walking out once work has begun is traumatic for client and consultant alike and destructive to the consultant's reputation.

Alternatively, the consultant who neglects to sign a contract may show up for work one day only to discover someone else doing her job, another consultant sent out by the broker who was willing to take a lower rate for the job, or is, perhaps, a low-paid salaried worker on the broker's payroll. Without a signed contract there is little a consultant can do in such situations.

Our friend, the sleazy broker salesperson quoted above, advises consultants to protect themselves from this situation by getting a contract in advance and suggests that you should "ask to see their blank contract up front, before the interview if possible. It shouldn't be a problem and may save you other headaches as well." A contract filled with damaging boilerplate is a tip-off that you are dealing with a broker of questionable ethics. A refusal to show you the boilerplate contract at all is a warning flag of real trouble ahead.

So, let's listen once more to what consultants have to say about the need for contracts:

"Never work without a contract."

"Don't ever do business with a broker without a contract."

"Never work without a signed contract."

"Don't work without a contract, ever!"

You get the point.

Rate Games

Another area of problem broker behavior revolves around rates. Brokers often tell consultants that the rate they are giving them is some stated fraction of the rate the client is paying. Sometimes this is true, but all too often the consultant discovers on the job that the client is being billed a rate far higher than what he'd been led to believe the broker was charging for his services.

This can cause not only the consultant to feel ripped off, but also the client. The client who is paying $100 per hour expects to be getting in return a quality of service that the consultant being paid $30 per hour isn't likely to deliver. However, brokers vehemently defend their right to keep rates secret, claiming that this is the only way they can prevail against competing brokers. The only way you can protect yourself against this kind of abuse is to do your market research and have a very good idea before you begin negotiations with a broker what kinds of money your skills command on the local market. And never take a job for a rate that you don't feel good about. If you do and end up feeling that you're being cheated and working for free, the client can't help but pick up on it. The net result will be only that you'll end up getting a reputation for having an attitude.

Bogus Standard Contract Clauses

Yet another way that brokers abuse consultants is to present them with boilerplate contracts including supposedly standard clauses that put the client at a severe disadvantage. Here are a few examples:

Quoting Rates for a "Professional Day"

The so-called professional day is an invention of large corporations who, having turned all their MIS staffers into contractors through downsizing, belatedly discovered that they must now pay contractors for all the overtime employees used to give them for free. To eliminate this problem, these companies may insist that all contractors get paid a daily rate, rather than an hourly rate, and that the day specified be a "professional day." Although this might sound prestigious, the professional day is defined as a day that includes as much unpaid overtime as the client wants. Under this arrangement, you get paid the same amount for working a sixteen hour day as you do for working eight hours, although, of course, as a contractor rather than a company employee you earn none of the brownie points employees earn for sacrificing themselves this way.

Although brokers may insist that this is "standard industry practice," it is *not* standard for contractors. If you are faced with a contract including this kind of arrangement, renegotiate it to become a standard hourly rate contract or, if you don't mind working twenty-four hours a day, negotiate a daily rate that takes into account the overtime hours you are likely to be giving the client.

Preacceptance Contracts

A preacceptance contract is a broker contract you sign *before* you go to a client interview. Often it includes highly restrictive noncompetition clauses that limit your ability to work for a company you interview with even if you do not take the contract you interview for. In some cases, consultants who have signed such contracts have then found themselves contractually bound to take contracts even though the contract turned out to pay less than the amount the broker verbally promised it would pay.

There is no reason to sign a preacceptance contract. Reputable firms do not use them. When they are used, they are usually part of a strategy of intimidating naive would-be contractors. Attorney Fred Wilf points out that, because no money changes hands at the interview stage, there may be some question as to whether such contracts are legally valid because there is no "consideration" involved, i.e., no benefit received. But even if this is true, should such a contract clause come under dispute, the expense of litigating is much too high for any reasonable person to risk signing one.

The only reason you might end up signing a preinterview contract of any type is if you will be reviewing confidential material of a sensitive nature as part of the interview process. In that case, it would be legitimate for a client to ask you to sign a nondisclosure form before attending the interview.

Stealing Clients

A final well-documented broker dirty trick is to collect resumes from consultants not because the broker has contracts to give them, but because the broker hopes to locate a new client for other consultants in their stable. As one consultant explains, "Employment ads are frequently posted as a ruse to get a list of prequalified leads—clients that use consultants—with there being no intention of ever employing the providers of such 'reference lists.' " This is not only unethical but can have serious repercussions for the consultant unlucky enough to be lured into the trap.

As one consultant who's been stung this way explains, "There is nothing to stress a good business relationship more than having a marketing rep call your client twice a month looking for opportunities when the client *knows* they got the name from you." The only way you can protect yourself from such pests is to be very careful where you send your resume and to refuse to work with any broker who pesters you for client contact information.

CONCLUSION

By now you may be wondering if working with brokers is ever worth the hassle. The answer is, yes. There are good brokers in the business too, not just the sleazeballs described here. Now that you've been warned about the bad ones, you are more likely to be able to locate a broker whom you can work with as an ally, whom you'll gladly call on when you need help filling your schedule with well-paid work, and whom you'll be happy to recommend to other capable consultants who've decided that brokered consulting makes sense for them.

8

GETTING TO
THE CONTRACT

The goal of your marketing efforts has been to find yourself potential clients. But once you've found them what do you do with them? How do you convince them to use your services? How do you use your early encounters with a client to build up the kind of long-term relationship that will attract the repeat business you need if you are to succeed as a consultant?

We'll turn now to what experienced consultants have learned about managing the opening stages of a nonbrokered relationship with a client. We'll look at that all-important first interview and the intermediate stages of the sales process: writing the proposal, clinching the deal, and negotiating the contract. Our goal will be to show you how to handle each step of the process so that the consulting experience can be a positive one for both the client and yourself.

MANAGING THE INITIAL INTERVIEW

Your first interview with a client will set the tone for all future contacts. Indeed, if you don't manage it well, there may be no future contacts. If you have gotten as far as a face-to-face interview, there's a good chance that the client does have a need that you could fill, but it will be up to you now to convince him or her that you can, in fact, fill it. Let's look now at how you go about doing this.

THE IMPORTANCE OF LISTENING

There's an old truism that real estate people often quote that says that there are only three things that matter when selling property, "Location, location, and location." Well, when it comes to dealing with clients, the three things that you must do are "Listen, listen, and listen."

No matter how good your technical skills may be, you will never get to use them unless you discipline yourself to listen to the client. Before you can provide satisfactory solutions to the client's needs you must listen closely, to uncover the client's real needs—which are rarely the ones he or she first describes to you. You need to listen, too, to determine the client's real attitude toward you, whether he or she has brought you in to solve their problems, or as often happens, for some less straightforward purpose. You need to listen for hints of the type of previous experience the client has had using technology and consultants, so you can address the client's unspoken hopes and fears. Both can have as much influence on the ultimate decision to hire you as the most well-reasoned, technically impressive proposal.

Listen well, and you'll be able to satisfy the client and build a long-term, satisfying consulting career for yourself. Fail to listen, and you'll end up with nothing to show for your contacts with the client but many hours of wasted time and effort.

If you come to consulting after years of being a technical specialist, learning to listen this way may be the hardest part of becoming a true consultant. This is because most technical experts find it far easier to talk than to listen, far easier to show off their knowledge than to relate to the knowledge levels of others, and far easier, too, to solve an immediate problem than to endure the lengthy, often boring, preliminary work required to uncover the problem that really needs to be solved. If you've spent your time until now as a technically expert employee, you may be used to having others run interference for you, managers and administrators who call on you only when a problem is defined and it is time for you to apply your skills. Now, as a consultant, you will have to do their work yourself and you will have to do it gracefully and with tact if you are to succeed in selling your services to the client.

What the Client Says versus What the Client Needs

If you've managed to get yourself in front of a client, the chances are good that the client has come up with at least one problem that is bothering him enough that he's willing to spend money to fix it. He may appear to have a good grasp of what his problem is, telling you, for example, that he needs a computerized accounting system, a new marketing database, or a few lines of code to finish up a project that is 95 percent complete. These statements may indeed summarize the client's needs quite nicely, but again, they may not.

Experienced consultants report again and again that the client's initial description of his problem is often very far from pinpointing the real problem that the consultant must solve if she is to satisfy the client. After more than a dozen years of consulting, Jeff Jacobs concludes, "Seventy percent of our clients really don't know what the problem is." Dorothy Creswell expands on this statement, adding, "The client often speaks in terms of symptoms and desires, rather than root problems and needs."

The client who tells you he needs an accounting system may be one whose small business has recently grown to where it has become too complex for his sister-in-law to handle the bookkeeping in her spare time. His real problem may be that his company needs a more professional accounting function, not just a computer system.

The client who asks for a marketing system may be hoping that bringing in a shiny new computer will magically bring in the shiny new customers her company needs so desperately, not realizing that her failure to craft a well-thought-out marketing plan first makes it unlikely that any computerized solution will help.

And the manager who tells you his project is "95 percent complete" may be hiding the fact that although he has indeed used up 95 percent of his allotted schedule, he cut corners in the design and specification phase and is now faced with thousands of lines of uncommented, partly debugged code that can't do the job. His real reason for calling in a consultant may be to find someone expendable on whom to pin the blame when it becomes obvious that the resulting mess cannot be cobbled together into a functioning system.

Thus you must approach clients' initial presentations of their problems with polite skepticism. Rather than responding to their statements by proposing an immediate technical solution, or by snowing them with your technical savvy and past accomplishments, you need to use the rest of this initial interview to probe for what the real needs might be so that you can propose a solution that will truly satisfy those needs. Only by doing this will you be able not only to win the initial assignment, but to complete it in a way that will result in a happy client, repeat business, and a flow of client referrals.

Using an Interview Worksheet

Clearly, then, before you can provide clients with effective solutions, you have to uncover their real problems and determine whether they are truly motivated to solve those problems.

Many consultants report using some form of interview worksheet to help them do an effective needs analysis that clarifies that client's problems. As consultant Werner Colditz explains, using such a checklist "will focus and structure the interview and make you look more professional. You won't be calling back an hour later with 'By the way, I forgot to ask you what products you manufacture.' " In his initial contacts with the client Colditz has found it useful to ask the questions summarized on the checklist shown in Figure 8-1.

- What are their expectations? How do they believe a computer will help them? (This should help you ascertain what it is that the client really would like to see change.)
- What is it that bothers them about continuing to do things the way they currently do them? (This pinpoints problem areas.)
- Where do they spend the most time? Where do they spend the most money? Where can costs be reduced to give them the most bang for their computer buck?
- How would they cope with a larger volume of business? (This question should also help bring out or confirm what their major problem areas are.)
- How do they think they could provide better service to their customers? Do they need better records? Faster access to customer information? More information about where to find customers?
- What are the unique characteristics of their business?
- Are they willing to adapt their procedures to fit in with general purpose software solutions or do they feel they have to have a custom solution?
- What is their existing investment in technology? How comfortable are they with it? How much can they afford to spend on changing it? How much are they willing to pay to improve matters?
- Who is the top decision maker who will make the call on using your services? Are there other people involved in the decision about the specific system you will be working with? What are all these people's feelings about these problems, and about using technology to solve them? How motivated are they to solve them?

FIGURE 8-1   Werner Colditz's checklist for interviewing clients.

Mich Kabay has devised a more streamlined set of interview questions. He asks clients, "If someone shook you awake at three in the morning and shouted, 'What is the single most profitable improvement you would like to make in your business?' what would you think of first?" He explains that the answer you get to this question usually leads to a fruitful discussion that reveals the client's values, perceptions, and the nature of his business.

The second question Kabay likes to ask clients is, "Why do your clients or customers buy your service or products?" This question helps him focus on the most important facets of clients' businesses and enables him to help his clients put their computer investment into improving critical functions first.

Consultant John Petry explains that the gist of what you need to ask your clients is this: "If we could sprinkle fairy dust on your business to improve just one thing, what would that be?" He also recommends asking, "What's the one thing you fear most happening?" both in their businesses or in the project under discussion. But Petry also suggests that when questioning clients about the changes they'd like to make in their businesses you ask them one last question, one many consultants neglect: "What things about your business do you want to remain *unchanged?*"

Petry reports that he used to use a formal list of questions in his initial interviews but stopped when he sensed that his clients didn't care for them. He suspects that they felt he was more interested in getting answers to *his* canned questions than he was in learning about *their* businesses. Now he says that in the initial phases of client contact he asks fewer technical questions and more "How do you feel about it" questions. He also asks more questions like "How did you do it before this?" or "Why did you change this procedure?"

Taking Notes

Consultants differ on how they help themselves track the client's remarks, but almost all report using some kind of memory aid to help them keep track of all that the client says both in the initial meeting and in follow-up contacts. Some consultants bring a notepad with them and make extensive entries while the client talks. Burt Johnson, who takes this approach, says that clients have told him that his assiduous note-taking in their offices helped convince them that he was serious and competent. But others report that clients also were impressed when they didn't take notes and still managed to remember previous discussions with precision. Embedded systems specialist Frank Bosso tries to tape record all pertinent technical discussions. He says, "There have been many times when a second hearing of the conversation produces a wealth of information that was just glossed over during the conversations."

John Petry takes yet another approach. He doesn't take notes but dictates a summary of the discussion with the client as soon as he gets back to his car after the interview. He transcribes this report when he gets back to the office and keeps track of each call he has to make back to the client as well as of the information that these calls produce. After a project is over, he's found it useful to review his original notes and subsequent contacts to see where it was that he missed things on the initial contact. He feels that this review procedure has helped him sharpen his interview skills.

QUALIFYING THE PROSPECT

Even if you don't use interviewing techniques like those described, it is important that early in the initial interview you get an answer to one of the questions touched on by Colditz in Figure 8-1: *You must establish whether the person you are dealing with has the authority to hire you.* You don't want to make the fatal business mistake of investing a lot of time and effort in a sales pitch directed at someone who is not in a position to buy.

If discreet questioning reveals that your contact is not in such a position, treat him with polite consideration and answer any questions he may have, particularly if his role is to screen you before letting you meet the people who do make the company's buying decisions. But keep your contact with him simple. Don't attempt to sell yourself to him hoping that he will then go to the person who can make that decision and talk her into hiring you. Instead, after you've established a comfortable rapport with such a contact, ask him politely but firmly for an introduction to the decision maker.

Experienced consultants suggest that a polite way to ask for such an introduction is to say something like, "I've really enjoyed talking with you and you've given me a really good sense of your department's database needs. Could you introduce me now to your project manager so that I can talk with her about some of the solutions we've discussed?"

ANSWERING COMMON OBJECTIONS FROM PROSPECTIVE CLIENTS

At some point in the initial interview with a person who is able to buy your services, or at least, at some time before the client commits to bring you in, you are likely to run into at least one stated objection. The client may express concern about the reliability of your one-person firm, the long-term wisdom of a solution you've proposed, or the fairness of the rate you've told him that you charge.

This can be disconcerting, but it is not a bad sign. Indeed, it is a normal part of the sales process, so when the client starts to pepper you with objections, there is no need for concern. Indeed, you should be much more concerned about the client who doesn't cross-examine you about something. The client who accepts everything you say without question, smiles and nods at what you say but doesn't come up with some kind of challenge, may be so complaisant because he's already decided not to work with you, or if you are particularly unlucky, he may be one of those whose motivation for bringing in a consultant is to find a scapegoat rather than a solution, and who needs nothing but a warm body to serve that need.

Let's examine the most common objections that the beginning consultant is likely to encounter and see how experienced consultants have learned to handle them.

The "Mortality Objection"

A very common question that the consultants who develop custom software hear over and over from clients is "What happens if you get hit by a truck?" With tongue in cheek, consultant Pamela Grycner has dubbed this the "mortality objection."

All consultants who encounter it—and most do—suggest that the best way of handling this objection is to assure the client that they have raised an important point, and one that you've already taken steps to solve.

Michael Stein suggests that you point out (if it is true) that there are other programmers who are familiar with your code and can support it, and that you emphasize that the code is written in a popular language that many local programmers know. If the client is very nervous, you might even offer to include the source code with the software at no additional cost if the client agrees to sign a legally binding nondisclosure form. Stein adds that he makes the point to the client that the problem inherent in the mortality objection doesn't just apply to one-person custom developers, but can occur with off-the-shelf solutions too. He reminds them that big software companies often decide to abandon products with no prior notice when they aren't selling well enough to repay support or when the company is bought out by another company.

Developer Rick Cosgrove goes one step further. Besides giving the client source code and a list of local developers who work in the same language as he does, he gives them the name of another developer with whom he maintains a business relationship in which each keeps up-to-date on the other's code.

Consultant Robert Barrentine suggests that, having taken steps like these, you should also ask the client what would happen to you if his firm gets into trouble, to emphasize that both of you are taking risk in a reciprocal relationship.

Software Escrow Arrangements

If you are not comfortable giving away your source code there is another arrangement you might mention to calm a client who worries about the fate of her code should you meet an untimely end: putting the software into escrow.

This involves putting your source code into the hands of a trustee—either an attorney, a bank, or a specialized software escrow company—and drawing up an agreement that specifies the conditions under which the trustee should hand that source code over to the client. Escrow arrangements protect the client not only in the case where you get hit by the proverbial truck, but also when you lose interest in your product and stop supporting it, or when your relationship with clients deteriorates to the point where they feel they cannot get adequate support from you, or when you decide to change careers, or indeed, in any situation where you are no longer able to provide ongoing support.

Escrow arrangements are not cheap. Consultants report being quoted fees in the neighborhood of $750 for the initial setup of such an arrangement with an additional fee of $800 a year being required to maintain it. But if you are talking about many thousands of dollars worth of software that the client will be dependent on for vital, strategic business functions, offering the client the opportunity to put the code into the hands of an escrow agent—*at the client's expense*—may reassure the client that they are doing business with a sound, responsible professional. You can find contact information for several software escrows firms in Appendix A.

"You Cost Too Much"

The client may well suggest that he's interested in your service but not at all happy with the rate you've quoted. This is a normal part of the negotiating process. If you were in a souk in the Middle East, when a potential client told you your price was too high, you would be expected to moan that if you took anything less your children would starve, and then prepare to walk away from the client, giving him a chance to call you back with an offer somewhere between what you'd asked for and what he wanted to pay. In short, everyone would know you were negotiating. But in our Western culture, it is much less clear when negotiating is appropriate and when it is not. As a result, many consultants find it extremely difficult to distinguish between a negative response to a quoted rate that truly is an objection and one that is a stab at beginning a normal negotiating process.

If the objection is an attempt to negotiate, remember that *you are not required to negotiate your rate.* This is especially true if you have taken the rate-setting steps described in Chapter 5 and if you have set a rate that falls within the range that prevails locally. It is quite permissible to smile and explain calmly and confidently that this is what you charge, suggesting by the way that you say it that if this client can't afford your services, there are others who can.

Burt Johnson reports that sometimes, when he runs into a client who objects to his rate, he finds that if he just shuts up and listens politely when the client starts talking about how expensive he is, the client may keep on talking and end up answering his own objection by mentioning that he'd used cheaper consultants in the past and that they'd messed up and that maybe it's worth trying a higher-priced one.

Other consultants deal with the objection that their rate is too high by making it clearer to the client what that rate will buy them. Consultant Rudyard Merriam explains to the client that the "hours" the rate applies to will be fifty to sixty minutes of *undistracted productive work*, not the diluted effort they are used to getting from employees. He also points out that he's an expert in the area he's working in who has done this kind of project many times before and thus can work more quickly and efficiently than someone who doesn't have a similar level of expertise. He also reassures the client that he will be reusing some existing code for the project and will not be developing the whole thing from scratch.

William Cohagen points out to clients that if they are comparing his work with that of employees, they should consider not only his much higher level of experience, but also the burdened cost of using an employee, a cost that includes *overhead expenses* like hardware and software, and is typically twice an employee's actual salary. If they compare his rate to the real cost of using an employee, they may wind up finding his rate a bargain.

But be careful. Often objections to your rate may hide other, more complex issues. Not the least of these may be that the client is assuming that the $75 per hour you are charging translates into an annual income of $150,000. This may challenge his ego and intimidate him because he earns far less, or it may make him feel resentment and envy that you earn so much more than he does. Some consultants have found it politic to handle this kind of covert objecting by gently explaining to the client who objects to "exorbitant" rates that the rate must cover *professional overhead*: insurance, up-to-date hardware and software, high marketing expenses, and of course that hefty self-employment tax. This can go a long way to removing this objection if it springs from envy or feelings of inferiority.

Avoiding Evangelism

If you cannot get past a client's problem with your rate, you may have to accept that you've just run into someone who isn't ready to deal with a consultant. Perhaps she really can't afford your rate. Many smaller businesses operate on such a tiny profit margin that they cannot, which is why few successful consultants concentrate exclusively on the very lowest end of the computer-using spectrum. Perhaps the client doesn't know enough about computers to understand what your expertise represents and really does believe that he can get the same quality of work from a moonlighting college kid paid ten dollars an hour.

Experienced custom developer Paul Ferrara points out that there may be little profit in casting yourself in the role of evangelist to such people. You will have to do twice as much work to sell yourself to them because you have to do two sales jobs. You must first convince them that they *need* a consultant and then convince them that *you* are the one they should choose. Ferrara has found it far more profitable to concentrate his efforts on companies that have already decided to retain a consultant, who only need him to sell them the idea of using him.

The "Dirty Little Secret" Behind Other Objections

There are other objections that you may run into, most of which you should be able to answer on your own. But if you keep finding yourself running into objection after objection when you believe you are coming up with good replies to each objection, and yet you sense that the client really wants to use your services, there may be an additional factor at work.

The client might be out of his depth.

When dealing with you, the computer expert, clients often put considerable effort into disguising their own ignorance about computers. As Dorothy Creswell explains, a client often confuses his own perfectly reasonable lack of knowledge about computers with stupidity—and no one wants to look stupid, least of all the kind of person most likely to rise to positions of leadership in an organization. As a result, explains Creswell, when talking with you and describing work that needs to be done, the client may often "cover up by grasping onto some fragment of information and presenting it as a 'requirement.' " The client who dots his conversation with technology-related buzzwords may know what he's talking about, but then again, he may just have boned up by reading an article in *Forbes* a few moments before you entered the office.

Consultant Steve Zilora gives a good example of this phenomenon when he says, "Often when I am interviewing with a new client, they'll ask me all about OOP, AI, and other frontier stuff and then ask me to do some FORTRAN programming."

It is quite possible that in trying to impress you with his technical savvy the client has gotten out of his depth and is now afraid to commit to a project because he's not sure exactly what it is that he's committing to, but is embarrassed to explain that he really doesn't understand half of what he's discussed with you. Often when this has occurred the only hint that the consultant gets of what is amiss is a sudden shift to a more confrontational tone in the client.

In such a situation your best bet is to offer to provide the client with a *simple, clearly written proposal* that makes clear the scope of the project and the approach you're going to take, before pressing him to make any kind of final decision about using your services. You might also offer to provide him with reading material relevant to the solution you're providing him so that he can improve his grasp of the technical matters you've been discussing without losing face.

It is often hard for those of us who eat, sleep, and dream computers to remember how alien they still seem to many otherwise intelligent professionals and to relate to their anxieties about technology in a compassionate, helpful way.

TELLTALE SIGNS OF THE PROBLEM CLIENT

While the thrust of your initial interactions with the client must be on determining the client's needs and making it clear how you can address them, in these early contacts you also should be paying attention to whether you feel good enough about a particular client to want to work for them. The sad truth is that some clients are bad news. Invariably when consultants have ended up working for one of these "clients from hell" they mention that they felt something a bit off, even in their earliest contacts with the client but that they ignored it or rationalized it away and plunged on with the relationship anyway.

Don't do this to yourself. Working for a bad client can be much worse than having no client at all. When you have no client you can use your time to market yourself and to improve your skills. But when you get tangled up with a bad client you can end up working full-time for weeks or even months without ever receiving a cent for your work, or you may end with a client who badmouths you to others in the business community and makes it difficult for you to find any further clients at all.

Unfortunately, there is no simple checklist you can use to screen out these troublemakers. But experienced consultants have come up with a few tips that might help you pick up on warning signs of danger lurking ahead. We'll look at some of them now.

Don't Become the Consultant Who Is Brought in to Fail

As we've mentioned before, clients don't always bring in a consultant because they want a job done. Sometimes they need a scapegoat, and no one makes a better one than the outside consultant. Consultants are called in to take the blame for a project that can't possibly make its deadline. They're also called in to implement policies that management doesn't want to see succeed, but which internal company politics require to be tested out.

One consultant who got caught up in a situation like this recalls, "We failed to get a contract renewal with a major bank because we delivered our stuff on time—seems the VP in charge really wanted to get rid of the system. After our delivery he replaced the project manager with an incredible yo-yo and kept the consultants whose code not only did not work but didn't even come close to meeting the requirements."

There is no foolproof way to avoid such situations, but you can eliminate some of them by being very leery of projects that show the signs of long-term mismanagement. If a project is way behind schedule, has no written spec, and is staffed by armies of bodyshop consultants, and if the suggestions you offer as to how to improve things seem to generate more obstruction than enthusiasm from the people in charge, you've probably stumbled into such a situation.

If your suspicions have been raised, don't hesitate to call people you know who work at the client company to ask them about any political issues that may be involved.

If, during an interview, you detect evasiveness in the client or an unwillingness to look in your eyes, be alert to the possibility that there is a hidden agenda involved.

Be wary of the client who is too eager to hire you when in your own estimate your skills may not be up to the job. Think twice about the client who doesn't question you about your background but merely sketches out the current project and rushes to conclude negotiations. If anyone will do in the given situation, there's a good chance that the function a consultant is being brought in to serve is political rather than technical.

Watch Out for Rate Chiselers

Experienced consultants warn you to be wary of clients who are overly creative with payment methods, in particular clients who tempt you into working for royalties on the software you develop for them instead of offering cash for your development work. As one consultant who has been burnt by such clients remarks, "Never do any work for anyone who says, 'You know the market is huge for a system like this! You'll be able to make a lot of money with this when it's done.' " This consultant explains, "What he wants is a free system and a share of your future profits for the privilege of 'making you rich.' This is a straight road to starvation."

Very few companies are able to market specialized application software packages successfully and most of those that do are companies that specialize in software development. The chances that an ordinary business client will be able to market a niche application for you in a way that generates significant royalties are close to zero.

Custom developer Martin Schiff's experience is typical. He explains, "I've written *lots* of custom applications, but only a couple have been sold more than once, and then changes were required." He says that the secret of his own success has not been reselling complete applications, but developing a library of routines that can be used for every new project. Therefore, while you may want to consider making provision for such resales when negotiating with a client, you must be very leery of the client who tries to get you to work only for the profits of such future sales.

Consultants who've been burnt by problem clients suggest that you watch out for the client who expresses surprise—or irritation—when you charge for things like hourlong support phone calls, site visits to explain material already covered in the system documentation, and other legitimate expenses. If you have made it clear what you will charge for, the client should be willing to pay for it. The client who constantly tries to extort free work from you is not one you need. You can sometimes identify these clients early in the sales process when they repeatedly try to get you to do significant amounts of work for free, or if they show irritation when told that you charge for all but the first meeting with a client.

Avoid Ego Hogs and Know-It-Alls

Another problem client that consultants warn against is the Ego Hog—someone who turns every situation into one where there is a winner and a loser. Burt Johnson explains that the client who fancies himself playing hardball "robs your time, gives you ulcers, and seldom pays off enough for the effort and pain involved." If you run into one, he says, "Say 'No thanks' and walk." The tipoff that you have encountered such a client usually comes during contract negotiations when the client shows inflexibility about modifying even the smallest of terms he's suggested. He may become aggressive and insulting, or attack your qualifications and abilities in a personal way when you don't yield to him on a contract point. This kind of behavior should make you rethink whether you really want the aggravation that dealing with this kind of person will bring, no matter how potentially profitable the work might be.

Another related kind of problem client is the know-it-all who responds to your initial stabs at solving his problem by shooting them down and snowing you with gems of information he's picked up from his brother-in-law or magazine articles he's read. This is the guy who is likely to lure you into designing a detailed proposal only to dismiss you, unpaid, after announcing that he can get a better system for $150 less from some obscure firm who advertises in the back pages of *Computer Shopper*.

There are many times when it is politic for a consultant to lay back and let the client be the star and win the glory, but this is not one of them. The client who sees your expertise as a challenge to be shot down is not likely to become a source of happy ongoing referrals.

The Client Who Is in a Rush

Another client that experienced consultants have learned to be wary of is the client who is in such a rush to have you work for him that he wants you to get started without a signed contract, spec, or any of the other "trivial" paperwork that might keep him from meeting his deadline. When another consultant asked on CONSULT if he should work for such a client, Greg Gorman responded, "Bells! Lights! Whistles! Don't rush into anything. *Every* time (and I do mean *every* time) we've seen a 'gotta get going on this right away' message from a new relationship, it's been something we should have run away from very, very fast. Why should you be making all the concessions if they're the ones who need you so badly?"

When you meet the "drop everything and do my job" client, you know from the start that you are dealing with a selfish, demanding client who has poor project management skills. Worse, this client often also turns out to be a rate chiseler who expresses shock when presented with your bill and takes a long time to pay—if he ever does. Gorman reports that one such client demanded that he supply three contractors who would work full-time including nights and weekends on his rush job, but when rates were discussed, the client refused to pay more than 10 percent of Gorman's standard billing rate. Gorman turned down the job after figuring that their rate would have been "within sight of minimum wage."

The client who is truly in a rush should be more motivated to cater to your needs and to pay extra (and in advance) for your attention, not less. Don't let a client stampede you into taking foolish chances.

Bigots and Fanny Grabbers

What do you do when a potential client makes snide remarks about your ethnic group? What should you do when you are grilled about your religious beliefs at a sales meeting? It may come as a rude shock to discover that equal employment law does not apply to situations in which you are working as a self-employed contractor.

Attorney Fred Wilf explains that, although there are laws that prohibit discrimination that do apply to independent contractors, they don't have the same force or effect as those that apply in employment situations. Therefore, if you are confronted with hints of bigotry or intrusive questioning about your day care arrangements or sexual preferences, you may have little recourse except to bail out. Why put yourself through the misery of dealing with a brutally insensitive client when the world is full of other clients who do not behave in this manner?

But sometimes it's a close call, particularly when a client may be unaware of his or her having crossed over the boundaries of taste and respect, or when you are dealing with an errant client employee in a corporate situation where discrimination is not supposed to be tolerated. Consultant Robert McAdams suggests that one way of handling discriminatory remarks in such situations is to have in place a company policy that states that employees of your firm are not to discuss personal matters such as religion or marital status with clients during interviews. If your corporation has minutes, put this policy in them too. Then, when faced with the sort of personal question that would be illegal in an employment situation you can simply state, "My company has a policy against discussing personal matters of that kind with potential clients." If a client has trouble with this, do you really need them as a client?

Sometime you may find yourself in a situation in which bigotry or harassment has gone beyond annoyance to abuse, from which you suffer demonstrable harm. In this kind of situation you may need the help of an attorney familiar with the law regarding independent contractors. Attorney Wilf tells of one situation in which a client canceled part of a project and refused to pay for work already completed because a woman consultant refused to sleep with him. Wilf sued on her behalf and she received a settlement, but the suit was based on the client's having personally interfered in the contract between his own corporation and the consultant's, not on sexual harassment.

THE INTERMEDIATE SALES PHASE: BEFORE YOU CLOSE THE DEAL

If you are lucky, an initial interview may be all it takes to convince a client to bring you in on a project. But many times clients hesitate to make a commitment and string out the initial phase of the relationship for weeks or even months before making a final decision. This is particularly likely when the project under discussion is large and complex.

This kind of client-inspired delay can be a normal part of a process that leads eventually to a mutually satisfying business relationship. But it is in this phase of the sales process that many beginning consultants get into trouble. They waste valuable time and, all too often, do significant amounts of work for free—work that a more experienced consultant would have been paid for, or not done at all.

To handle the phase of the sales process that follows the initial interview properly, you will have to combine a willingness to reassure and interact with the client with an ability to *set limits.* You will have to understand the sales process and establish clear-cut goals for every step you take as it proceeds. Only that way will you end up getting the firm commitment from a client that must be the basis for a satisfactory ongoing relationship.

KNOWING WHEN TO START THE CLOCK

One thing you must understand when dealing with new clients is when it is proper to start the clock—when you should start charging the client for your problem-solving services. Both during the interview and afterward, new consultants are tempted to rush in and do their darndest to solve every problem that the client presents them with—long before they've gotten any commitment from the client to pay for these efforts. Although providing such free assistance may delight the client, it by no means ensures that the client will subsequently pay you for more work. In fact, quite often the opposite is true. As one consultant wryly sums it up, "I have found that giving out a lot of free advice invariably leads . . . to giving out more free advice!"

This isn't because clients are exploiters. It is just a normal human instinct to see what we can get for free and only to pay for what we absolutely have to. But because clients will gladly allow you to do work for them for free that they can't bring themselves to pay for, successful consultants must pull off a delicate balancing act. They must suggest to clients that they can solve their problems, without actually solving these problems until clients agree to pay for it.

Which is not to say that you won't do some work for free. Almost all successful consultants accept that they have to devote some unbillable time to clinching a deal. Most consultants give clients a free initial consultation lasting anywhere from one to three hours and many invest more unpaid hours in drawing up formal proposals for potential clients.

But successful consultants also know that they must set clear limits on how much unpaid time they will devote to the client. Consultant and developer Larry Finkelstein explains how he handles this challenge, saying, "Generally speaking, I do not bill for the first meeting with a prospect." But he adds, "I also do not give any *real* advice in such a meeting either. Once we've gotten past the first meeting and agreed to the terms of the contract then *all* the work that I perform related to that client is billable."

Another consultant, Dave Yates, echoes Finkelstein when he says, "Giving away the store! I know the feeling well. We just *love* to solve the problems and talk about the latest and greatest toys. I was so proud of myself last week because in talking with [a potential client] I was able to impart the knowledge that I knew what their problems were likely to be, some possible solutions to the problems, and had the expertise to implement these solutions. And I did it all without telling her a single solution!"

Yates explains that, having learned to do this the hard way, he now gives potential clients one or two hours of free time in which he explains his services and shows them how he might be able to help them. Then he explains that for any concrete and in-depth analysis, they'll have to pay.

Though experienced consultants emphasize the need to set strict limits on the amount of free time they spend on any client, new consultants often fear that they can't get away with this kind of behavior because of their lack of experience, and think that giving away a free sample of their work might be a more effective way of landing a new client. But oldtimers emphasize that this is almost always a mistake. If you don't act as if your time is valuable when confronting clients, why should they?

So it is important to make it clear that you expect to bill for your solutions. It is equally important to let the client know when the billing clock will start ticking. "I got into several situations where the client stayed longer than I felt necessary for the first meeting and started asking advice," says consultant John Mueller. He adds, "I follow a strict policy now of the first hour is free. After that, all time is at my normal rates. I make sure the client realizes this before I even go in for the first meeting. It makes a big difference if the client knows up front that you don't want to be taken advantage of."

FOLLOWING UP WITH PROSPECTS

Even before you go into the first interview you should know how you plan to follow up on it. If possible you should set the client up for that follow-up in the concluding stages of the interview.

One technique many consultants find useful is to hold something back when asking the client questions about his company. As David Gannon explains, "I have found that if I touch on all the questions, there is little chance of the call backs for more information." He likes to save a few questions until after the interview is over, so that he can have a good excuse to call the client a few days later and so continue the relationship.

Another useful technique is to invite the client to see a demo of your software. But if you do this, Paul Ferrara warns that it is always best to insist you hold the demo in your office—on your turf—both for the psychological advantage it gives you and because it is much safer to demo anything on your own system rather than attempt to install it on a client's potentially fluky system.

Another approach Ferrara has found valuable with potential clients who show interest in his custom software is suggesting they talk to, or preferably visit, one or more of his satisfied customers. He finds that if they won't make this effort, "they probably aren't interested, regardless of what they say, and that if they do do it, completing the sale is a piece of cake."

Consultant and software developer Frank Cook has found that the best approach for him is to design a *multistage follow-up*. He explains, "We used to send out a huge packet of information early in the cycle. Then we were stumped on what to say on the next call. We changed strategy and now we send out one piece of literature. On the next call we ask if they got it and have any further questions. The first piece doesn't say much, so we can then say we'll send a second piece. We also made up a questionnaire that helps determine what their needs are and that's another thing we can send. After they return it we can call and talk about what they answered."

Consultant Anthony Mayo takes a similar approach. He says, "I work to end each call with an understanding of what the next step will be and a promise to check in with them at a certain point. What information are they waiting for? Whose advice are they seeking? Whose approval do they need? This not only gives you something specific to follow up on, it may help you make more progress on the first call." He also follows up on every phone call with a letter and then sends postcards every week or ten days to active prospects. All these contacts keep his visibility high.

PREPARING PROPOSALS

Beginning computer consultants, particularly those who have read a few general purpose books about consulting, often wonder whether they need to follow up the initial interview by preparing a formal proposal for presentation to the client.

The answer, surprisingly, is no. Unless the client specifically asks for a proposal, most computer consultants find that all that is necessary is to mail a brief letter that recapitulates the points that were discussed during the interview.

But sometimes a client does ask for a formal proposal, and it is here that beginning consultants are most likely to get into trouble, because it is all too easy to misunderstand what a proposal is—and provide the client with something else instead.

A Proposal Is Not a Spec

The danger of preparing a fat, beautifully bound proposal that looks like the kind of proposal used by management consultants is this: The consultant who spends an unpaid day or two on a customer site collecting the information needed to do a detailed proposal for a client may well be giving away the store, since a professionally conducted systems analysis is often all that the client really needs.

Many a budding consultant has presented his potential client with a beautifully formatted, twenty-page proposal detailing the exact nature of the work he plans to do, including a list of specific hardware and software he'd use for the job, only to have the client thank him, dismiss him, and go out on his own to buy the exact hardware and software the consultant has specified. Even worse can happen. One consultant reports, "One of my prospects actually Xeroxed my proposal and sent it to my competitors."

The key to avoiding this kind of situation is to make it clear both to yourself and to the client what the difference is between a proposal and a spec.

A proposal is a selling tool. It describes what you are going to do, what it is going to cost, and how long it is going to take, but does not give any but the most general description of how you are going to solve the problem.

A specification, on the other hand, *is a design document.* It describes how to provide an actual solution in detail and can be implemented by anyone, not just the person who drew it up.

Therefore, if your clients want more than a brief summary of how you'll solve their problem and insist on getting brand names, configurations, and information of that nature in a proposal, you must explain to them that what they are asking for is not a proposal but a spec. You must make it clear that such a design document is the end product of a significant amount of consulting work—a deliverable and that if this is what they really need, they should expect to pay you for it.

The Format of a Computer Consulting Proposal

Successful computer consultants agree that the kind of proposal that is their most effective selling tool is brief—often two or three pages and almost never more than ten. It is frequently little more than a follow-up letter reconfirming points made during the face-to-face meeting with the client. Even if it is a bit more extensive, it rarely attains the size or complexity of the hefty, expensively bound proposals favored by management consultants.

The purpose of the proposal is to *communicate* to clients that you understand their problems and to *sketch out* approaches to solving them. Dorothy Creswell explains, "A proposal is like the artist's sketch of a new building, which shows the general form. It's not the floorplan, the detailed blueprints showing the electrical systems, nor is it the final product."

Charles Miller agrees: "We don't solve the client's problem in the proposal. In most cases, we only detail an understanding of the problem together with an approach to solving it. You know, 'You can't get employee stats easily, so you need an automated HR system which we think is a DBMS application, and we propose six people—resumes attached—using Oracle for six months to write this HR system.' "

Michael Stein points out that it is often very useful to include in such proposals not only a list of what work is to be done, but also what he calls "negative specification"—an indication of work that is *not* going to be included in the project. Doing this establishes *clear boundaries to the project* at hand. Burt Johnson also includes this kind of negative specification and adds to this section of his brief proposal as the project continues and the client discovers other things that would be nice to have but were not in the project as originally agreed upon. He makes these excluded items the impetus for a "phase two" to be sold to the same client as the project nears completion.

Michael Stein explains that he has learned over the years that the most effective proposals are those in which he does a lot of "showing off how well I understand their problem, spitting back at them what they have told me about the problems that they are now facing." John Genzano agrees. "When I do a proposal," he explains, "I try to remember that the person reading it is probably very busy. So I make sure that the benefits of what I am proposing are in an executive summary which will not be longer than one page."

Genzano adds, "The requestor doesn't really care whether I'm going to use Paradox on a PC or XYZZYG on a MILFER, as long as he is going to have his problem solved and get benefit worth the cost." What the requestor *does* care about, he explains, is himself. "So I tell him how his life and job are going to be so much easier when I get the job done. I leave all of the technical 'how' stuff out of the proposal ('That's just a detail!') and I put in a lot of 'what' and especially 'why' stuff."

Here is a quick list of points to be included in a brief proposal:

- The problem to be solved
- How you will approach solving the problem
- The date when the work can begin and the length of time expected to complete it
- Billing and payment procedures, including a ballpark estimate of project cost

If you are tempted to prepare an elaborate proposal, keep in mind this observation made by a seasoned consultant: "Time spent on preparing detailed proposals apparently does not increase a consultant's win/loss ratio. After thinking about the implications of this statement, I have come to the realization that I have been preparing proposals to *impress myself!* I have no doubt in looking back on my many systems designs that I am my own most appreciative audience."

You may well need to do some detailed analysis before taking on a client to assure yourself that you can indeed solve his problem and, just as important, that you can make a profit doing so. But there is no reason to share the fruits of this more detailed work with the client until he has made a commitment to work with you and to pay you for the work.

Protecting Your Ideas

If you do feel you must include detailed information in a proposal in order to convince a prospect to hire you rather than a competitor, it is wise to take a few precautions to prevent the client from handing your solution over to a competitor. Computer consultants have found several techniques helpful in doing this. One is to use a legal-sounding declaration that what is included in your proposal is proprietary information.

Consultant John Flanigan includes the following text on his proposals:

This document contains information proprietary to [my company name] and as such this document may only be used by [prospect] for the purposes of evaluating the suitability of the design proposed by [my company]. No other uses are permitted.

Consultant C. Blaise Mitsutama uses similar wording and then adds the following:

[Company name] has used its resources and knowledge base and has expanded time and effort in preparing this proposal and is providing this proposal at no charge to [prospect]. In consideration of this fact, [prospect] may not provide this document, or any part of this document, as reference material to any other prospective contractor. Nor may [prospect] use this proposal as the basis for evaluating any other prospective contractor.

Another strategy is to sprinkle copyright notices liberally throughout your document. While it is not legally necessary, placing a copyright notice prominently on each page helps remind the client that he doesn't own the information you've included in the proposal. Along with a copyright notice in the form, "© company name," some consultants include the additional text:

The information in this proposal remains the property of [company name] and may not be reproduced, stored in a retrieval system, or transmitted in any form without the express written permission of [company name].

How to Get Paid for Writing Detailed Proposals

If the client's need is fairly clear cut, the brief, free proposal described so far may be all that is needed. But sometimes when a client presents you with a complex problem it may not be possible to sell your services without providing a convincing detailed spec. In this case many consultants find that the most effective sales strategy is to use a staged approach. They present the client with a free, brief proposal that suggests that the project be broken up into several phases, the first of which is a detailed analysis of the problem. This analysis phase is designed to terminate with the delivery of an extensive project document that includes detailed specifications and provides the client with reliable time and cost estimates for the rest of the project.

In accepting this kind of proposal the client commits to pay for the initial analysis phase. However, as a gesture of compromise, many consultants who are otherwise unwilling to work on a fixed-fee basis will do this preliminary requirements analysis phase for a fixed price. This is often necessary because many clients, particularly less sophisticated ones, simply won't let an unknown consultant do a detailed needs analysis on an open-ended hourly basis.

Many consultants confess that in such situations they often end up earning far less than they might had they billed time that they spent on the analysis at their usual hourly rates. But they do it because they figure that providing the detailed analysis will eventually lead the client

to give them a much larger, more valuable piece of work. They are, in effect, *discounting their work* up front in the hopes of being able to sell
the client the entire project.

Even though with this approach the consultant may end up earning
only a few hundred dollars for many hours of work, the fact that the
client is paying for that work is still extremely important from a psychological standpoint. If nothing else, the client's willingness to pay
distinguishes him from the freeloaders and tire kickers. As one consultant explains in describing a project where the effort it took to write the
proposal was far in excess of the $500 he charged for his work, the
client's willingness to pay him at all showed him that the client considered him a serious contender for the project. It let him avoid the situation he'd encountered elsewhere where the "prospects have
contacted half a dozen companies for proposals and you're really in
there just to increase the statistical base of their evaluation and you
never really had a chance."

To the surprise of many beginning consultants, clients who are serious
about solving their problems usually will agree to pay for detailed specifications. Consultant Anne Pruitt states, "I always charge for my specs."
During the initial interview with her client she explains to the client why
a spec is needed and that she typically charges from $100 to $300 for such
work. Pruitt explains, "I make the point to my prospects that they are actually *getting something* for their money. In one or two cases I've mentioned that if for any reason they don't proceed, the spec will serve as a
good starting point in the future and that *anyone* can use it, not just me."

It is often necessary to help the client see the value of doing a detailed
analysis at the beginning of a project. Consultant David Yates points out to
his clients when attempting to sell them an analysis for which he charges
a flat rate of $500 that if they buy this analysis, "because we understand
their needs so well, we can probably do the detailed configuration work in
'only *x* hours instead of *y* or so.'" He adds, "This way the client knows that
he will recoup some of his investment in the needs analysis."

However, it is not always necessary to discount the analysis phase of
a project. Many consultants insist on doing preliminary analysis at their
regular hourly rate. Consultant Daniel Opperman explains, "I go on the
clock at my normal hourly rate to do the analysis phase. I make it clear
to the client that they will receive a detailed requirements document
that they are free to use to secure bids from others. I almost always get
the subsequent contract but even when I don't, at least I've pocketed
three to five thousand dollars for my time."

The crucial thing to keep in mind here is that *you should set the tone*. If
you respect your own abilities and have confidence in the value of the
work you do for a client, the client is more likely to respond positively to
your assumption that you deserve to be paid for doing this valuable work.
If, instead, you project a sense of uncertainty about the value of your work

(as many beginners do) and if you hesitate to ask for payment for things like a detailed spec, your behavior suggests that you are not sure your work is worth paying for, and that it will be up to the *client* to decide if your work is of value or not. Such an unprofessional approach is not likely to convince the client that bothering with you is worth his time.

COMPETITIVE BIDDING SITUATIONS

As should be clear from some consultants' comments regarding billing and bidding, it is very important for you to be aware of how seriously a client is taking your bid for a job before you decide how much work to devote to preparing it. It is frustrating to discover that you've lavished days or weeks of work on winning a project where seven other companies have also been invited to submit bids. Many established consultants are reluctant to invest their time in preparing proposals for projects that resemble "cattle calls" unless the client is willing to assure them that they are going to be seriously considered.

Burt Johnson explains that he's found the simplest way to deal with these situations is to ask a direct question. "I used to play the coy business negotiator," he says. "Now I ask, 'Are you considering others for this? If so, what do you need to see from me to make me be your choice?' " Johnson says that he won't pursue a contract unless he gets a response from the client that assures him that, presented with a reasonable proposal, they will award him the job.

Many other consultants share his view. Consultant Anne Pruitt reports that she's found dozens of clients without having to participate in competitive bidding situations. Indeed, competitive situations are rarely encountered by the one-person consultancy working on smaller projects, but are only likely to become a factor when you grow your consulting business to a multiperson shop bidding on extensive corporate and government projects.

Beginning consultants often wonder whether it is worth their time to respond for requests for proposals (RFPs) for government work that are published in the local newspaper. These almost always turn out to be an extreme case of the cattle call situation. They attract dozens, if not hundreds, of consultants. Consultants who have responded to these proposals report that they demand much more work than is justified by the chances of winning the assignment.

CLOSING THE SALE

Once you've met with the client and the client has asked for a proposal or a price quote, and once you've presented the client with either, it's time to move to the final and most intimidating phase of the sales cycle. Until you've been asked for a proposal or quote you've had to walk warily, touching bases with the client, perhaps calling with interesting tidbits of information to keep the relationship going, and waiting for the client to make their move. But once the client has made that move, the ball is in your court and you must act aggressively.

As Dave Yates explains, "If you have given the prospect a quote, then there should be no such thing as 'touching base.' When the presentation is made, ASK FOR THE SALE. (And yes, it's written in capital letters on the wall of our back room.) If you have answered all of their objections but they cannot commit for whatever reason, ask when you should contact them to close the deal. When you call don't be shy. Ask them if they have reached a decision."

Yates emphasizes again the importance of acting like a professional, pointing out that while copier salesreps and people selling office supplies might "pussyfoot around like they're looking for crumbs from the office budget wars" as a computer professional "you are an important businessperson, dealing with other important businesspeople, and don't have time to be strung along just 'checking in.' "

Ask for the sale, and if you don't get it, don't be shy about asking the client politely why you didn't. Do this not so you can come back with a hard-sell follow-up, but because what you might learn about why you failed in this situation can help you make another, perhaps better, sale.

There is nothing shameful about losing a contract. Indeed, no consultant gets all the contracts he or she bids on. But if you listen to what clients tell you throughout the selling process, if you carefully qualify your prospects in the initial visit and screen out those who are just tire kickers, experienced consultants suggest that after a few months of practice you should be able to land anywhere from 75 to 85 percent of all contracts in which you've invested significant effort.

THE INDEPENDENT COMPUTER CONSULTANT'S CONTRACT

Whew! You've got a deal. The client has told you that you've landed the contract. Now all that remains is to nail down the piece of paper that will make it legal. Or does it?

Do You Need a Legal Contract

A small but vocal minority of independent consultants insist that drafting a complicated legal document to formalize the business relationship is an unnecessary complication, and one that may undermine the relationship with the client at the very start. Paul Ferrara says, "I've operated a multiperson consulting company doing custom programming for ten years on just handshakes and, very infrequently, letters of agreement. It's always worked for me."

Canadian Midrange specialist, Tony Toews, is another consultant who dislikes using written contracts. He explains, "In the event that there are difficulties, no contract, lawyer, or courts will ever help out." But he also points out that he works in a region where community ties are close and where people know each other. He says that if at some future time he should find himself "wronged," he's confident that he can deal with the situation by letting "everyone else in town know my side of things."

No-Contract Nightmares

But before you let yourself become swayed by these arguments, you should know that such consultants are a minority. For every consultant who visits the CompuServe Consultants Forum to brag about trouble-free no-contract experiences, there are dozens who post messages like the following: "I did a month of work for a client who now claims I did not do what he asked me to do and refuses to pay. Unfortunately, I didn't bother to get a contract and have no way of documenting what the client asked me to do."

Indeed, no-contract horror stories abound. One consultant recalls, "We made our worst mistake with one client. We had a vague agreement about what was to be done, with absolutely nothing in writing. After five months of work done for a fixed price of $2,500, he never paid us." Other consultants tell tales of neglecting to get a contract and then showing up at a client site for the first day of what was supposed to be an extended stint of work, only to find that the client had replaced them with a cheaper consultant.

The problems that can afflict the consultant who doesn't have an agreement in writing include tardy or missing payments, disagreements about the nature of the work to be done, lack of clarity about when the work is to be considered complete, misunderstandings about the consultant's responsibility for ongoing support, and conflicts about who owns software that the consultant developed for a client as part of the project.

Attorney Fred Wilf says, "I know that many contractors don't like written contracts, and many clients are turned off by them. Regardless, I still recommend written contracts in much the same way that computer consultants recommend regular backups."

Consultant Art Ellingsen recommends that you get a contract *before you need one.* He points out that even when you have an excellent relationship with a client you must still prepare for the day when "budgets get cut, or a [company] president or administrator gets hired, or a new board gets elected." It is not unheard of for the person who brings you into a large company to lose his or her job before your work is complete. If this happens and you've been relying on an oral contract, it may be impossible to convince the new person in charge that they are committed to pay what you are owed for work you've completed for their predecessor.

Attorney Lance Rose gives his reasons for suggesting that a consultant have a contract: "Limitation of liability, disclaimer of warranty, acceptance provisions, and timing of payments." He also points out that it is often effective to use a contract to make the client aware that you are going to be working against a set spec and that if the client changes that spec they will have to pay more for the work.

Do You Need a Lawyer to Draft Your Contract?

In many cases after you agree to work for them, clients will present you with contracts their lawyers have drawn up. This may lead to problems, particularly if the client is a small businessperson not accustomed to dealing with computer consultants, who has merely modified a contract that he has developed for use with general contractors such as plumbers or electricians. Such contracts often include clauses requiring you to provide large amounts of liability insurance of a type that is difficult for consultants to find (see Chapter 4 for details on how to handle this), and they may neglect to cover important points such as ownership of software to be developed under the contract (see Chapter 7 for guidance on this problem).

If you are presented with such a contract it is well worth a consultation with an attorney specializing in intellectual property law and computer applications to make sure that you aren't inadvertently committing yourself to something dangerous or expensive. If you are concerned about the expense of such legal aid, one approach that is useful when you foresee doing several contracts with a single client is to ask the lawyer to help you and the client arrive at a *general services contract* that covers a year's worth of work, and allows you to add an addendum for each individual piece of work you do for the client, rather than requiring the negotiation of an entire new contract for each job.

Steve Zilora finds this approach useful. As he explains, "The addendum is the project spec. The contract covers secrecy, payment, and all the litigation stuff." He adds, too, that he's found his clients to be "quite flexible" when it came to negotiating these contracts.

Should You Use Off-the-Shelf Contracts?

For the consultant who is disinclined to spend money on the services of a legal professional there is another alternative: using a "canned" contract. You can buy legal forms containing contractor agreements, neatly shrinkwrapped, at your local business supplies superstore. If this isn't enough for you, you can buy software that tailors template legal documents such as original equipment manufacturer (OEM) agreements and licensing agreements for software publishers.

Is this a good solution?

Attorney Lance Rose says such agreements can be useful, with one major caveat, explaining, "If you modify a form contract, you may be venturing into uncharted territory as far as the legal effect is concerned. Forms designed with blank lines are one thing; changing boilerplate language without a strong sense of the legal effects can lead to 'interesting' legal consequences." When one of his clients brings him a contract he's modified himself, Rose says his thoughts often go something like, "Whoops—there goes the limitation of liability. Whoops—there goes the control of project changes through change orders. Whoops—there goes the exclusion of consequential damages" and so on.

Fred Wilf draws another consulting analogy when he suggests that using form contracts without a lawyer is like installing Netware without an experienced computer consultant. Sometimes it works, and sometimes it doesn't. In addition, he points out, Netware doesn't change from one state to another, but the law does.

Therefore, if you are going to use off-the-shelf contracts, you should limit yourself to "filling in the blanks" and not get creative with the legal wording. But the experience of most consultants who have managed to stay in business for the long term suggests that economizing here is a mistake. *It is worth paying for expert legal advice.* In the long run it will cost you a lot less than one really expensive do-it-yourself mistake. As one consultant says, waggishly, "All lawyer jokes aside, the peace of mind I get from their benediction on my wild and crazy deals is worth the bucks."

The Contract as an Educational Tool

Perhaps the greatest benefit to the independent consultant of negotiating a contract with the client is that it enables both parties to sanity check that they share the same view of what work is to be done and how. This is particularly useful when the contract involves work to be done for a client who has little or no experience in dealing with the software development process. Clients who are used to buying nothing more complex than fixtures or plumbing services are entering new territory when they decide to purchase computer services and custom software.

The client who doesn't understand up-front that custom software must be debugged and that there will inevitably be some problems that can only be flushed out in acceptance testing, is not going to be a satisfied client, no matter how good the software you deliver. The client who doesn't understand that no computer system no matter how well specified is going to solve all his business problems the day you unpack it from its boxes is likewise not one who is going to send you glowing referrals.

Few technically unsophisticated clients understand the need for a well-crafted specification, or the impact that a few tiny, last-minute changes can have on delivery dates and the quality of the ultimate product. Few of these clients understand the need for training that they will encounter when they first install new, complex, off-the-shelf software, or the hassles they may run into when new releases of old familiar products must be installed.

The contract negotiation stage is an excellent place to spell out for such clients exactly what you intend to do and to be sure that you and the client are, indeed, working with shared expectations. This is the time to hew out what conditions must be met for the client and you to consider the software completely functional and to make sure that the client understands that a seemingly simple change in the spec will necessitate more, possibly expensive, work from you.

Contract negotiations can be nerve racking. It may only be when faced with the need to formalize the hitherto genial business relationship in a legal document that clients come to terms with their own anxieties, or reveal to you the damage done by previous unpleasant experiences with consultants who could not deliver what they promised.

But difficulties encountered at the contract-drafting stage should be thought of as being like problems discovered when writing a high-level spec. They may be nasty and irritating to deal with, but it is a lot better to flush these problems out at the start and to solve them before work begins than to encounter them later in the process when they can be far more damaging.

CONTRACT CLAUSES AND WHAT THEY MEAN

Chapter 7 discussed the contract clauses you are likely to encounter when dealing with a broker. Now we're going to discuss some other kinds of clauses that can come up when you deal directly with clients. Some of these clauses also occur in brokered contracts, but may not have as significant an impact on you in the brokered context as they do when you are working without an intermediary. In light of the importance of getting expert legal advice when crafting such agreements, it is not my intention here to tell you how to write such clauses. Our goal here is only to familiarize you with the details that lawyers will be concerned with and to help you understand the kinds of situations these clauses cover and the underlying issues they reflect. You'll find the model consulting contract recommended by the Independent Computer Consultants Association in Appendix C.

Payment Terms

The contract is where you spell out exactly what you expect to be paid, and just as importantly, when you expect to receive your money. This second condition is far more important than most beginning consultants, accustomed to receiving regular paychecks, may imagine. The tendency of most businesses is to hold invoices unpaid as long as possible to enjoy the use of the money involved, and as an independent contractor you may find yourself with almost no leverage when your client's accounting department continues to assure you that your invoice is being processed, but no check appears in the mail.

As a result it is always wise to specify that the client must pay you within a specified number of days after receiving your invoice, two weeks, for example, or at most thirty days.

Consultant Kaye Caldwell urges consultants to make sure that they don't let payment lag more than a month after billing, and suggests that you enhance the chances of the client taking you seriously by writing the contract in such a way that if payment is not made within thirty days the consultant can discontinue working for the client until the payment is received. As she points out, on a six-month contract, "If [the consultant] bills monthly and is not paid for sixty days he will be nearly halfway through the contract before he sees that there might be a payment problem. Too many big companies take advantage of small companies by stretching out their payments to ridiculous lengths."

She also suggests, and many other consultants agree wholeheartedly, that if possible, you ask the client to *pay you a certain amount up front* before you begin work, as proof of their intention to pay. Suggested amounts for such advance payments include one month's worth of billing, 10 percent of the total cost of the project, or even as much as 25 percent of the estimated cost of the total project.

In the United Kingdom, Consultant R. H. Warden reports that it is customary to bill clients at the end of the month, after which they have a thirty-day settlement period. However, he finds that even his "good" clients often make him wait sixty days or more for payment.

If you do find yourself working on a fixed-price contract, negotiating fair payment terms is even more important. The client may often expect to pay you only when the job is complete, but this is almost always unacceptable. Consultants and VARs who work under fixed-cost terms advise that the only way to manage such projects is to demand a percentage of the total up front, and to then establish checkpoints throughout the project where, when mutually agreed upon terms are satisfied, the client pays a further percentage of the project cost.

One consultant gives as examples several different arrangements he's worked out in such situations. For one deal with a large client he required 25 percent up front, two more interim payments at 25 percent, and one final payment when the system was ready to certify. This, he explains, gave the customer control of the project while giving him interim funding and allowing him to monitor the client's ability to pay promptly. For a contract that involved the purchase of significant amounts of hardware for a new client this same consultant required 75 percent up front, and the final 25 percent on delivery of the hardware.

By far the biggest payment problem consultants encounter is the client who doesn't pay the very last payment due after the project is complete—when a consultant has lost the ability to stop work on the project as an inducement to payment. One solution to this problem is to include a clause in the contract that specifies that if source code is included in the deal it not be transferred to the client until all payments have been made. Another solution is for the consultant to retain ownership of the code and *the right to resell it elsewhere* until final payment is received.

Guarantees

Clients often attempt to write into contracts stern wording that penalizes the consultant who doesn't deliver a satisfactory product or who doesn't meet a deadline. Very frequently the client who demands this kind of a guarantee most loudly is one who has been burned in the past by an incompetent consultant. You must negotiate these clauses carefully to avoid being put in an untenable position. But you must also be very careful that in negotiating them you don't add to the client's fears or act as if you are indeed trying to provide an escape clause that will allow you to take advantage of him.

An example of such a client is the one who told a consultant that he'd been burnt badly twice in the past and said, "When I am ready to proceed, not one cent will pass to the computer person until *everything* is running to my satisfaction." Twice-shy clients may demand money-back guarantees or clauses that specify a per-day penalty for every day that the consultant is late on delivery. They may even go so far as to insert indemnification clauses that specify conditions in which the consultant must reimburse the client should the project go seriously awry.

All experienced consultants encounter these kinds of clients, and most of them have learned that they must be handled with great tact and sensitivity. Clients do have a right to be assured that they will receive what they expect for their money and that they won't end up paying for substandard junk. As consultant Michael Scriven points out, "Today even garages guarantee their work."

But many experienced consultants have also discovered that the client who is utterly inflexible about negotiating these kinds of demands and is unwilling to accept *any* risk when beginning a new relationship with a consultant may be sending out one of the telltale signs of the problem client.

Here are a few solutions that experienced consultants have found can mollify the nervous client in such cases and lead to a mutually satisfactory arrangement.

- *Staged Guarantees.* If a client insists on a money-back guarantee, break the project into a series of smaller steps and limit the scope of the guarantee to a single step. Once the step is signed off on, the guarantee expires. Consultant Michael Kibat stresses that it is very important to get the exact nature of each milestone to be met in writing when taking this approach so that the client cannot weasel out by saying "this isn't what I wanted."
- *Retention of Ownership.* If you agreed to a money-back guarantee, specify that if the client does exercise the guarantee, the software or system you've developed for them belongs to you alone once you've refunded their money and that you are entitled to all revenues that it might generate, past, present, and future. Consultant Andy Harmon suggests that this kind of arrangement will prevent the client from claiming a system is "unsatisfactory" to avoid payment when they fully intend to use it.
- *Rebates.* Offer to rebate the final payment if the client isn't 100 percent satisfied. For the past ten years consultant Bob Clements has done this, promising clients that they can retain the final 25 percent payment on a fixed-price job if they aren't completely satisfied with the results. He reports that he's only run into a few clients who exercised the option of retaining the final payment and that in each case he went out of his way to make the unhappy client happy, and that these people remained his clients.
- *Incentives.* If a client insists on a cash penalty for late delivery, negotiate for a corresponding bonus for early delivery or write into the contract a cash incentive for on-time delivery. However, many consultants warn that it is never wise to agree to a penalty clause covering late delivery unless you are in complete control of the project. Lateness may well result from incorrect specs supplied by

the client, failure of client hardware (not installed by you), strikes, hurricanes, and illness of key personnel.

- *Bonding.* Offer the client the option of using a performance bond to cover your work. Such bonds are purchased from insurance companies. Unfortunately, they are expensive enough that most consultants who have suggested them to nervous clients have also insisted that the client supply the money to pay for them.

The hallmark of all such successful compromises is that neither party in the agreement ends up carrying all the risk. It is also important to confine all penalties and guarantees to situations that you, the consultant, can reasonably expect to control. If during negotiations you run into a situation where, after good-faith attempts to modify a specific clause, you are still uncomfortable with the level of risk involved in it, it may be a sign that this isn't a deal you want to pursue further, no matter how otherwise tempting it might look. Stepping away from such situations may be wise. You are the one who will end up paying if things go sour, and the amount of anxiety that such a clause can generate may be much more than you should have to live with for months, or even years of your future. More than one consultant has discovered, after coming to a painful decision not to accept a contract with a deeply disturbing clause in it, that, when pushed to the wall, the client will drop the problem clause rather than begin the search for a new consultant.

Nondisclosure Agreements

There are two different kinds of nondisclosure agreements you need to be concerned about when negotiating a consulting contract: the one that protects the client's trade secrets and the one that protects your own. Clients take the clause protecting their own trade secrets very seriously and you will almost always have to agree to some version of one. Such clauses are written to keep you from passing on to competitors the details of how a company processes its data, or to keep secret its development plans and marketing strategies.

The important thing to keep in mind when considering such a clause is that there be a clear definition of what information is actually covered and under what conditions that information may be disclosed. Some clauses define the material covered as being anything that the client stamps "Confidential" or otherwise identifies as being proprietary. This is perhaps too restrictive, as it wouldn't cover things you overheard relative to the company's strategy or marketing plans. Others are so vague that they might cover anything related to the company's business. Accepting such clauses might interfere with your ability to work for other clients in the same industry as the client they cover. Attorney Lance

Rose recommends redrafting any such agreement to specify that confidentiality applies only to those things that are likely to be truly secret.

A nondisclosure clause can protect you, the consultant, too, particularly if you use your own libraries of previously developed code when working for the client. A nondisclosure clause would prevent the client from turning over your source code to another consultant or from revealing your client list to competitors.

Just remember that a nondisclosure clause will not in and of itself prevent an unscrupulous client from passing information or code on to a competitor. It merely gives you a basis for demanding expensive legal redress when such violations occur. If you have serious concern about keeping your materials private and have any question about the trustworthiness of a client, it is best to work out another way of keeping the client from getting access to your confidential material.

Who Owns the Code

Another important issue that you should settle at contract writing time is that of who will own the software you develop under the contract.

Legally, you, the independent consultant, retain the copyright and ownership of any code you develop for a client unless you specifically sign over your rights to the client in writing. However, very few clients realize that this is the case, and most assume that the work you do for them on their dime is theirs. Rather than sign over their rights to their code, many independent consultants prefer to give the client a license to use the software they've developed, since they know they can sell the same code or modified versions of it to a multitude of clients.

It is therefore very important to make sure that if you intend to retain the copyright and ownership of your code for future use and potential sales to other clients your client is aware of this.

If you are a custom developer who reuses portions of your own previously developed code when developing new systems for clients, you need to be particularly careful of boilerplate clauses in client-written contracts that specify that you assign to them "all inventions, discoveries" and the like. Cross these words out and explain to the client that you have to retain ownership to the software toolkit that will be an integral part of the product you will deliver to them as it is the basis of your ongoing business. Consultant Guy Scharf has found that though there may be resistance from "the client's bureaucracy" to such demands, the problem usually fades away "after you reach someone who actually can make decisions."

Although you legally retain copyright to your work in the absence of an agreement to transfer that right, Attorney Fred Wilf suggests that you always put a copyright notice in your software. Doing this will prevent any infringer from arguing that they did not know that your work was copyrighted. Wilf warns that if you register your software with the government's copyright office, depositing the required fifty pages of your code could invalidate any claim you might want to make that the code was a trade secret and thus covered by nondisclosure agreements. There are alternative deposit rules that you can use to get around this problem that you can learn from the copyright office or from a lawyer who specializes in such work.

Source Code

The consultant who is selling a license to use his code rather than the code itself faces another decision when drafting the contract: whether to let the client have the source code for the system or whether to deliver only the object code.

There is no unanimity on this topic. Some consultants refuse to turn over source code, fearing that the client will turn it over to a competitor or bring in cheaper consultants to modify it, whose sloppy work may negatively impact the original consultant's reputation. Others argue that their clients, fearful of their going out of business or otherwise becoming unavailable, will not work with them unless they agree to turn the source code over. This issue is one that again brings you into contact with your client's insecurities over your reliability, and so must be approached with more than ordinary tact and diplomacy.

Here are a few solutions that consultants have found for working out equitable agreements concerning source code:

- If you do not want to release the source code to a client who is worried about what might happen to his system should something happen to you or should you cease supporting the code, offer to put the source code into escrow, as we discussed earlier in this chapter.
- If a client is concerned about paying for you to develop something you will then be selling to another client at some future time, recast this to show that this way of working has benefits for this client too. Consultant Michael Stein explains to clients that, "the reason they are paying what they are for the program, and not three times as much, is because the development of a lot of the code was paid for by earlier custom projects."
- Offer to let the client buy the source for an additional charge. One consultant reports including the following clause in his contracts: "Source code is available for an additional 1.5 times the final cost of the completed system." He reports that so far none of his clients has exercised this option.

- If you plan to resell the software, offer the client who is paying you to develop it a commission on your subsequent sales. However, one consultant who used this approach with what has turned out to be a very popular vertical package cautions you to limit the client's commission to a limited number of sales, or perhaps to an amount that represents his total investment in the project. An open-ended commission arrangement can prove very expensive on a successful software product.

Arbitration

A final clause that may save you a lot of grief is one that specifies how disputes between the parties to the contract will be handled. Be careful not to accept wording that makes you liable for the cost of all litigation that grows out of the contract—even litigation you win. Such unfair clauses may be unenforceable. L. J. Kutten, a lawyer who publishes frequently on computer-related law, points out that in many states, by statute, "if X has a contractual right to attorney's fees for anything from Y, then Y has a similar right to attorney's fees from X. Y's right to collect need not be expressed in the contract."

Some consultants report very good experiences using clauses that specify the use of binding arbitration as an alternative to litigation. A typical arbitration clause should include wording like the following:

> Such arbitration shall be conducted before an arbitrator(s) selected by, and in accordance with the rules of the American Arbitration Association. The decision of the arbitrator(s) shall be final and binding to the parties. The arbitrator(s) shall have the discretion to order that the costs of arbitration, including his fees, other costs, and reasonable attorney's fees, shall be borne by the losing party.

Using binding arbitration to solve disputes is almost always cheaper and quicker than going to court.

CONCLUSION

Once again, it is becoming clear that the key to success in the early stages of your relationship with the client is how well you communicate. How well you listen, how well you respect the client's needs, and how compassionately you deal with the client's fears will have a lot to do with how likely you are to win the client's trust and go on to build a fruitful business relationship.

9

ON THE JOB

The work you do as a consultant may end up being much like work you've done before. But because you will be doing it as a consultant, you will be doing it in a very new way. To succeed as a consultant you will have to *develop a consultant mentality*. You will have to learn to take responsibility for things you used to leave to others, like creating a productive work environment and getting paid. At the same time, you'll have to learn to ignore things that you may be used to treating as important, like taking credit for your successes and judging your results by an absolute standard.

CREATING A PRODUCTIVE ENVIRONMENT

Beginning consultants who come to their first consulting assignments fresh from years of salaried work are often astonished to discover that clients who don't bat an eyelash when asked to pay them $50 an hour, may balk at providing them with a telephone, a desk, or even a computer on which to do their work. But this is often the case, even when clients insist that consultants do all their work on-site. Experienced consultants frequently find that they must put considerable effort into creating a conducive work environment for themselves if they are to be productive and meet their clients' needs.

The Physical Environment—or Lack of It

The experience of one mainframe systems programming specialist is typical of what almost all consultants experience at one time or another. He reports, "When I started my last assignment there was no desk, no telephone, no terminal, no userid. It took about four weeks to get my own desk, but all of the drawers were already full. The terminal on that desk did not work. It took another three weeks to get it fixed."

When equipment is provided it is often located at an inconvenient spot. On a recent assignment another consultant reports having no problem getting a working terminal. But the terminal he was given sat on a credenza behind the company controller's desk—where the controller continued to work for the length of the assignment. Other consultants have found themselves expected to do their work on whatever computer was currently not being used by company employees who were having lunch, attending meetings, or out sick. Some have had to work in unheated warehouses, and one even recalls working with seven other contractors in what had recently been the shower room of a county detox center.

You will not last long in consulting if you can't handle such situations with aplomb, or at least with the kind of calm problem-solving skill exemplified by the deskless consultant who solved his problem by turning a large wooden wire-spool he found in the client's warehouse on its side and using it as a desk.

Some consultants have found that the best way to deal with this kind of problem is to provide clients with a Day One Checklist a few weeks before they plan to begin work on-site. They explain to their clients that they can save themselves considerable expense by providing such things as a desk, a phone, security clearances, valid userids, manuals and documentation, and an organizational chart.

Other suggest that at the time you sign the contract, you ask the client whether there are other documents you will need to sign to gain access to the corporate systems and data you will be working with. They report that clients at large corporations appreciate you showing this kind of foresight, although they may not always be able to expedite the needed paperwork. Even when they can't, because you've made that extra effort to help out, you can relax and feel less anxious when you find yourself forced to spend unproductive, billable hours waiting for necessary equipment and approvals.

If you will be using the clients' hardware and software, it is also a good idea to explain that you can get a lot more accomplished in a shorter time if the client ensures that the release of the software you need is installed on a working system before you show up. In case this kind of preparation isn't enough, many experienced consultants routinely bring their own laptops, modems, and software manuals along with them to the client site, as well as their own tape, ministaplers, and paperclips.

Ensuring Access to Client Employees

Another common problem consultants encounter on the job is difficulty in getting to vital client employees. It is very frustrating to report for a new assignment only to discover that the only person who knows the details of the system you've been called to work with has just left for a two-week vacation. Even when such employees are available, consultants are often expected to wedge discussions with them into bits of time left over from the employee's other responsibilities.

Consultant Darrel Raynor points out that it is vital to have important client employees understand they must give you blocks of time in which to discuss the situation away from ringing phones and secretarial interruptions. When he has had difficulty getting them to schedule this kind of time, he has found it useful to ask the higher-ups who brought him in to lend their names to a procedure memo requesting that all employees give him this kind of consideration.

Working On-Site versus Off-Site

Because of the chaos that can prevail at a client site, most consultants prefer to do as much work as possible at their own offices. But client concerns about security often result in corporate policies that discourage or even forbid off-site work, especially in large corporations. Clients may be reluctant to let you dial into a mainframe or access a PC using remote access software because of fears of exposing themselves to hacker break-ins or viruses. Others may be nervous about letting an unfamiliar consultant bill for time spent out of sight and may require that you spend at least a certain proportion of your time on-site so that they can keep tabs on your progress.

Experienced consultants have developed several techniques for convincing their clients to let them work in their own offices. Some give the client a *cash incentive*, setting their rates so that the client pays less for work performed at the consultant's own office than work done on-site. Burt Johnson charges 20 percent more than his usual hourly rate when he has to do more than 10 percent of the work on a project at the client site. John Genzano justifies charging clients a higher rate for hours worked on-site by explaining that this additional cost compensates him for time spent traveling and for the opportunity cost of not being able to respond to other clients' emergencies. However, if you take this approach, be sure that your client is aware of this policy before you begin work and that your different rates are set out in the contract.

Other consultants appeal to the client's desire to keep costs down by explaining that they are more productive working in their own environments with their own software tools. They also point out to clients that when they work out of their own offices the client saves additional money by not having to find them office space and equipment.

Another useful approach is to explain to clients that you cannot work on their premises for extended periods of time because doing so prevents you from supporting your other clients. Paul Ferrara says his new clients appreciate this stance because they know that in the future they too will be needing his support and are glad to see evidence that he takes pains to make that support available.

But it may be that you won't be able to talk the client into letting you work off-site. If that is the case, don't judge yourself too harshly. In many niches it simply isn't possible. "If I had made a policy of refusing on-site work, I would have been out of business long, long ago," says one consultant with more than twelve years in the business. The large mainframe shops and defense industry engineering installations that make up his clientele rarely let anyone work off-site. If such firms are your target customer, you will have to live with on-site work. If you are concerned that working on-site might threaten your ability to claim independent contractor status, try to be sure that you never work more than a few days a week on-site for any single client and keep more than one project going at a time.

DEVELOPING THE CONSULTANT MENTALITY

Many new consultants have difficulty grasping the shift in attitude they must make to work successfully as a consultant. Employees develop a host of attitudes and behaviors that help them succeed in the workplace. But many of these attitudes and behaviors no longer work when they return to that workplace as a consultant. The reason for this is simple. Although the work consultants do may resemble that of employees, the rewards they can earn from doing that work are very different. Consultants don't earn promotions or get raises, no matter how good the job they do. They don't get to stick around to admire what they've done, nor do they triumph from backing the winner in internal political wars.

Consultants come in, do a job, earn their fee, and if they play things right, they get called back to do other assignments or get referrals that lead to other work.

The consultant who goes into the workplace looking for other kinds of satisfaction, for acclaim, admiration, or for power, may be in for some tough times. Because the single most important thing that you have to understand about being a consultant is that the consultant is—and must remain—an outsider.

Maintain Your Status as an Outsider

This is the central truth you must keep in mind if you are to develop an appropriate consultant mentality: *Your outsider status is your greatest source of strength as a consultant.* It is what lets you come in and propose solutions unlimited by the political concerns that may hobble long-term employees. *But it is also your greatest liability*, because as an outsider, you have no power base, little leverage, and no protection from whatever political pressures might prevail. Your only connection to the company you are working for will be the people who brought you in, and your loyalty must be to those people, not to the company itself, or to an abstract idea of how a job should be done.

In effect, your ultimate loyalty must really always be to yourself and to your own growing consulting practice. A consultant mentality is one that keeps the client at an emotional arms' length. You must treat clients ethically and give them your best, but you must also always keep in mind that every situation that comes up must be evaluated from the standpoint of how it will help or hurt the growth of your own consulting practice.

Bob Bosché, who has been an independent consultant for more than eight years, sums up very well the way that a consultant must operate very well when he advises new consultants, "You should take a very helpful but subtle approach. Your presence as an outsider alone will create enough insecurity and resentment." The consultant, Bosché warns, must operate in the background and show "a good healthy 'team spirit' attitude with the primary goal of making the employee project partners successful through subtle direction rather than any attempt at *management*."

Consultants must focus on making the client look good, not on making themselves look good. As Bosché points out, "If you are good and add real value to the project, they will allow you to become the de facto leader, as long as you operate in the background. If you are good, all the right people will know it."

But you must stay in the background. You must not, as all too many consultants do, get sucked into feeling so comfortable that you make the fatal mistake of acting like an insider, because doing this inevitably brings a backlash from employees who are the real insiders, who will rightly resent having an outsider lording it over them or taking what they feel are the employees' own perogatives.

You Are the Client's Guest

One consultant claims that the best single piece of advice he's ever been given about consulting came in the words of a company receptionist. "I was griping to one of the people I worked with at a client site about the resistance that some of the local staff had to working with me," he recounts. "I must have been out of line because the receptionist overheard me and flew from behind her desk to remind me. 'You are a guest here and don't you ever forget it!' "

An employee can bitch about the lousy coffee in the company cafeteria. A wise consultant will not. Nor will a wise consultant allow himself to be lured into making slighting remarks about company policy or the quality of any of the company's employees. Just as family members may joke about weird old Uncle Ernie but will soundly defend the old sot against slurs made by someone outside of the family, employees can complain about things that you, the outsider, cannot bring up without causing offense.

Take Nothing for Granted

Another important part of the consultant mentality is developing a heightened instinct for self-protection. Because you are an outsider you can't know what is going on when you enter a new work environment. You must tread warily and never make the mistake of acting on assumptions about how a client does things without first checking each one out.

At the abstract level, you can't assume that clients will always behave sensibly, or even that they will do what is in their own best interest. At a more mundane one, you can't assume that the client's staff are competent, or that the client's existing hardware and software are correctly installed and function properly.

Clients frequently give their least competent staff members the job of orienting a new consultant because it causes the least disruption to their projects to pull such people off them for a few days. So experienced consultants accept whatever help they are offered in a respectful way, but they double-check anything that could later cause them trouble. They take the time to verify hardware configurations and software release levels, and they test out the client's software to make sure it is working correctly before they begin making any modifications to it.

Consultants who develop code for clients warn that it is very important to ask to see a copy of the client's *coding standards* before you begin your work. Many clients care only that the code you write works, but others may demand that data-names follow a specific convention or may be fanatic about capitalizations and indentations in code. In some cases company policies make it impossible to release code into production unless it conforms to a host of rigid and often meaningless standards that you may not hear a word about until you complete your systems testing.

Even seemingly familiar stuff must often be approached with caution. A mainframe consultant reports that he only discovered that his client had saved a few bucks by omitting to install a mainframe security software package found in almost every mainframe site when the client informed him that a test run he'd submitted into a test queue had just

printed an entire run of real checks. Just because something is so dumb
that ninety-nine companies out of one hundred won't do it doesn't
mean that your client won't give it a shot.

The biggest mistake that many beginning consultants make is thinking that if they ask too many questions they will look unprofessional
and jeopardize their image as an expert. Nothing could be farther from
the truth. Unless you ask a lot of questions when you start out a new assignment you are likely to make expensive stupid errors that will mark
you forever in the client's mind as a bungler. So while at the start of a
new assignment you may be eager to begin achieving results and impressing the client, you are much more likely to achieve this goal if you
take the time to ask the questions you need to ask and put some time
into investigating the environment in which you find yourself.

Clients who are heavy users of consultants report that they generally
give any new consultant a week or two to get up to speed before they
begin to judge their performance. They know that no one can walk in off
the street and know all the ins and outs of their businesses. So even
when dealing with a naive client who expects you to have almost mag-
ical powers, it's worth remembering that some ramp-up time is always
needed.

Assume nothing, ask questions, and document what you are told. As
consultant Payson Hall quipped when asked to give the gist of effective
consulting procedures, "Trust everyone . . . and cut the cards. Keep
written records of important discussions and include key points in your
regular written status reports to your client."

COMMON PROBLEMS WITH CLIENTS

There are some common client-posed quandaries that virtually all consultants run into at some time during their careers. Let's look at a few of
these now and see how experienced consultants deal with them.

The Client Wants Something Dumb

One of the thorniest problems consultants encounter is how to handle
the client who wants them to do something the consultant knows is a
mistake.

The issue might arise over something minor, like when a manager
asks you to redesign your software so that it no longer interrupts data
entry operators with "tedious" error messages. Or it may involve something major, like a client's decision to install a cheap networking solution that you know is not capable of supporting the number of users the
client hopes to put on it by the end of the year.

This kind of situation confronts consultants with the delicate balance they must maintain at all times between being the expert and being the client's ally. Handle it wrong and you may keep your clients from making expensive mistakes, but only at the cost of your ongoing relationship with them. If clients come away from the experience feeling bullied, or sensing that you look down on them for their lack of judgment or expertise, your victory will be an empty one.

The key to dealing with such situations is to *stay focused on your relationship with the client* and not let your determination to be right overwhelm you to the point where you forget that your primary goal is to satisfy that client. No matter how good for them your solutions might be, you can't cram them down clients' throats if they don't want them. Just as you must remember that you are a guest, you also have to recall that a guest would never force something like health food or vitamins on a host, no matter how good for them they might be.

You can only suggest. *You cannot insist.* And if you are to succeed at consulting, when you run into a situation where clients would be well advised to change course, you must figure out a way to manage the situation so that clients come away thinking that they, not you, were responsible for making the change of direction.

Longtime consultant Carl Brown suggests that when clients approach you with requests that you do something you believe would be a mistake, you tell them that you are confused and need to have the rationale behind the request made clearer. This way you force clients to give their decision more thought, but you do it in an unthreatening way, since you've made it clear that the reason you need clarification is to clear up your own "confusion" rather than because you are sure the decision is wrong.

Brown also suggests that you ask questions that might allow clients to reach on their own the conclusions that you've already come to. For example, in the case of the client who insists on the cheap network you might say, "I'm not clear on how you plan to get around the fact that BudgetNet can only handle a maximum of ten workstations. Did I misunderstand something or did you decide that it wasn't necessary to support all fifty users you originally specified?"

This approach not only saves the client's ego, it keeps you from looking like an obnoxious fool in the situation where you have missed something and haven't grasped the client's very good reason for doing what she wants to do.

But even after you've made clear your concerns, a client will often proceed with what you consider an inadvisable course. In such cases, particularly one in which you see the possibility of serious problems occurring in the future, it is advisable to put your reservations in writing.

Consultant Anne Pruitt explains that she handles this kind of situation by putting a notice on her invoice saying something like, "I have made x, y, and z changes, as requested by you. As we discussed, this could lead to problems a, b, and c. You must prevent these problems by always making sure that the gramlit is sprogged in the martee."

Other consultants don't wait until the work is done, but send their clients a letter stating the exact nature of the work they have been asked to do, the ramifications of the work and potential problems that lie ahead if it is undertaken, and then ask the client to sign off on it.

Once the work has been done, you are not yet done with the need to act diplomatically. Consultant David Moskowitz warns that if the solution does indeed end up causing the problems you've predicted, "The worst thing you could do is say, 'I told you so.'"

Many consultants worry that their reputations will suffer if they let themselves be overridden by a client. They fear having their name associated with what ends up being a failed project—and this point is worth considering. There are situations in which you may have to back out of a project rather than work with a client who is pursuing what you consider to be a foolhardy course. This would certainly be true if a client wanted you to cut corners in a way that could eventually cause harm to others. If your client ends up getting sued and your product or services are involved, you might find yourself learning firsthand how terms like "liability" and "malpractice" are interpreted by the courts.

But it is important to maintain a sense of proportion here. You are rarely likely to encounter the client who wants you to do something negligent or dangerous. More often the dumb thing that the client wants is something that, though it might not be the optimum solution to his problems, might still be a solution.

Consultant David Arnold points out to the consultant who worries about damaging his reputation that, "If you *object* to doing what they want, *that* will get a reputation." He cautions that it can be more dangerous to be perceived as negative or obstructive than to be involved with a less-than-perfect solution.

Regardless of the solution you implement, the only way you are likely to succeed as a consultant is if the end result of your work is a satisfied client.

The Obstructive Client Employee

Another common problem that almost every consultant runs into at one time or another is that classic consulting nightmare, the obstructive client employee. Problem employees range from the highest of top executives to the lowliest clerk. What all of them have in common is a deep desire to impede a consultant's progress and the means to pull it off.

The problem employee may be a user who refuses to sit down with you to help clarify the spec, or a production services functionary who refuses to give you access to necessary files. She may be a manager who insists you fill in multiple timesheets covering every fifteen-minute period that you've worked or another programmer who intentionally gives you bad test data.

There are many different reasons why employees become obstructive toward consultants, but the key thing to remember is that this obstruction rarely has anything to do with you personally. Almost always it originates in problems that existed long before you showed up and it is only your outsider status that makes you its target.

Thus, if you run into an obstructive employee, you should try to keep in mind that the manager who is giving you the hard time may fear that her department will be eliminated if your project succeeds. The user who refuses to discuss the spec with you may be someone who earned a reputation for being the local "computer wiz" until you showed up and showed that his amateurish solutions were costing the company unnecessary dollars. The programmer who gave you the bad data may have just been denied a raise in spite of putting in lots of overtime and may find it intolerable that the company is willing to pay you so much in view of what they are paying him.

Sometimes, too, an employee's obstructive behavior may be an attempt to comply with the hidden agenda of a company bigwig who has his own reasons for seeing the project fail.

Only if you keep encountering obstructive employees on assignment after assignment should you begin to consider the possibility that your own behavior might be contributing to the problem. Perhaps in your zeal to get the job done you have not been respectful enough of the people whose help you need to get that job done. Perhaps you have forgotten your guest status and are offending the company's staffers by behaving as if you think you are their manager. If that is the case, you should start putting some serious work into improving your "bedside manner."

But even when the problem is not of your own making, dealing with obstructive employee behavior requires infinite tact.

Should You Alert Management to the Presence of the Problem Employee?

New consultants frequently wonder whether they should alert higher levels of management to the presence of an obstructive employee. The answer to this is a qualified "maybe." As Hawaiian consultant Nanette Geller points out, whether an appeal to upper management will be successful depends on your relationship with upper management. Geller says she has found that "If they brought you in then they will take you more seriously. If they never heard of you until the project went sour, it's harder, but still not necessarily impossible."

Paul Ferrara concurs: "I'm often working at the detail level of a pro-

gram with someone several notches below the person that actually re-
tained me. So let's say the bookkeeper asks for something really asinine.
I'd make my point and if it's not resolved at that level, I'd bring it up to
the controller. Normally the latter and I are going to share the same
view, but if not, I'd do it the way he wanted."

No matter who you appeal to in dealing with this kind of problem,
you must always exercise caution. You must never assume that the executive you are appealing to will share your assessment of the problem
employee's motivation or of his effect on the project. For all you know,
the problem employee is his son-in-law—or his best friend. However irritating he might be to you, the problem employee may be very valuable
to his employer for reasons you know nothing about. For this reason, if
you force the client to choose between you and an employee, you must
be prepared to hear that you are the one who is going to go.

State the Problem Impersonally

Consultants who have dealt with this kind of problem warn that if you
do appeal for help when dealing with an obstructive client employee,
you must be careful to state the problem in noncontroversial terms.
Rather than saying, "Joe Blow is doing all he can to make this project
fail," say instead, "I foresee problems ahead in this project unless we
can get middle management to be more committed to our goals." Management can then ask you to clarify the problem or let it go. If they let it
go, it isn't necessarily because they missed your point, but it may just be
that they are aware of the situation but don't feel it is worth antagoniz-
ing the problem employee.

If you feel a need to get more specific about a problem, Geller suggests
that you be careful to use a nonaccusatory way of describing it and say,
"Such and such happened," not "*X* did it." She suggests that you state
your concern in a memo, not in conversation, because it is much easier
to maintain the standard to tact in a memo than in a conversation where
you may easily be lured into saying more than you meant to.

Graceful Exits

If a troublesome employee does succeed in torpedoing your project,
there may be nothing you can do but find another assignment. In such
situations, experienced consultants report that it is a good idea to resist
the temptation to defend yourself even when you get blamed for the
failure of the project. Instead, when leaving the project, try to maintain
a friendly, professional, confident manner that leaves the door open for
a future relationship.

A good way to handle the solution is to send a cordial exit memo that
doesn't defend your actions but simply states that should the company
change its mind about whatever it is that has been the problem em-

ployee's primary objection to your work, you'd suggest that the client do such and such. This leaves open the possibility of reopening the relationship should the problem employee, as often happens, eventually be recognized for what he or she is and be removed.

When stymied this way, you may find it an even better strategy to do nothing at all. One consultant who found himself caught in a project dead-ended by the negative attitude of a manager who was later removed reports, "We elected *not* to speak up because we didn't know the internal politics. We were probably correct." He's since gotten other projects at the same company and feels that little would have been gained by making an issue of the employee's opposition.

Problems with Other Consultants

Another thorny problem you may run into is what to do when you find that a client is dealing with—or has dealt in the past with—another consultant whom you consider to be incompetent. David Moskowitz describes one way to cope with this dilemma, saying, "I've talked with some clients who are convinced that consultant X is great when I think that X is just this side of a $%^&* (pick your own low-life word). I refuse to say anything bad about another consultant to a client. If they think he's great, if he's always done the job for them, if he always comes through for them, etc., it doesn't make *any* difference whether I think the person is good or bad."

Sometimes it is the client who describes another consultant to you as a $%^&*. Sadly , it is all too common to run into potential clients who at the drop of a hat will pour out invective about the consultant who burned them on a past project.

Caution! The other consultant may indeed have been a prime jerk— but he may not have been, so this is a situation where it pays to listen carefully.

Does the client believe the consultant is a jerk because he insisted on a written spec? Because he couldn't deliver on an unreasonable schedule? Because the software evinced a few bugs after installation? Because he wouldn't make extensive changes for free after the software was installed?

For every consultant who has burned a client, there is a client who made life hell for some consultant. So when you encounter a stranger who displays a high level of emotion about a previous consulting relationship, you should take steps to make sure that you too, after months of unpaid work, don't end up painted by him as yet another rip-off.

Paul Curtis makes it a practice to ask clients for permission to contact the consultants who they say burned them. This way he not only can learn about trick stuff in the system, but he can also evaluate what it was that really caused the previous client/consultant relationship to go sour. He's found surprisingly little resistance to this request. In fact, he has even found that interacting with both parties in such a dispute has at times allowed him to arbitrate it and clear up the preexisting problem to everyone's benefit.

Clients Who Don't Understand the Software Development Process

Clients who report being burned by a consultant are all too often clients who purchased computer-related services without understanding what they were getting into. Clients are often woefully innocent about the amount of effort they will have to invest in learning to use the best-designed computer system. They are often unprepared for the finicky nature of software and the propensity of supposedly standard hardware to develop incompatibilities as software and hardware evolve.

The bug that is only a minor, and expected, irritation to the consultant may look to the client like proof that she has thoughtlessly squandered thousands of irretrievable dollars on a worthless piece of junk that will never work properly.

Often, then, the consultant who earns a poor reputation is not one whose solution is necessarily bad (though unfortunately, many of those do exist) but is instead one who did not adequately relate to the client's psychological needs or who failed to give the client a realistic sense of what to expect at the project's outset.

Consultant Chris Hawkinson reports that in his first five years in the business, most of his clients hired him to " 'fix a mess' the last consultant left." In all of these cases, Hawkinson eventually found that "the biggest problem was communication."

When custom software is involved, the difficulties are multiplied a hundredfold and client education becomes even more important if a project is to succeed. One lighthearted but telling illustration of the challenge consultants face is the sign one consultant reports seeing in a colleague's office that said:

SOFTWARE DEVELOPED

- Innovative Designs
- Low Prices
- High Quality
- Fast Results

Pick any two and let's talk.

To avoid the kinds of misunderstandings that can emerge and poison the client/consultant relationship, experienced consultants suggest that you take the time to make your clients aware of the following truths of software development:

- *Obsolescence Is Inescapable.* The dizzying pace at which computer technology advances means that no matter how state-of-the-art your solution is today, there will always be something new showing up in a few months to make your equipment and software look old hat. The important thing to get across to clients is that even though this happens, it shouldn't matter if the original solution solves the problem it was bought to solve.
- *Support Is Required.* No matter how user friendly a system is, if the user has not worked with computers in the past it is going to take some time and some formal education to get up to speed on any system. Consultants should make sure that naive business users understand that they should not even consider buying a system unless they are willing to invest in the support and education it will take to enable them to use that system effectively—or pay lavishly for other people's help.
- *Careful Design Is the Key to Success.* Building a piece of software without a carefully designed spec is like erecting a skyscraper without a blueprint. The client needs to understand that every hour put into designing the system properly eliminates ten hours that would otherwise be needed to jimmy functions into "completed" code.
- *Midproject Changes Are Expensive.* All time estimates are based on the requirements that the client has made known at the time the estimate was given. Clients must understand that if they make significant changes to the spec a new estimate must be made.

But what if you try to educate the client about the nature of technology and he won't be educated? One consultant explains such an experience, saying, "No matter what I did to try and educate him about the software development cycle, he could not seem to comprehend. I am afraid that I had to count my losses minimum and get out of the project before the hours got racked up too high." In such a situation, you may not have any other choices. Just remember, consultants who stay in business are those who create satisfied clients. It is not likely that this kind of client can ever be satisfied.

PROBLEMS CONSULTANTS CREATE

The consulting challenges we've described so far were those posed by client behavior. But consultants themselves also cause some of the problems they run into without any outside assistance.

Handling Mistakes You've Made

Sooner or later, while working on a client's system, no matter how good you are, you are going to make one stinker of a mistake. Perhaps you'll erase a data file that turns out not to be as backed-up as the client thought it was. Perhaps you'll purchase and install a piece of hardware that turns out not to be able to handle the job it was bought for.

The hallmark of consummate professionals is not that they don't make mistakes. It is instead the way that they handle them once they have been made. When they do make a mistake, professionals are *honest* with the client about what has occurred and offer to *fix the problem without charge*.

For example, when he realized that his client's billing system was generating incorrect reports because of a mistake he'd made when rebuilding a clobbered file, a consultant who specializes in accounting solutions says, "I turned to the client and told him what the problem was. I also said, 'this visit is on the house.' And that was that. He appreciated my honesty and the fact that I made good on my mistake."

Where many beginning consultants get into trouble is deciding when to classify time spent on troubleshooting activities as legitimate activity and when to attribute it to their own blundering.

For example, one consultant who found himself putting in over sixty hours studying a new client's undocumented system wondered whether to bill for these hours, asking, "How much of that time was [spent due to] my own stupidity and how much was real enough that the client should pay for it?" You may have similar questions when you find yourself spending a day or two hunting down bugs in code you've written or scrambling to deal with hardware incompatibilities you knew nothing about when you ordered a hardware configuration for the client.

In such cases it is easy to err toward taking too much on yourself. Experienced consultant Dorothy Creswell warns that it is best to be cautious in applying an arbitrary standard of professionalism and to be careful before jumping to the conclusion that your own stupidity causes you to spend the time you do on a project. Software does need to be debugged. Hardware incompatibilities are a fact of life. Although you may be able to imagine a perfect consultant who would not have to spend the time that you do on solving these problems, if the chances are good that other reasonably competent consultants would have to put in similar amounts of time to solve a similar problem, you are probably justified in charging for your time.

If you really aren't sure whether to charge in a borderline case, discuss the issue with your client, explaining what you've done and why you had to do it. The consultant who spent so much time learning the undocumented system did just that, and the client agreed to pay for his time since he knew that he'd cut corners by not paying for adequate documentation when the system was developed.

Charging for Ramp-Up Time

Another dilemma new consultants face is whether to charge clients for the time it takes them to learn the ins and outs of a new language, operating system, or off-the-shelf application.

If you've sold yourself to the client as an expert familiar with a specific language or piece of application software, clearly it would be wrong to charge the client for time spent familiarizing yourself with how it works. But many times clients bring in familiar consultants to work with new software because they have been happy with their previous work and would prefer to deal with them than bring in an unknown expert, no matter how good.

In this situation many consultants do charge their full rate for the time they spend learning the new software, arguing that their skills are in enough demand that the time they spend working for the client learning something new could be spent on other billable work.

But other consultants, mindful of how important it is to maintain cutting-edge technological skills, take another approach. Although they charge their standard rate to learn the ins and outs of an obscure piece of software they are never likely to use again, they may *charge a lower fee* for ramp-up time when a client brings them in on a project that will give them experience using a hot new piece of software or a development environment, like Windows NT or Delphi, which, when mastered, will add significantly to their appeal to subsequent clients. Thus this lower rate gives their steady clients an incentive to give them an opportunity to keep their skills up to date.

Whatever you decide, the most important thing is to make sure the client understands the ground rules you will be using when billing for your learning time.

Dealing with Missed Deadlines

Missed deadlines are another potentially troublesome issue for consultants. As an employee you've undoubtedly participated in many projects that made their dates by redefining the deliverable or pushing significant amounts of incomplete work into the next project phase. Such dodges might do a lot for the careers of corporate managers, but as a consultant you cannot afford to employ that kind of strategy when schedules go awry. Being anything but up-front about the status of a project that is not going to make its dates is a sure way to permanently alienate your client.

David Moskowitz explains, "I don't think that missing a deadline, per se, is that much of a killer. However, if you tell the client that you're on time and *then* miss—look out!" He suggests that when unforeseen problems emerge you *inform the client of the impact on the schedule immediately* and then do as much as you can to reduce that impact. Consultant Guy Scharf adds, "Whether or not missing a deadline is important depends on the project." He's had clients who felt that delivery date was a critical component and who preferred to adjust price and features rather than miss the original target date. But other clients faced with a schedule problem may choose to absorb the delay in order to get what they originally asked for.

The important thing here, again, is to *communicate with the client.* If your delivery schedule runs into a problem, don't attempt to second-guess what they want, but give them the chance to set the new priorities.

When You Get into a Jam

Sooner or later you face the ultimate consulting nightmare—a technical problem you can't solve on your own. Perhaps you can't get a new release of some off-the-shelf software to install, or you can't get a new printer to print in any font except Old Gothic. The client is looking to you to solve the problem but you're stumped. How do you handle these situations?

Ninety-nine percent of the time the answer is, by using your modem.

Asking for On-Line Help

A wealth of technical expertise is available on-line twenty-four hours a day to anyone anywhere in the world who can log into the Internet. It is a very good idea to become familiar with the resources available on-line before you need to call on them for help, so that you'll know where to turn when technical disaster strikes.

As you go exploring the on-line resource you'll discover that each public bulletin board has its own personality and is best at providing a specific kind of information. You'll have to do some experimenting to find out which on-line environment fits in best with your own needs and your own personality style. A board that may be one consultant's favorite place to get help may strike others as a waste of time. Because it can be expensive and time consuming to explore the on-line world when you are new to it, it is also a good idea to ask other consultants and computer professionals to recommend the boards they find most useful.

Paradoxically, the explosion of interest in the World Wide Web in 1996 has made it more difficult for consultants to find on-line help quickly. Throughout the 1980s and early 1990s, hardware and software vendors maintained support forums on Compuserve and these forums provided a centralized meeting place for professionals who needed help. A query posted on the message board of the appropriate forum would often receive an informative reply within minutes.

But with the success of the Web, many vendors moved their support services to their own Web sites. In some cases this has meant that the vendor replaced the interactive portion of a forum with a searchable database of problems and solutions, leaving the visitor who cannot find a quick solution with no choice but to e-mail tech support. In others, the vendors have established their own news groups, or even established news servers of their own where visitors could discuss technical problems, as is the case with Microsoft.

Unfortunately, consultants looking for technical help from newsgroups may now have to wait days for a reply, since that can be how long it takes a newsgroup message to propagate through the Net. With the dispersal of support services through the Web, it can also take more time to locate vendor sites and screen out the worthless ones. As the Web matures, it will become easier to cope with the multiplicity of resources available. But for now the consultant must often navigate a frustrating maze of index and newsgroup search engines before finding the help he or she needs.

Still, it's worth persisting. Help is available on-line. And when you do find a useful on-line resource like a newsgroup devoted to your favorite platform, make the effort to contribute. Many consultants don't realize that the key to getting the most out of on-line help is to participate. You may get some good answers if you log in once every few months to post a question that has you stumped, but you are likely to receive a lot more help if you maintain a presence on one or two well-chosen boards and establish yourself as someone willing to help others. By doing this you can build up the kinds of relationships with other experts that will ensure that when you need help these people will go that extra mile to help you solve your problems.

Bringing in a Subcontractor

Sometimes when you find yourself confronting a task that is outside of your area of competence, the best solution may be to bring in a subcontractor who has the needed technical skill. To do this effectively you will have to spend some time networking within your local consultant community, so that you can get referrals to people who have the skill and professionality you need.

If you do this, be sure that you make it clear to the client that you will be bringing in a subcontractor. Consultant Theresa Carey explains how she handles such situations: "Every so often I run into a situation with a client that is either outside of my areas of technical expertise or is a request that I can't handle in a timely manner due to workload constraints. I'll tell the client about that and suggest one of two things—that they find another consultant to do the work, or that they have me sub-contract that portion of the work and supervise the subcontract. Each time I've had this happen, the client has chosen to have me select and supervise the contractor, because they have grown to trust me over time to do the job for them."

Ethical Issues of Importance to Consultants

Alas, I wish I could say that if you don't run your business ethically, you'll soon be out of business, but I can't. There are plenty of computer consultants practicing in the real world whose ethics leave something to be desired. You'll run into them when you bid for jobs, and often, when you start working on them. And as your career progresses you'll constantly encounter clients whose suspicion and distrust are the result of having been the victims of such unethical consultants.

Not all the unethical consultants you will run into have chosen to cast their lot with the scummy sleazebags and weasels you might be tempted to lump them with. Some are just people who don't know enough to know that their skills are not adequate for the kind of work they've taken on—the proverbial fools who rush in where wiser men—and women—fear to tread. Others may not be aware that they are violating ethical principles.

But it is important that you know. Figure 9-1 is a list of general prin-

---

Ethical consultants engage themselves:

- To place the client's interest ahead of their own
- To keep information about the client confidential and take no advantage of that knowledge
- To accept no commissions in connection with the supply of services to the client
- To hold no directorships or controlling interest in any business competitor of the client without disclosing it
- Not to invite an employee of a client to consider or apply for suggested alternative employment
- To inform clients of any relationship and interest that might influence the consultant's judgment
- To accept no assignment which exceeds the scope of their competence
- Not to work when their judgment might be impaired by illness, misfortune, or any other cause

---

FIGURE 9-1   Ethical ground rules for all consultants.
(From M. Kubr, ed. *Management Consulting: A Guide to the Profession.*
Geneva: International Labour Office, 1978. ISBN 92-2-101165-8, p. 50.)

ciples of ethics appropriate for all consultants. In addition to these general rules, there are a few areas in particular in which new computer consultants are prone to run into ethical difficulties. We'll look at them briefly now.

Promising What You Know You Can't Deliver

Consultants who misrepresent their skills to clients make it harder for everyone to make a living consulting. Saying you will do something in half the time and for half the cost that you know it will really take, may get you the job, but it is unethical, and it does nothing but reinforce the public's view that all consultants are shysters. Ethical consultants are honest with clients and present themselves as experts only in areas they have good reason to believe they have mastered.

Taking Commissions, Finder's Fees, etc. That May Influence Your Recommendations to Clients

While it is appropriate for vendors to offer commissions to dealers and distributors who sell their wares, it is not right to call yourself a consultant if you get commissions for recommending a particular brand of hardware or software to your clients or for suggesting that they use the services of another professional. Taking such commissions compromises your ability to make objective recommendations. If you do it, you should represent yourself to clients as a dealer, not as the kind of consultant who is an objective source of advice. Independent computer consultants may participate in programs that give them discounts on software that they use for their own training, or special access to tech support, but if you do participate in such vendor programs you must make very clear to clients your relationship to the vendor and that you do get benefits from this association.

Condoning the Use of Pirated Software

Using illegally copied software is a crime. Consultants have a responsibility to make it clear to clients who may not know this that using such software is illegal. The consultant who proposes a system that saves the client money by using illegally copied software is suggesting that his client participate in illegal activity. Attorney Lance Rose reminds you that the consultant who helps a client set up a system that he knows calls for the use of software copies that the client will be creating illegally will be considered a "contributory infringer" should the company be audited. The Software Publisher's Association has been very aggressive in pursuing companies that make use of illegally copied software.

10

MANAGING THE CLIENT RELATIONSHIP ONCE THE JOB IS DONE

Once you've completed a project for a client you face some important decisions. Your best source of referrals for new clients is your satisfied clients, so it's clear you want to maintain a strong positive relationship after the job is complete. At the same time, many consultants report that in keeping old clients happy they wind up spending too many hours of unbillable time on work-interrupting phone calls and visits.

CLIENT SUPPORT IS A MAJOR PROFIT CENTER

Consultant Mike Ballentine explains that you can look at doing ongoing support as either a bottomless pit or an unending well. Done right, he says, ongoing support can be one of your greatest marketing tools. It can turn disgruntled customers into super customers. It can tell you exactly what the next version of your software should contain. And it can do all this while making you money. But, he adds, "the puzzle is to figure out how to price it."

For many consultants, the key to setting a fair price on such support is distinguishing between bug fixes (things that were supposed to work in the original deliverable that don't) and the hand-holding, petty enhancements and other kinds of support that do not stem from failures in your original work.

If you can make this distinction, you may find, as do many experienced independent consultants, that providing ongoing support to old clients may earn you anywhere from a quarter to one third of your income in any one year. This is true whether or not you are a VAR who sells boxes with turnkey software solutions installed or a custom software developer.

Getting involved in ongoing support has other obvious benefits. Maintaining a steady stream of brief and friendly contacts with old clients makes it much more likely that they will call on you when they need new work done, and that they will think of you when friends ask them to suggest a consultant to help them. Then too, the service call is a great time to pick up leads, because that is when you are most likely to hear about other projects that are just getting off the ground.

PREVENTING BUG FIXES FROM EATING UP YOUR TIME

But the key to making support a profit center is to *make sure that the support you do is billable.* This requires a lot of conscious preparation on your part before the original project is over.

Clients rightfully expect that when you've completed a project the solution you have delivered will work. If it doesn't you will have put in whatever time it takes to resolve it—for free. But you must also spend time educating your client to ensure that they don't confuse bug fixes with other kinds of support that you must be able to bill them for. You must make them aware early in your relationship that once their new system is installed they will have to pay you for hand-holding, training, and adding new functions to their system that weren't included in your original deal.

Here are some strategies that experienced independent consultants have found useful in satisfying their clients' support needs in a way that builds a strong relationship without leaving them working for free:

- Be sure to establish clear and mutually agreed-upon standards for certifying when the system you have delivered will be considered complete and functional. The best way to do this is to work from a detailed written specification and to set up with the client an explicit set of acceptance criteria that, when met, will result in a client sign-off. Once the client has signed off on this acceptance testing phase, the project should be considered complete and the client should expect to pay you for any further time you must invest in it.
- Assure clients from the beginning of your relationship that support for your clients' existing systems takes priority over new work. When you attempt to win new clients it is important to let them see that you won't win their business at the price of ignoring other clients' calls for after-the-sale support. If they see you give good service to your existing clients rather than abandoning them when new clients come along, clients are much more likely to be willing to pay for such service when their time comes.

- Make it clear to clients that once acceptance testing is complete, you will fix any emerging bugs for free for a limited period, for example, ninety days. Explain to them that all systems have a certain number of bugs that only emerge after the system has been used heavily and that this is why you offer a limited term of free support.
- Use a sliding scale for response time. For example, you might make it clear to the client beforehand that you will respond within twenty-four hours to a problem that comes up during the first month after installation, forty-eight hours to those that come up during the second, and ninety-six hours to those that come up in the third. This allows you to pursue billable work first and take care of problem resolution in your spare time after the software's initial break-in period has passed.
- Make sure that the client understands the difference between a bug fix and training. Many clients will not make the effort to read documentation or to educate themselves in how to use computer hardware and software. If you have provided them with clear documentation and startup training it is important that they realize that if they can't get the software to work it is up to them to at least read the manual. If they prefer to have you supply answers immediately, they should expect to pay for this kind of service.
- Develop high-end user training to train a trainer for the client and include this training in the project price. Encourage the client to appoint one person to be your sole contact so that they, not you, have to deal with problem users and repetitive questioning.
- Create support checklists. Determine the most common problems your clients encounter and document how to solve them. This resource will be valuable if you need to train others to support your software. If may also help you pinpoint problem areas in your software and improve your product so it does not require as much support!
- Cross-train with another consultant so he or she can back you up and provide emergency help in cases when you are not available. The alternative may be working ninety-hour weeks and giving up vacations for the duration of your consulting career.

METHODS OF BILLING FOR SUPPORT

Once you've established that you will bill clients for ongoing support, there are several different ways of doing this. Some consultants bill only for actual support while others prefer to set up inclusive service contracts. We'll look now at how such arrangements are handled.

Billing for Actual Time Used

As you saw in Chapter 5, many consultants bill clients at their usual rates for even the shortest telephone call. Whether you can take this kind of approach depends on the strength of your client's respect for you, the demand there may be for your particular kind of skill in the marketplace, and your own personal resolve. Many consultants who have tried this approach have found that it did not work well for them because their own fear that the client would balk at being charged for a minute or two of phone support led them to give away too many un-billed hours that they'd spent on the phone.

Consultant David McNish is one consultant who is comfortable billing his clients for a fifteen-minute chunk of his time when a phone call takes as little as one minute. He defends this policy by saying, "I've never gotten any complaints and I figure it costs me this much just to bother making the call, making a record of what was said, and the trouble to bill for it." Another consultant who bills this way, Aric Rosenbaum, also reports few complaints from customers. But he says that he has run into clients who mentioned that they hate being charged in this manner by other consultants and would much prefer to pay a fixed amount every month.

Billing Support as a Percentage of Software Development Cost

When supporting custom software, another way to structure the support agreement is to bill the client for an annual maintenance fee that works out to 15–20 percent of the software's original price, excluding training and analysis costs. This fee covers any necessary fixes and minor modifications, but not enhancements.

One consultant describes how a firm he worked for managed this kind of arrangement. The company's typical system cost around $300K, with $200K of that amount being the actual cost of the software, so the typical support contract cost $35K a year. This fee included four site visits a year. Any further visits were at the client's expense—a nontrivial specification as many of the firm's clients were overseas. The contract also included design and installation of any changes made to the system, but not the costs of developing the actual changes, which were priced separately. A hidden benefit of this kind of arrangement is suggested by the consultant's remark that, "It takes a few years for the customer to realize they are paying fees and expenses for you to come four times a year to sell them stuff."

Setting Up Support Contracts and Retainer Agreements

Consultants who allow their clients to pay a fixed amount for support usually do so by setting up formal support contracts. There are many different ways to structure such arrangements, but most of them share the common characteristic that *the client pays in advance for a predefined number of support hours at a discounted rate.* If the client needs more than the agreed-upon hours, the contract specifies a rate at which such hours will be billed—usually one that represents a discount over the consultant's usual rates.

Michael Stein includes the price of such support in the price of the custom systems he develops. As part of the original contract—and figured into the cost of that contract—he provides clients with a limited number of hours at 50 percent of his normal rate. He usually sets the number of support hours at a figure that represents 10 percent of the total number of hours he estimates for the project.

Stein says, "A great advantage of this policy is that it has eased the tension that sometimes emerges when there is a dispute about whether a request is a bug fix or a modification. Rather than reading the spec with the eye of a Talmudic scholar to see whether the change should be free or cost $X, we can take the Solomonic approach, and cut the child in half for $X/2$." Stein sends his clients a periodic accounting of how much time has been used and how much is left, and reports that though he is only billing at half his usual rate, he ends up profiting because he ends up being able to bill for a lot of time spent on things like short phone calls that he might not otherwise have been able to bill for at all.

VAR Eric Hart sells his clients support contracts guaranteeing them a specified number of hours, anywhere from 10 to 200, at a rate that is approximately 30 percent cheaper than his usual rate. His clients find it easier to buy support in big chunks this way because they don't have to get purchase orders for every call and visit. The support hours he sells can be used for on-site or in-house work, phone support, research, hardware repair, or whatever the client needs.

Frank Cook, whose company sells a vertical market product for the funeral industry takes another approach. He charges $360 a year for 800-number telephone support. He says that most of this support is spent helping clients with problems that they could have solved by reading the manual supplied with the software, but he feels that the goodwill he earns by supplying the unlimited phone support is worthwhile. Even at this low figure, he also estimates that support earns him about 25 percent of his total revenues.

Instead of calling this kind of an agreement a "support contract," other consultants call it "working on retainer." Under this arrangement you and the client agree that your services will be needed for some prespecified number of hours. You then agree on an hourly rate, and the client pays you that amount in advance for the contracted number of hours. Under this kind of *retainer arrangement*, as in most support agreements, if you end up working less than the agreed-upon number of hours, the client still must pay you the entire retainer. If you work more than the agreed-upon number of hours under a retainer agreement, you bill the client at the agreed-upon rate for each subsequent hour.

There are other less common ways of setting up such arrangements. You may contract to do specific tasks on a monthly basis for a *flat fee*, for example, backing up client data once a week for $100; or you may, as consultant Paul Van Geel does, charge a flat rate of several hundred dollars a year that entitles the client to a predetermined discount on any hours they choose to buy during that year as well as a guarantee that he will be able to devote those hours to them.

The advantage of any such an arrangement for the client is that it ensures him the use of the agreed-upon amount of your time and prevents you from becoming too busy to work for him. It also locks in a rate for your work and protects him from unforeseen rate hikes. The advantage for you, the consultant, of course, is that you have a predictable cash flow and that you can devote yourself wholeheartedly to working for the client.

Consultant Bob Paul who worked on retainer to support a real-time manufacturing system he developed for a client found it a very positive way of structuring the relationship, saying "I have felt free to give 110 percent attention to their problems when they come up—particularly important because what few problems do come up are usually related to some operational issue, or equipment problems either with the system itself or their own manufacturing machines. Without the retainer, one of us would surely feel cheated in a situation like this."

Some consultants who use this arrangement allow the client to carry over unused hours to the next retainer period but most consultants treat them as expiring at the end of the retainer period unless some extenuating circumstance made the client unable to use them.

Don't Become a Part-Time Employee

There is only one pitfall to keep in mind when negotiating for such support agreements. If you are concerned about maintaining your independent consultant status and not being reclassified as a W-2 employee by the IRS, you must avoid signing any contracts that commit you to spending hefty hours working on-site for a single client for long periods of time. The client who cannot persuade you to become an employee will often propose just such a contract as a substitute, asking you to work for them at a reduced rate, for many hours a week, on-site, for an indefinite period of time. Such contracts may indeed cause you to look like a part-time employee to the IRS and may jeopardize your independent contractor status. (See Chapter 3 for more information on this problem.)

CONTRACT PROGRAMMERS AND ONGOING SUPPORT

It is also important to understand that all discussions of support arrangements in the preceding sections apply only to relationships established by independent computer consultants. If you are a brokered contract programmer, you should be very careful to never sign a contract that includes any provisions requiring you to work for free to fix bugs in any code you provide a client. Unscrupulous brokers sometimes include such clauses in their contracts, and a few unlucky consultants have found that the brokers subsequently invoke these clauses to compel them to work for free or to justify nonpayment for work already completed.

Ethical brokers and clients will always pay a contract programmer for every hour worked, without respect to what type of work those hours were spent on.

SOLVING PAYMENT PROBLEMS

One of the toughest things about being your own boss is that it brings with it the need to be your own bill collector. As an employee you took it for granted that if you did your work you would receive your paycheck on time and for the correct amount. But when you become a consultant, collecting what is due to you can be an ongoing headache. Almost every long-term consultant has at least one tale of "the one that got away"—money owed them that they were never able to collect from the deadbeat clients, check bouncers, and bankrupts who stiffed them, sometimes for many tens of thousands of dollars.

Experienced consultants know that payment can be a problem and take steps to prevent these problems from occurring or at least try to limit their scope. They've learned to recognize the warning signs of payment problems and they know what to do when payment problems do arise.

Differentiating between *Slow Pay* and *No Pay*

If you are about to start working with a client you will have to readjust your expectations of what prompt payment is. Even your best customers are likely to hold onto your invoices for a few weeks. This is standard corporate accounting practice. Even consultants who've made the effort to negotiate terms into their contracts that specify payment "net 30" or "net 15" find that it is a rare client who pays them promptly on that schedule without some previous arm-twisting.

Large corporations can often be the very worst in this regard. One consultant reports waiting ten months to receive payment from GE and going a full two years before receiving payment for "net 30" invoice sent to Wang—and that was long before Wang ran into financial difficulties.

Indeed, it is because they run into this kind of payment delay that some very competent consultants choose to work through brokers and are willing to accept a lower rate in exchange for biweekly payment (as discussed in Chapter 7).

If you intend to remain independent, you will have to learn to live with a certain amount of slow payment. As consultant Steve Zilora says, "Big companies may be slow to pay, but at least they *do* pay. I used to be upset that in spite of *their* contract saying net 30, it was usually net 45. However, in the past couple weeks we've heard all kinds of stories about not getting paid at all. So now I'm quite happy."

REMEDIES FOR SLOW PAYMENT

If chronic slow payment problems are jeopardizing your cash flow here are some steps experienced consultants report have improved the situation for them.

Check Credit Before You Begin Work

There are several ways you can check a new client's credit. One is to *ask for trade references.* This means getting information that allows you to contact other vendors who do business with the client. For example, if you plan to sell software to a client, a hardware dealer who regularly supplies that client might be an appropriate reference to check. Ask the dealer whether he has experienced problems getting this client to pay on time, and if he has, be particularly vigilant in your dealings with this client.

It is also possible to *get credit reports* on your clients from credit reporting agencies like Dun & Bradstreet Information Services and TRW.

You can locate these agencies through your local yellow pages. TRW Credit also maintains an on-line service on CompuServe (GO TRW) that allows you to request a copy of the client's credit report for a charge of less than $50.

However, experience has taught some consultants that even a good credit rating is no guarantee that they won't run into payment problems with the client further down the line.

Approach Collection Proactively

Another solution is to get actively involved in the collection process. Michael Stein gives a good example of how a bit of extra effort may significantly improve the speed with which clients pay. He says, "We never just send the bill and wait for the check anymore. We usually deliver the bill in person when we are on-site anyway, or messenger it. The next day we call, verify receipt of the bill, ask if it was in line with what they expected, or if there are any problems we need to clear up. If they say everything is fine, we ask when we should expect payment. For large checks, we ask them to hold the check rather than mailing it— we send a messenger. If payment is even a day or two later than the date they gave us, we call. This nips the 'check is in the mail' syndrome."

Offer a Prompt Payment Discount

Offering discounts has worked for some consultants. Steve Zilora says his firm offered major clients a 10 percent discount for all billings greater than $100K, provided the invoice was paid on time. As a result of this offer, his accounts receivable went from forty days to twenty-five days very quickly. Carl Brown says that this strategy can also be effective when dealing with government contracts. He's found that government agencies will pay more quickly if he provides a 5 percent discount for payment within thirty days, because contract administrators must justify failure to take advantage of such discounts.

But this strategy doesn't always work. Some consultants report that accounting departments in large corporations often take these discounts and still pay the invoices weeks or months after they are due, knowing that vendors heavily dependent on their business are not likely to be able to do much in protest.

Enforce a "No Pay, No Work" Policy on Clients

Consultants who have suffered through serious problems with deadbeat clients in the past often take a more draconian approach to slow payment. They argue that they have found it impossible to distinguish between the kind of slow payment that eventually gets paid and the kind that turns out to be the first sign of what turns into a no-pay situation. So their solution now is to make it clear to all clients, via contract clauses, that if the client gets behind in paying them, they will stop work until they get caught up. Burt Johnson explains how he implements such a policy, saying, "I warn the client that I *never* work on any project where I have more than two invoices open." If more than two bi-weekly invoices go unpaid, Johnson says, he lets the client know that he will do no further work until the account is brought up to date.

Johnson points out that one benefit of this system is that it keeps the invoices smaller, and thus less overwhelming for the client. Another important benefit is that with such frequent invoicing, there is less money still due when the project is complete, which is when clients are most likely to avoid payment.

Charge Interest on Past Due Bills

Many consultants wonder whether they can charge interest on money that is owed them for many months. State law varies on whether you may do this, so it may not be an option for you. But in states where it is legal, some consultants have found that including interest clauses in their contracts is a good way to motivate clients to pay on time.

Make Sure Slow Payment Isn't a Sign of Client Dissatisfaction

If a client keeps dragging his feet on paying you, before you assume that he's getting ready to rip you off, you might ask yourself whether the slow payment is a form of nonverbal communication that is signaling that the client is unhappy with your work but is not quite able to bring himself to discuss it. Sometimes the client may be disturbed by some unexpected charge that appeared on the invoice, but feels uncomfortable bringing it up. Michael Stein has seen this happen, and says, "You'll be amazed at the number of times clients will act surprised that you billed them at all for this or that." Often he's found that when he's called about an overdue bill for $10,000 or more the client has replied, "Oh yeah, I needed to call you about this $49 item." If this is the case, flushing out the client's unspoken concerns may be all that is needed to speed payment.

Take Hostages

Since 90 percent of payment problems involve final payments for software and hardware that are already delivered and installed, it is wise to structure your relationship with clients so that you still have something you can hold over their heads if final payment is not forthcoming. This is of particular importance if you are working under a fixed-bid agreement where the last payment represents a significant proportion of the cost of the whole project.

Peter Schulz is a developer who usually works under contract terms that specify one-third payment on signing, one-third on completion of coding, and one-third on delivery. He has learned to deal with final payment problems by refusing to hand over the source code for his applications until the client's final check has cleared the bank.

Other consultants have found it effective to refuse to answer support calls for clients who have withheld the final payment.

WHEN CLIENTS WON'T PAY

The client who pays slowly can make your life miserable. But the one who refuses to pay at all can put you out of business. Consultants who have continued to work in the face of a pile of unpaid invoices, trusting the client's assurances that the checks are in the mail or that he'll pay as soon as his next big contract comes through, often find themselves in dire straits. But many other consultants find that their nonpayment problems don't come from the single spectacular client who runs up a huge tab, but from the slow dribble of clients who try to worm out of paying final payments on software or systems that are already installed in their offices, or who unilaterally renegotiate a contract to say that they owe less money for the work already done than they originally agreed to pay.

There are some things you can try in such cases, before investing in a full-fledged lawsuit. The most effective is to look as if you are willing to begin such a suit.

Have Your Lawyer Send a Letter

Sometimes acting like you are going to sue can be as effective—and a lot cheaper—than actually suing. One consultant who has tried this approach explains how it works: "I have only used a lawyer once, and that cost about $100 for the consultation and the letter he sent. I collected in full after the letter. In other cases I sent my own letter stating that if an agreement were not forthcoming I would take appropriate legal action."

This strategy is most effective if you do have a written contract, and hence a clear-cut legal claim. But a consultant who has used this strategy warns, "You have to be careful not to threaten legal action if you do not intend to go through with it."

Take Your Case to Small Claims Court

If you do decide to sue and the sum involved is relatively small, you may be able to pursue your claim in small claims court rather than having to pay a lawyer to pursue a full-fledged suit. However, to use this strategy, the amount owed you must be less than the maximum permitted under your state's definition of "small claim." These limits vary widely from state to state. In California, you may sue in small claims court for an amount up to $5,000, while in several other states claims must be less than $1,500. Attorneys warn that you usually can't get around these limits by suing separately for individual open invoices, either. Most judges will treat this kind of behavior as an attempt to circumvent the purpose of the small claims court and may respond by throwing out all your claims.

To determine whether the money owed you can be recovered in small claims court, phone your local small claims court clerk and ask. They are usually friendly and helpful and if you qualify they will explain to you how to pursue your claim.

Hire a Collection Agency

Another approach that may also work is to call on the services of a collection agency. One consultant who has resorted to this alternative describes his experiences this way: "I've only needed them twice in ten years, but they do all the work. They charge a fixed percentage of the money they collect. You have to negotiate that percentage. I pay 18 percent of all money collected before it goes to court. If it goes to court I pay 25 percent. I have no fees for attorneys or anything else. The collection agency won't charge until the debt is paid and they assess the customer 18 percent interest. If the collection agency can't get any money, I pay nothing."

You can locate collection agencies in your yellow pages, but it would be a good idea to ask for local references before getting involved with one.

Get Cash for Bad Checks

One consultant reports that he found a good way to deal with the situation when a client paid him with a rubber check. When the check was rejected by his own bank for insufficient funds, he contacted the client's bank and inquired whether there now were any funds available in the client's account. When the bank told him there were, he explained that he had a check drawn on the account and asked that a hold be put on the funds. Upon presentation of the bad check the client's bank wrote him a cashier's check for the full amount due him.

Don't Work for Promises

It is not unheard of for clients who run into financial difficulty in mid-project to inform a consultant that they've just decided to renegotiate the contract. For example, one consultant ran into this with a client who let several invoices go unpaid and then informed the consultant that he'd decided to change the contract from an hourly basis to a fixed-price contract and that he wouldn't pay the consultant anything further until the work was complete.

When faced with this kind of demand, more than one consultant has let hope overwhelm good sense and has completed the project only to discover when payment was finally due that the client had no intention of paying.

Experienced consultants warn that it is never a good idea to do any more work for the client under any arrangement when payment has already been shown to be a problem. If a client wants to renegotiate terms, they suggest you insist on getting full payment for any work you have already completed before you discuss renegotiating the rest of the deal. And you should never allow a client to renegotiate a contract in a way that removes his own incentive to pay.

That the penalty for ignoring this advice can be stiff is shown by the testimony of one consultant who says that, faced with nonpayment combined with promises, "I went ahead and did more work for them; they then filed bankruptcy and left me sitting with a $25,000 bad debt that I couldn't collect a dime on."

Even if you do eventually manage to collect, experienced consultants have found it a good idea to handle with care clients who have a history of payment problems. Some report that they make it a practice to require that such problem clients pay them a retainer, up front, before they will agree to do a new project for them. If the client won't go along with these demands, these consultants advise you to cut your losses and find new, paying clients. As one consultant who learned the hard way warns, "It very seldom pays to work for deadbeats."

WHEN CLIENTS CAN'T PAY

The collection strategies we've looked at so far work as long as the client actually has the money he owes you. But what if he doesn't? Unfortunately, most of the time, if a client really doesn't have the money, no matter what he owes you and how well you can support your claim, you're out of luck.

Consultants have sued clients at their own expense and have had judgments awarded by the court, only to find that if the client's bank account is empty, the judgment is worthless. "I got a judgment and couldn't collect" is an all-too-common summary of such relationships.

The situation can be even worse if the client who owes you a significant sum declares bankruptcy. Once he takes that step, no matter how much money is owed you, you become one of the horde of unsecured creditors whose claim against the bankrupt is only satisfied after everyone else he owes money to gets their share. At best you may receive a few cents on the dollar. One consultant discovered that bankruptcy laws in his state even required that he *give back* a payment he'd already received from a bankrupt client within ninety days of the declaration of bankruptcy so that he not be considered as having received "preferential treatment" compared with other creditors.

Can You Repossess?

Many consultants think that in a case like this they can protect themselves by repossessing the systems they've sold the bankrupt client. But such is not the case. Even when the client owes you for tangible assets—software and hardware—you can rarely take things into your own hands and repossess them, even when they haven't been completely paid for.

Consultant Lee Lammert tells of a particularly harrowing experience he had in such a situation: "I once had a client purchase a system, net 30 days, and when they were three months past due they sent me a hundred bucks. The net result was that they forced me to accept $700 for a $2,500 PC. When I repossessed the computer directly, they called the cops to report a theft! I had to give *my* computer back to them to keep from being thrown in the clink." Lammert was chagrined to discover that "a past due invoice does not give you any claim on assets, even if you sold them. Once you make delivery and tender an invoice, those assets are not your property anymore and you no longer have any claim to them, unless you have filed a UCC-1 [an installment payment form] against them, which you almost never do for normal accounts as they are designed to protect assets secured for time payment purposes."

Another consultant ran into a related disastrous situation when a client went bankrupt and the bankruptcy court ruled that the consultant's software package, which had not yet been paid for, was legally to be considered an asset of the client. This meant that if the developer resold the software, the proceeds of the sale would go to the bankrupt client, not the developer!

In view of these cases it is wise to protect yourself legally by writing into contracts wording that specifies that title to software and hardware you are selling to the client will not pass to client until the consultant has received full payment for them.

What about Software Bombs?

Some consultants wonder whether they can protect themselves from deadbeat clients by coding "time bomb" routines into their software that will cause it to lock up or do things like erase files unless these bombs are disabled by a keyword supplied by the programmer. These consultants reason that if the client doesn't pay, they have a right to withhold the information that will disable the bomb and so keep the client from using software that they haven't paid for.

However, courts have almost universally taken a dim view of such arrangements. In a case involving an Oklahoma trucking company, an injunction was granted barring the activation of such a bomb. Other developers whose bombs have detonated as a result of client nonpayment have also faced hefty lawsuits.

The only situation in which courts might permit you to get away with such a strategy is when it has been made clear in advance that a software license must be periodically renewed, and where the software is designed to stop working when this renewal has not been made. Even so, you can do this only if your contract with the client clearly states that the software will cease functioning unless the license is renewed.

CONCLUSION

If this chapter has struck you as unduly depressing, don't let it disturb you. Most clients are not problem clients. Most pay, many show up with more work they will pay for, some rave about the work you do for them and do recommend you to other, responsible clients.

Because our aim has been to get you started successfully, we've focused here on the problems you are likely to encounter as you begin to work with clients, rather than on the satisfactions and successes that are just as likely to occur. But now that you've been made aware of the worst things that can happen, you are no longer naive—and no longer as likely to damage your newly begun consulting career by plowing into one of these situations unaware.

I wish it were possible to devote as much time to describing the pleasures and successes that wait for you too, because these satisfactions, not the problems, are the heart of the client–consultant relationship, and they are what make computer consulting worthwhile over the long haul. But it is not possible to do this. Each happy business relationship, like all happy human relationships, is unique and grows out of the way your own skills, abilities, and personality mesh with those of your clients. But now that you've been shown the ropes and warned of the dangers that lie in wait for the unwary, you are much more likely to go on to discover the joys and satisfactions of participating in a mutually satisfying client relationship on your own.

11

GROWING YOUR CONSULTING BUSINESS

At some point even the most successful consultants realize that there is an inherent limit on how successful they can be selling what is, after all, a limited quantity—their own time. Because there will never be more than twenty-four hours in a day, when you are selling the client the right to use your time, the extent of your success will be limited to how much you can charge for each individual hour. So it is clear that consultants who are to grow their practices beyond a certain point will have to find some way of leveraging their work.

There are several ways to do this:

- You can invest some of your time into developing products that can be sold over and over again, like software, books, or seminars.
- You can bring other people into your business and use your expertise and connections to profit from the sales of their services as well as your own.
- You can move from selling your services into selling other people's hardware and software products and become a dealer.

Consultants who do not branch out and grow their practices in these ways often find that after the first exciting years of their careers, they hit a plateau where they may still make a good living, but lose their zest for what they are doing.

This is natural. Successful computer consultants tend to be bright, creative, internally motivated people who need to find new challenges to keep them satisfied, no matter how healthy their bank accounts. So it is wise to keep in mind that expanding and diversifying your consulting practice is not only necessary to increase your earning power, but also to ensure that you build a consulting career that you can enjoy for years to come without burning out.

SOFTWARE DEVELOPMENT AS A SIDELINE BUSINESS

The consultants who appear to be the happiest with their long-term consulting careers appear to be those who move from selling their own services into developing sideline businesses that involve selling something else. The obvious choice for this something else would appear to be a turnkey or shrinkwrapped software product. But surprisingly few computer consultants ever develop such products, although at the start of their consulting careers many custom developers assume they will.

Why Consultants Rarely Develop Successful Software Products

The reason for this is explained by custom developer Martin Schiff: "I think that everyone that writes custom software has it in the back of their mind that one of the projects written for a client will become the next great vertical market package. But most of the time it does not work that way. The reason that the client is doing custom development is that no packages on the market meet their needs, and usually the needs are quite specific."

Schiff's most successful stand-alone product so far has not been one he developed for a client, but instead a shareware time and billing program, Time Is Money, which was designed to serve his own needs and those of other professionals like himself who sell hourly services.

Consultants have also found a measure of success through reselling code libraries and utilities they have originally developed for their own use. Consultant Egberto Willies did just this when he launched his COMM-DRV software product, a library of serial communications routines and device drivers.

Preserving Your Rights to Resell

Consultants who have succeeded in marketing their own software products point out that it is important to *retain the copyright* to as much of your own code as possible.

As discussed in Chapter 8 on contracts, when you develop software as a consultant, you retain the legal rights to your work *unless* you specifically sign over these rights to the client. But, as you may also recall, many clients, particularly large corporations, insert wording into contracts that assigns the rights to your code to them. If you plan to release a product of your own someday, it is essential that you reject any clauses that transfer the right to reusable code libraries you may have used in constructing an application for a client. If the client insists on ownership of code you believe has resale potential, you must either negotiate an agreement that allows you to remarket the software under some kind of joint agreement, or you must make it explicit that the client's rights pertain only to the completed application you provide them, not to the code libraries you used in creating it.

This should make it clear that anyone who has any hopes of developing a major software product should *never negotiate any contract involving software without calling on the services of an attorney* experienced in computer-related intellectual property law. Royalty and marketing arrangements are simply too complex and dangerous for an amateur to attempt to negotiate them unaided. If you must save money early in your practice, do it elsewhere. A mistake in negotiating rights to software with serious resale potential could end up costing you millions.

Getting Your Product into the Marketplace

Once you have developed a product that has market potential, you will have many decisions to make about how to publish it. It is a good idea to spend some time networking with other developers and learning how the software business works before you sign anything a software publisher might offer you. Software authors as a group are extremely active on public bulletin boards and networking with them on-line is the single best way of learning what you'll need to know to market a product successfully.

One common truth that such developers are likely to point out to you is that the terms of a deal a software publisher may offer you may sound attractive, but individual publishers vary greatly in the attention they give the products they acquire. As successful developer Scott Sharkey pointed out when a budding developer asked him about a seemingly generous offer an obscure publisher had made him, "Five percent of one million is better than fifty percent of a dollar."

Sharkey went on to explain that when dealing with publishers you must look at the figures they project for your product's sales and then ask for a piece of the profit on those sales up front. Sharkey also warns, "If they want perpetual, exclusive rights to market, and most do, be sure to charge them something up front for that too. Otherwise they may never sell a copy, and you'll be out of everything."

Experienced developers also emphasize that you must consider other things besides royalties when negotiating with a company that wants to market your software. For example:

- Who will do installation support?
- Who will be responsible for bug fixes to the existing code?
- Within what time frame will bug fixes have to be provided?
- Who will be responsible for coding up product updates?

If the answer to these questions is "you," you may wind up with burdensome commitments to maintaining a product even when it isn't selling well or earning you significant royalties. This kind of commitment can eat up your time without providing additional income. Here, too, the advice of an attorney experienced in negotiating such contracts can be of great value.

Some consultants take another approach and market their commercial products directly, without using a publisher as an intermediary. Egberto Willies claims to be making a "healthy profit" on his communications library product, which he markets himself using advertising placed in a number of magazines that target programmers, like *Dr. Dobbs* and *C Users Journal*. Willies also advertises his software in mail-order card decks like Programmer's Powerpack and sells his product through resellers whom he gives a dealer discount.

One last method many consultants use to distribute their products is to release them as shareware. Despite a few well-publicized shareware success stories, almost all consultants who have taken this path emphasize that it is not the quick road to easy wealth. As Karl Thompson, the author of the shareware product, Solvelt, wryly puts it, making "half of a good living" from a shareware product can be "nearly a full-time job." But if you could be happy earning an additional couple of thousand dollars a year from a product that would otherwise be earning you nothing, the shareware channel may be worthy of investigation.

One good way of learning more about how to succeed as a shareware author is by participating in the SHAREWARE forum the Association of Shareware Professionals (ASP) maintains on CompuServe. Another resource is shareware author Bob Schenot's excellent guide, *The Shareware Book*, which is itself downloadable as shareware from many bulletin boards.

Another publication that many developers recommend enthusiastically to any consultant who would like to expand their software development efforts is the *Software Success* newsletter. You'll find a listing of contact information for this and other useful publications in Appendix A.

SEMINARS AS A SIDELINE BUSINESS

To the surprise of many budding computer consultants, the seminar business, rather than software development, is the sideline business that computer consultants are most likely to pursue and succeed at. There are several reasons for this. One is that, as we've emphasized throughout this book, successful consultants are very good communicators. Their ability to communicate combined with their high level of expertise makes these consultants much more likely than the general population to excel at teaching and lecturing. Another reason why consultants are drawn to the seminar business is that they know giving seminars will not only earn them money, but can also be a very useful way of expanding their base of contacts and clients. Experienced consultants treat a well-designed seminar not only as a profit center but also as a *marketing tool for their other consulting services.*

Some consultants get into the seminar business on their own, presenting training at client sites or renting a room in a hotel or other business locale and doing their own advertising. Those who have tried this report that to be able to make any profit from giving your own seminars, you must be able to charge at least $100 per participant, and often much more.

Working with Seminar Houses

Other consultants who make holding seminars a significant part of their careers prefer to present their seminars under the aegis of one of the large seminar/training houses, such as Digital Consulting or Data Base Management, Inc. (DBMI). This frees them from the need to handle the logistics and marketing of their seminars and frees up the time such activities would take for other billable work.

The advantages of working with a well-known seminar house include having the seminar house take full responsibility for and absorb all costs of marketing, scheduling, advertising, and presenting the seminar. The consultant's only responsibility is to develop the seminar and its associated materials and to travel around, usually to a number of different cities throughout the United States and Canada, giving the seminar to the people the seminar house attracts.

In order to be able to give these kinds of seminars, you will have to have a credential that would establish you as an expert in the eyes of a seminar house's mostly corporate clientele. Such a credential might be having held a position in the past as a top MIS executive in a well-known company or having published a book on the subject you plan to lecture about.

The rewards for this kind of work can be considerable. Expert consultants who have given seminars for large consulting houses on "hot" topics like CASE reengineering or object-oriented development strategies report earning anywhere from $750 to $1,000 a day. In addition, they can also earn royalties of as much as $250 a day for every day that another of the seminar house's instructors teaches a course that they've developed. Less distinguished consultants report earning in the neighborhood of $300 a day teaching more mundane subjects like "C Programming" or "How to Use WordPerfect."

Consultant and seminar presenter Sharon Podlin suggests that you ask any seminar house you are considering working with to provide you with the phone numbers of other consultants who have worked with them, and that you contact these people and ask them how they were treated. She also suggests that when signing a contract with a seminar house you make sure that you get reimbursed for travel and hotel expenses, beyond the daily rate you get for teaching the course. Because seminar houses can be very slow at paying she adds that it is also a good idea to insist on "net 30" terms for any contract you sign with them.

Honing Your Presentation Skills

If you decide to move in this direction, it is important to realize that teaching is an art. Try to get some practice in doing public presentations before you sign up to do a big seminar. Consultants who have built up seminar sidelines advise that you practice your lecturing skills at Toastmasters clubs and by giving talks through local high school and college extension services. These extension services are usually eager to have professionals present courses as short as an hour or two on subjects of interest to the local business community. If you have trouble with public speaking, consider taking a class on the subject at your local junior college, or take a few voice lessons with a local instructor.

Security expert Mich Kabay, who has extensive experience lecturing, explains that the key thing to keep in mind when preparing a talk is "what the audience ought to be able to *do* after the talk that they can't do, or maybe can't do as well, before the talk."

Using Seminars to Market Your Other Services

It is also important to take steps to maximize the contribution that seminar giving can make to the rest of your consulting practice. Sharon Podlin warns that you should never sign a global noncompetition agreement that excludes you from taking on consulting assignments with the people who attend a seminar you give for a seminar house. You may agree not to teach other classes to these people on your own, but you should retain the right to provide them other services, like systems analysis, strategic planning, or programming.

When you give a seminar, you can often generate consulting work by aggressively following up on your attendees. Systems analysis expert Rich Cohen explains that he's found it useful, when faced with a question from an attendee for which he doesn't have an immediate answer, to offer to get back to them later. Cohen makes it a point to get contact information from his questioner after the presentation and calls them back with the answers he's dug up. Some lecturers also report that they find it useful to offer to mail out additional materials to those who express an interest in having them.

Consultant and shareware author Bob Schenot reports that he's often been able to turn the follow-up calls that result from these requests into consulting assignments, because when he calls a few weeks after a presentation, seminar attendees have often decided that they need more help using the technology he's been presenting and are often eager to turn to him for that help.

WRITING AS A SIDELINE BUSINESS

Another important sideline business for consultants is writing. While you can earn significant amounts of money writing for a professional audience, the main contribution of writing to your consulting career isn't the money you will earn but the fact that *publishing a book or article on a well-chosen topic is the single easiest way to promote yourself to expert status.*

The Benefits of Writing

A professional book that sells 2,000 copies may earn you only $4,000 in royalties, but if 80 percent of your two thousand readers are corporate CFOs and your topic is data security, you may have just become Mr. Data Security to a significant proportion of the people who are the chief market for your services. Once you've established yourself as an expert in a niche this way, you are much more likely to be able to command thousand-dollar lecture fees and the enormous hourly fees that the true expert can command.

Writing a professional book may significantly enhance your existing consulting practice even if the book is not all that successful. One author whose book on OS/2 earned little more than its original $10,000 advance claims that the year after the book came out he received $80,000 in new contracts that were due entirely to his authorship.

Learning the Ropes of Publishing

If you are interested in pursuing publishing, it's a good idea to read up on the subject and to talk to as many authors as you can before you invest much time in actual research or writing. Publishing is a business, albeit a rather odd one, and the more you know about it before you get involved with it, the more likely you are to succeed.

The how-to books that will best help orient you to the publishing world are those that discuss how to market nonfiction. Nonfiction publishing works quite differently from fiction and genre publishing, so only books that explicitly discuss nonfiction publishing will give you an accurate idea of how this kind of publishing works. Judith Appelbaum's classic *How To Get Happily Published* is a good place to start your orientation to the publishing field. Several other good books for would-be nonfiction writers are listed in Appendix A.

If writing book-length works is more than you want to get into, but you still would like to do some professional writing, you might consider writing articles for the business trade press. This kind of publishing can also be an effective way of establishing yourself as an expert consultant.

There are dozens of limited-circulation magazines targeting the PC and MIS community and many of these are eager to find new contributors who understand the needs and concerns of their specialty audiences. The best resource for locating information about these magazines is *Ulrich's International Periodical Index*, which should be available at the reference desk of your library. *Ulrich's* lists just about every trade magazine in the world sorted by subject matter. It also gives audited circulation figures and contact information, and may indicate whether a publication is open to freelancers.

If you aren't familiar with a given publication, it is appropriate to write a brief letter to the editor mentioning your professional credentials and indicating that you are interested in doing some writing for them and would therefore like to see a sample copy of their publication. When you get the sample copy, study it closely to determine what kinds of articles its editors publish, their tone, the skill level of the target reader, and the kinds of subjects that get the most space in its pages.

Once you have a good idea of a given magazine's style, send the feature editor a brief letter describing the article you'd like to write for them and include copies of any of your published work. If you have never published before you may have to write the article before querying, to demonstrate that you are capable of doing a professional job.

When considering any writing you might do, it is important to choose your topic carefully. It is always better to write specialized articles targeting the people who make up your potential client group rather than more generic articles to be read by others, no matter how large that audience of others might be. Try to choose subjects that demonstrate your expertise in an area related to the services you sell your clients. The more specialized your topic and the more closely tied to the services you sell your clients, the more likely a book or magazine article is to enhance the rest of your consulting career.

Treat Writing as a Profit Center

Because many trade publications and publishing houses differentiate between "consultants" and "freelancers" it is important to make it clear to editors that you want to be treated as a freelancer. Editors presume, quite rightly, that most consultants will be so thrilled at seeing their name in print that they won't need to be paid cash money for their work. Therefore the rates they pay professional freelancers are often double the rates they pay a consultant for the identical article. Professional writers usually get better advances from book publishers too than do consultants, whom the publishers know expect to reap significant career advantages from having a book published.

So it is always a good idea to make it clear to any editor you deal with that you are treating writing as a profit center and not as just an occasional method of advertising your consulting services.

Typical freelancer rates for magazine articles are $300 to $1,000 for a one-thousand- to four-thousand-word article. Typical advances freelancers receive for writing computer-related books are $3,000 to $15,000.

The easiest way to break into many magazines is by writing software reviews. Unfortunately, there is a reason for this. Nothing eats up as much time as installing and exercising a new piece of software. Many now sadder-but-wiser consultants have found themselves spending weeks doing the work necessary to prepare a single $200 review. Unless you are already very familiar with the software involved, approach invitations to write software reviews cautiously. Besides their potential as a time sink, reviews rarely pay well and having your name on a software review does not contribute significantly to establishing your credential as an expert. Feature articles and opinion pieces give you much more visibility and are usually much easier to write.

SELLING HARDWARE

Although moving from consulting into product dealership seems like a logical course for a computer consultant to take, in recent years it has become increasingly difficult for computer consultants to move into retail hardware sales.

With the price cutting that rages between hardware superstores and mail-order companies, few consultants find that they can make hardware alone a significant profit center. Consultants who have tried to make the move report that getting involved with selling hardware brings on a whole new set of headaches:

- Bookkeeping becomes significantly more complex as consultants must keep up with local and state tax reporting requirements.
- The question of who is responsible for hard disk problems or monitor failures involves consultants in ongoing, tough-to-resolve conflicts with wholesalers.

- Consultants often find themselves unable to return hardware they've purchased for resale that turns out not to work with a client's configuration.
- Potential clients take up hours of their time having the hardware dealer explain the meaning of the specs for a particular hardware solution only to go out and buy the identical configuration from a mail-order vendor who advertises a rock-bottom price.
- Consultants who become hardware dealers find themselves dealing with more frequent collection problems. As one rueful consultant puts it, comparing collection problems he ran into as a consultant with those he faced as a hardware dealer, "It is one thing to be stiffed mowing a lawn and quite another when they keep the lawn-mower."

Most experienced consultants who've dabbled in hardware sales advise that the only way that hardware sales can be profitable is if you have access to clients likely to make high-volume purchases. Otherwise, the expenses involved in phoning around to find the best price and terms on a system to be resold—or to get support and service when that system fails—can easily eat up any profit you might make off of the sale of one or two systems. This is what consultant Arylnn Poczynek calls the "four-weeks-on-the-phone-for-five-dollars syndrome."

Furthermore, the dizzying speed with which hardware prices and specs change means that to stay current with the marketplace you must be prepared to read literally reams of material every month.

Many consultants who decide to deal in hardware or software do it not because they see it becoming a profit center for their consulting businesses, but because *it is a way of increasing their value to the client.* They view it as a courtesy service that makes their other moneymaking services such as training, installation, or customization, easier to sell.

But because of the headaches involved, many experienced consultants find it easier to refuse to resell hardware at all, and instead to confine themselves to offering clients advice on how to purchase from superstores or mail-order sources.

If you decide to move toward becoming a dealer, you will need to establish a relationship with computer equipment wholesalers. Consultants who have done this advise that the first time you deal with a distributor you should plan to buy several items. Know how much you want to spend and be prepared to buy if the price is right. They point out that the wholesaler is accustomed to dealing with callers who order twenty to one hundred items and may find a new client who dickers and calls several times about the purchase of a very small order not worth bothering with.

Expect to pay COD for your first order and don't try to put purchases on a personal credit card. Your goal is to have the distributor offer to send you an application for a credit account with them. Experienced hardware resellers warn that you will have to pay for purchases you make from a distributor with checks drawn on business, not on a personal bank account.

SELLING THE SERVICES OF OTHERS

At some point in your consulting practice, you'll have far more business than you can handle on your own. At this point you'll have to make a decision about whether you want to grow your consulting practice by adding employees. This is not an easy decision to make. It is true that when you bring in employees you begin to leverage your own work, and there is a potential of earning significant amounts of money for yourself from selling the services of people who work for you. But for every consultant who attributes her ongoing success to bringing in new staff members, there are a few others who have found this kind of expansion to be destructive to their businesses, or at least to their peace of mind. As one long-term consultant explains, "I have had as many as twelve people on my staff and I prefer working alone instead of refereeing personnel problems and fixing their screw-ups."

Avoid Trying to Clone Yourself

If bringing in employees is to be a positive experience, you'll have to put some serious thought into exactly what kind of employee you should bring in. Consultants whose practices have taken off to where they are working what one such consultant has called "a 3,000-hour week" often give in to the temptation to try to clone themselves. They try to hire an experienced person whose job will be simply to do the work that the busy consultant can't fit into an already jam-packed schedule.

But this rarely works, for the simple reason that a person who really is your peer isn't likely to show up looking for this kind of salaried work. If they are interested in salaried work at all, they are likely to look for it in huge, wealthy corporations that can offer them high salaries, job security, promotion opportunities, and cushy benefits packages. If they are drawn to consulting, they are much more likely, as you were, to want to work for themselves.

So the people you are likely to encounter when you attempt to hire someone to help you do your own job are the ones who, no matter what their skills, are not going to be very good at it. Typical is the experience of the consultant who reports, "I brought in another consultant to offset the workload only to have my client call me each day. They let him in the door because I sent him, but would always say, 'he's a nice guy and everything, *but. . . .*' "

Hiring Clerical Staff

Consultants who have successfully expanded their practices by bringing in employees suggest that instead of attempting to duplicate yourself, you try to find people who can do much of the low-level work that now eats up your time, and thus free yourself to put more time into the expert work that is what made your practice succeed in the first place.

There are several approaches to doing this. One is to analyze your situation to see if you are wasting significant amounts of time on trivial, nonrenumerative tasks that are eating up what could otherwise be hours billed at high consulting rates.

One consultant who did this kind of analysis reported: "I tend to spend too much time doing idiotic busywork. I never get invoices out in any reasonable amount of time. I spend half my day playing phone tag with vendors making sure that my parts were shipped when they were promised and if they weren't, why they weren't."

If this is what you find when you look at your own situation, the best solution may be to hire clerical help. Consultant Stephanie Allemann did. As she explains, "I went to Accountemps and hired a temporary worker so that I wouldn't have to do all the paperwork. It worked out fine and I ended up hiring her myself after twelve weeks. When she moved away I then hired someone myself by placing an ad in the paper. It's amazing how many good people there are out there looking for work. Many of them are mothers. Thus part-time, flexible hours are preferred."

Hiring Programmers

However, clerical help is not the answer for all overburdened consultants. Consultant Glenn Abelson speaks for another group when he explains that at a certain point he realized that "I would have to either program or sell. I was a very good programmer but an extremely good salesperson." Faced with this choice he decided to hire a programmer since he found that "programmers are easier to find, less expensive, and easier to work with than salespeople."

But bringing in a skilled professional employee like a programmer requires that you, the consultant, make more of an adjustment to the way that you do business than would be the case when bringing in clerical help. Jeff Sachs, who has successfully expanded his business to include a number of programmers, says, "The key to the whole thing is to have a willingness to delegate. If you won't delegate, you'll never get beyond that which you can do personally." Sachs adds, "Delegating was tough to do. I mean, you have to really trust someone's ability to do as good a job as you would do—and, of course, there is no one who can do that! You learn to live with it and find good trainable people."

Consultant Emerick Woods backs up Sachs's advice when he explains, "Usually I've opted to use very bright but fairly junior people in terms of programming. There is a penalty on the front end in terms of getting them up to speed as programmers but usually they grasp the application fairly quickly and can usually work without much direction from me once I spec out the assignment."

Woods explains that you have to expect some problems to come up when you bring in hired programmers. He's found that "they make lots of mistakes," which limits the kinds of things he can set them to work on, and they usually lack the same commitment to quality and effort as he himself brings to his business. But Woods explains that he's avoided bringing in senior people because of worries about compatibility problems and problems "managing levels of expectation." He's observed that bringing in people with too high a level of experience has been a significant factor in the failure of other consultants he's known who have tried to expand this way.

Paul Ferrara explains that he's succeeded with the programmers that he's brought in as employees because he looks on the relationship he's establishing with them as being one of "trainer/trainee." His goal is to try to make them as good as he is and he accepts that at some point they may want to go out on their own. This seems to be a realistic approach and one that is likely to ensure that your relationship with employees stays a positive one.

Hiring Sales Staff

When a consulting practice has expanded to the point where it makes sense to bring in additional help, it is very tempting to consider bringing in a salesperson, particularly since marketing is a task that few consultants claim to enjoy. To determine whether your business could support its own salesperson, you need to look at what a salesperson could realistically expect to make selling the services of yourself and other people working for you.

Frank Cook, who has hired salespeople to help him market in his software and hardware business explains that "here in Indiana I can hire good salesmen if I guarantee five or six hundred dollars a week for two or three months to get them going and establish a commission structure that will allow them to get into the thirty-to-forty-K range in a reasonable time." Only if your own business can realistically be expected to generate commissions that will attract competent salespeople in your own region, should you consider hiring one. If you do, it is also important to make sure that the salesperson you hire has a background in selling a product or service that is fundamentally similar to yours both in the kind of client who buys it and in the nature of the sales cycle it takes to sell it.

Becoming a Broker

Many consultants wonder what it would take to expand their one- or two-person shops into consulting brokerages. The answer, according to one man who has built up such a brokerage, is a thick skin, top-flight sales skills, and a great deal of money. This broker points out that when large consulting companies open a new branch office, they typically invest from $250,000 to a million dollars. His own experience has been that "a small firm will ultimately spend that much too, though they may spread it over a longer time."

That money pays for office expense, high phone expenses, and the cost of advertising, as well as the salaries of a sales staff who will probably not be producing much in return for that salary for the first six months to a year the broker is in business.

This broker points out that successful brokers see themselves as a service provider to clients, not as agents for consultants. Their work involves "zillions of phone calls, and lots of rejection." At the start, "everything is a cold call." Success in cold calling means only that the broker has located a client who has a need. Then the broker must be able to find someone to match that need. This is rarely easy in the very competitive market in which brokers operate. This established broker estimates that the average broker—even those who get called by clients with job orders—can only fill a quarter to a third of the job orders they receive.

Another peril that the would-be broker may face—and one that can scuttle a broker firm—is one consultants are already familiar with: becoming overdependent on one or two good clients. Consultants who branch into brokering usually are those who have a relationship with a big client that leads to their placing others there. But reliance on such golden clients can lure the would-be broker into thinking they have established themselves rather than realizing they have gotten a lucky break. When that client dries up, the broker who has not mastered cold calling and built a visible presence in the local business community may be ill-equipped to compete with other area firms. Our experienced broker friend also warns that losing control over cash flow and relying on overly optimistic sales forecasts are the biggest perils that lie in wait for the would-be broker.

Alternatives to Expansion

Before you rush out to hire employees, it is worth considering whether expansion is your only option. Consulting work flows in a feast-or-famine pattern, and it is often worth resisting the urge to expand, at least long enough to determine whether your current overload is merely a blip or whether it is likely to continue.

One consultant contributes the following story as a warning. "I knew someone who was consulting at the same company as I was. Since it is a large company, he was overjoyed to get the account. The company paid regularly, ordered extra hours, etc., until he kept escalating what he could deliver. He tried to add more resources by hiring more and more programmers but their quality varied and some were quite contentious. Ultimately he lost the account and had to scale back the company to about 10 percent of its size. Knowing when to say no to more business is very tricky, but it is important to survive."

Expansion for the sake of expansion can be a mistake if what you really love about consulting now is the technical work you do. Promoting yourself to upper management may increase your income, but at the cost of filling your day with an increasing amount of managerial and administrative work. Becoming an employer can be expected to bring a whole new set of stresses into your life, and they may be more than you want to deal with. If this is so, there is nothing wrong with admitting that you don't want to worry about meeting a payroll and taking responsibility for the welfare of other people who will be dependent on you for their incomes.

CONFRONTING BURNOUT

If, like the majority of people who enter computer consulting, you do not find some way to subtly shift the direction of your business over time, if you don't keep adding to your technical skills so that you can take on new and challenging assignments, or if you can't move the focus of your efforts from selling your own services to selling those of others, or selling stand-alone products, it is very likely that you will eventually face burnout.

Burnout is when you wake up one morning and realize that you hate what you're doing, that you're sick of dealing with client problems, and that you're tired of playing catchup with a technology that seems to change beyond recognition every time you take ten minutes out to go to the bathroom.

But burnout is not something to be afraid of. It is not a reason to avoid beginning a career as a consultant. *Burnout is a natural part of the ca-*

reer cycle typical of most computer consultants. In almost every case where it comes up, it doesn't signal the end of the consultant's career, or even represent a failure. It only means that it's time for the consultant to take a radically new career direction.

The truth is that only a handful of consultants make it past the tenth anniversary of a continuous consulting practice. For most computer professionals, consulting turns out not to be the end stage of their career, but rather a single phase in a cyclic career pattern.

Why Consultants Burn Out

Consultants burn out for a variety of reasons, most of which point to the next steps that consultants must take to keep their careers going.

Many consultants report that over time they get tired of the *social isolation* that comes with working for themselves. Being a guest at the client site gets old, and after a few years of consulting some consultants—even successful ones—yearn to give up the outsider status they must maintain as consultants and get involved with projects they can feel more deeply involved with. This kind of burnout may be a sign that the consultant's network of peers is not as strong as it should be. The answer to it may be to get active in organizations in which the consultant may become an insider. Or this kind of burnout might signal that it's time to put in a stint as an insider again, working as an employee and building new connections with professionals and people who may become clients for a future consulting phase.

Another reason for burnout is the *monotony* that results when a consultant gets stuck in a niche that doesn't offer enough challenge. "My clients think I walk on water," complains one busy consultant. "But so what?" Showing users how to back up their work on diskettes gets boring. Recovering erased files loses its appeal too, even if it thrills the client. This kind of burnout may be a warning signal that the niche you've chosen, though busy, isn't forcing you to keep up your skills and learn the new things you'll have to master if you are to be able to attract clients in a few years when the technology may have advanced to where the things you are doing now are no longer needed.

The *advance of technology* itself may be causing your burnout. It is hard to wake up one morning and admit that the technology that you've been living off of for a decade is no longer able to bring in enough clients to keep you busy. But this happens to even the most successful consultants. Artificial intelligence, mainframe systems tuning, and aerospace engineering support are all specialties that consultants report earned them $100,000 a year for many years before evaporating when the marketplace made a radical shift in direction. If you are burning out because marketing is taking up more and more of your time, the answer may not be to keep throwing your energy into an increasingly frustrating task, but to address the underlying career problem and do what it takes to rejuvenate the skills you have to offer potential clients.

First Aid for Burnout

If you find yourself starting to show the telltale signs of burnout, there are a few things that other consultants have done to give themselves some breathing room and rejuvenate their own careers.

Cut Back on Commitments

The first thing to try is to cut back on your commitments. The marketing momentum you have built up over years of building up your practice may be a mixed blessing if you find yourself working sixty-hour weeks and can't recall when you last took a vacation. Consultants who are burning out because of overwork report that it often helps to work out arrangements with other local consultants that allow them to cover for each other when emergencies arise. Having done that they often take the step of formally scheduling time off.

If you alienate some clients by not being available eighty hours a week, take comfort from the fact that you'll be a lot happier replacing these clients with more reasonable ones in the future.

Another alternative to taking off a large block of time is to cut down on the number of days that you work each week. Remind yourself that the point of consulting was supposed to be having more, not less, control of your work life.

It may be worth examining whether you've been encouraging clients to demand too much of your time through using lax billing practices or showing too much willingness to respond immediately to their every hiccup. Remind yourself that there are consultants who manage to stay in business even though they take vacations, see their kids, and spend some weekends away from their computers.

Become Selective about Accepting New Assignments

Another approach to heading off burnout is to make it a hard-and-fast rule to turn down assignments that duplicate work you've already done. Hold out for projects that let you learn new things and try new approaches. You may not make as much money in the short term but you are likely to regain your original excitement about the work you do, which must happen if you are to be able to continue at all.

Raise Your Rates

If you're working too many hours, perhaps you're not charging enough for what you do. Some consultants have found that raising their rates is another way of ensuring that the new assignments they take on are more challenging. Raising rates may cut down the number of hours you work and give you time to get further training in areas that you'd find more interesting than your current area of specialization.

Move the Business Out of the House

Many consultants who work out of home offices find that one of their biggest problems is that they end up feeling that they are always at work. They sit down at the computer after dinner to make "one tiny change" only to have the whole evening disappear as they get sucked back into their latest project. Renting an office outside of your home and doing all your work there, rather than in your home, may help you re-draw the boundaries between work and the rest of your life and may force you to put more effort into rebuilding the emotional relationships you may have been avoiding with your workaholic behavior. Having an office outside of the home may also help you be more productive during your official work hours, as you won't have the temptations of TV, the latest magazines, friendly phone calls from neighbors, or the refrigerator, to distract you.

Plan for a New Career before You Need One

Most consultants recognize the need to stay aware of developments in their own niche and make heroic efforts to educate themselves, so that they can continue working in their field even as technology changes, but few people ever prepare for the day when they might become thoroughly sick of their entire niche. To avoid this problem, it is a good idea to always be on the lookout for new areas you might study that are only tangentially tied to your current consulting specialty. Ask yourself "What would I do if the demand for what I do now completely evaporated?" and come up with a long-term plan that ensures that you will have more than one option should that happen.

Consider Salaried Employment

Too many times consultants let the strong if unspoken contempt for people who are employees rather than entrepreneurs prevailing among some consultants blind them to the advantages that they might reap from a stint in the salaried work force. If you are sick of having to be constantly marketing yourself, and tired of the isolation of the consulting life-style, why not look for a situation in which you could exercise your skills in a less stressful context?

Sometimes people who have been consultants for a long time believe that this will render them unattractive to employers and that even if they wanted a job they wouldn't be able to find one. But this is simply not true. In the age of downsizing and nearly continuous corporate restructuring, employers have become accustomed to encountering highly experienced personnel who have changed jobs frequently and mixed consulting with other kinds of employment. If the work you've done as a consultant demonstrates that you have the skills and capabilities needed to fill a job, your having been a consultant should not prove a barrier to your being considered for it.

Moving Out of Consulting

Unofficial estimates by consulting organizations suggest that fully one-quarter of computer consultants leave the field each year, although the number of consultants remains fairly constant as departing consultants are constantly replaced by newcomers. But it's worth giving some thought to where these disappearing computer consultants go.

In almost every case, computer consultants who have been able to sustain themselves as consultants for more than three years leave consulting not for the unemployment line, but for high-level salaried jobs that offer them a chance to refurbish or redirect their skills, and do things that they cannot do as a consultant.

For an experienced consultant, there are times when making the shift back into salaried employment is a much better career move than to stick with a consulting practice that has stagnated. As employees, ex-consultants can rebuild a network of satisfying interpersonal relationships on the job, and they can tap back into the client's point of view by, basically, becoming "one of them" again. Often it is only as an employee that a consultant can get the hands-on training required to pursue a new emerging technical specialty that will later provide the basis for a new and more successful phase of consulting. Indeed, one of the hallmarks of those most skillful at managing to lead a lifetime career in a technological specialty is that they know when to make the switch from a consultant to employee, so that they maintain their viability in both environments over time.

Consultant Burt Johnson has interspersed his consulting career with stints as a manager of engineering at several different firms, including a well-known high-tech manufacturer. After putting in over a dozen years as a consultant specializing first in aerospace applications and then in artificial intelligence, consultant Jeff Jacobs greatly enjoyed taking a salaried position in the training division of a major software vendor.

Many contract programmers find themselves offered full-time work by clients whose systems they've become familiar with. And many, having sampled the company's style as contractors and having decided they are comfortable working with it, take these salaried jobs and quickly find themselves moved into managing the very projects they used to code on.

It is important therefore not to make the mistake of thinking that once you are a consultant, you must always be a consultant. If, after you've made a success of it, consulting does start losing its allure, it is almost always a mistake to suppress your growing feelings of unhappiness in what you are doing and to force yourself to keep on working.

Such feelings of dissatisfaction are signs that, heeded properly, can help you reconsider your position and force you to take the steps needed to ensure long-term satisfaction with your work life. To ignore them can lead to disaster. More than one consultant reports that when he continued to push himself to work at a consulting career that had lost its appeal, he found himself eventually sabotaging himself as his subconscious did what it could to force him to quit—by screwing up projects, angering clients, missing deadlines, and destroying the good reputation the consultant had invested years in building up.

So if you find yourself feeling the stirrings of burnout, take them as a sign that it is time to make a change. Look for ways you can ease the pressures on yourself and analyze what it is about your current situation that is causing your burnout and what kinds of changes it suggests that you need to make. The vaunted flexibility that a consultant needs to have must include the flexibility to not be a consultant anymore.

Making the Transition from Consulting

If you do decide that it is time to leave consulting, there are a few pointers to keep in mind that will make the transition easier. A very important one to remember while job hunting is that you must translate your income into a "salaried equivalent" when asked what your previous salary has been.

If you tell an interviewer that your "previous salary" was $50 an hour, you aren't likely to get hired into a job that pays $60,000 a year because the interviewer/employer may do some rough calculations and assume that you are used to taking home $100K a year.

Instead, when asked about previous earnings, tell the interviewer what your net earnings were after you deducted what you had to spend on insurance, overhead expenses, and self-employment taxes. This net figure, which is what you really earned, is much more likely to be in line with what an employer would pay.

Another important point to keep in mind is that it is important to reassure a potential employer that you will make a commitment to his company and his job. Employers worry that consultants will go back to consulting the moment they get a call with a juicy contract offer. To counteract this fear, let the employer know that you are willing to commit to working for them for a period of several years.

When you look for a salaried job after years of consulting, don't underestimate the level you should hire in at. After many years of running your own business and serving clients, you have made yourself into a relatively high-level employee. So don't make the mistake of applying for the kinds of jobs you used to have before you started consulting—jobs that require only middling amounts of experience. Look instead for positions that involve technical or managerial leadership. These take longer to find than lower-level jobs, but these are the jobs that successful consultants reentering the salaried work force most commonly land.

The best place to look for jobs is with the clients you've most enjoyed working with. Don't be shy about asking a favorite client whether they might have a position that you'd fit into. You may, however, want to ask these clients to treat your request as confidential information if you don't want word getting around to other clients that you are thinking of leaving consulting.

Finally, whatever your current level of burnout, if you do go back to salaried employment try to *select a job that prepares you for a future consulting phase.* As sick as you may be of consulting now, the chances are that in a few years, if you've learned new skills and built a new network of contacts, you will be eager to have another shot at going out on your own. Many consultants report only getting the hang of consulting on their second or even third try at it, when they've finally mastered a body of expertise sufficient to sustain a long-term consulting career.

If possible, choose a job that will give you access to training that will be useful to you if and when you go out on your own again, rather than one that emphasizes management skills or intracompany politics. Jobs with the potential to give you lots of exposure to people who might make excellent future clients are also highly desirable, particularly if marketing difficulties have been what has taken the fun out of your current stint of consulting.

CONCLUSION

When asked about the secret of what let him succeed in computer consulting for more than a decade consultant and consulting firm principal Stephen Kent replied, "I burn out every few months." He explained what he meant by saying, "Every now and then I get overwhelmed and feel as if there's no end in sight." At those times, he's found he has to refocus and plunge on. Kent has discovered that consulting success is not a plateau but is instead a dynamic state. He has had "to learn something new every week." He's lived through "putting our tech eggs in the wrong basket" several times. But after ten years of calling himself a consultant, he says, "I can't think of any other way I'd want to live. I'd go crazy in a conventional job. The variety of this life is my life. I love it."

And so, with luck, will you.

APPENDIX A

RESOURCES FOR CONSULTANTS

BOOKS

Consulting

Arnoudse, Donald, Paul Ouellette, and John Whalen. *Consulting Skills for Information Professionals*. Homewood, IL: Dow Jones-Irwin, 1988. ISBN 1-55623-121-0

Barcus, Sam W. and Joseph W. Wilkinson. *Handbook of Management Consulting Services*. New York: McGraw Hill, 1986. ISBN 0-07-003658-6

Bellman, Geoffrey M. *The Consultant's Calling: Bringing What You Are to What You Do*. San Francisco: Jossey-Bass, 1992. ISBN 1-55542-411-2

Feingold, Norman and Leonard Perlman. *Making It on Your Own*. Austell, Ga: Acropolis, 1991. ISBN 0-87491-941-X

Hentzen, Whil. *The 1997 Developer's Guide*. Milwaukee: Hentzenwerke Corporation, 1996. ISBN 0-9655093-1-1

Holtz, Herman. *How to Succeed as an Independent Consultant*, 3rd ed. New York: Wiley, 1993. ISBN 0-471-57581-X

Ruhl, Janet. *The Computer Consultant's Workbook*. Leverett, MA: Technion Books, 1996. ISBN 0-9657116-0-5

Schiffman, Stephan. *The Consultant's Handbook*. Holbrook, MA: Bob Adams, 1988. ISBN 0-937860-93-X

Shenson, Howard L. *Shenson on Consulting*. New York: Wiley, 1994. ISBN 0-471-00925-3

Shenson, Howard L. *The Contract and Fee-Setting Guide for Consultants and Professionals*. New York: Wiley, 1990. ISBN 0-471-51538-8

Weinberg, Gerald M. *Secrets of Consulting*. New York: Dorset House, 1985. ISBN 0-032633-01-03

Weiss, Alan. *Million Dollar Consulting*. New York: McGraw-Hill, 1994. ISBN 0-07-069102-9

Zoghlin, Gil. *From Executive to Entrepreneur: Making the Transition*. New York: AMACOM, 1991. ISBN 0-8144-5010-5

Legal Aspects of Consulting

Brandon, George I. and John K. Halvey. *Data Processing Contracts*, 3rd ed. New York: Van Nostrand Reinhold, 1990. ISBN 0-442-23320-5

Dunaway, Robert and Daniel Remer. *Legal Care for Your Software*. Berkeley, CA: RDS Publishing, 1993. ISBN 0-9636256-0-8

Fishman, Stephen. *Software Development, A Legal Guide*. Berkeley, CA: Nolo Press, 1994. ISBN 0-87337-209-3

Gilman, Joel B. *The Professional Programmer's Software Copyright Handbook*. Seattle: Specialized Systems Consultants, Inc., 1991. ISBN 0-916151-45-X

Ridley, Clarence H., Peter C. Quittmeyer, and John Matuszeski. *Computer Software Agreements: Forms and Commentary*. Boston: Warren, Gorman & Lamont, 1993. ISBN 0-685-69655-3

Salone, M. J. *How to Copyright Software*, 3rd ed. Berkeley, CA: Nolo Press, 1989. ISBN 0-87337-102-X

Steingold, Fred S. *Legal Guide for Starting and Running a Small Business*. Berkeley, CA: Nolo Press, 1992. ISBN 0-87337-174-7

Sales and Marketing

Baber, Anne and Lynne Waymon. *Great Connections: Small Talk and Networking for Businesspeople*, 2nd ed. Manassas Park, VA: Impact Publications, 1992. ISBN 0-942710-80-0

Burnett, Ed. *The Complete Direct Mail List Handbook: Everything You Need to Know about Lists and How to Use Them for Greater Profit*. Englewood Cliffs, NJ: Prentice Hall, 1988. ISBN 0-13-159278-5

Dawson, Roger. *The Secrets of Power Persuasion: Everything You'll Ever Need to Get Everything You'll Ever Want*. Englewood Cliffs, NJ: Prentice Hall, 1992. ISBN 0-13-799362-5

Fisher, Roger, William Urey, and Bruce Patton. *Getting to Yes: Negotiating Agreement Without Giving In*, 2nd ed. New York: Penguin Books, 1991. ISBN 0-14-015735-2

Good, Bill. *Prospecting Your Way to Sales Success: How to Find New Business by Phone*. New York: Scribner, 1986. ISBN 0-684-18620-9

Holtz, Herman. *Speaking for Profit: for Executives, Consultants, Authors & Trainers*. New York: Wiley, 1987. ISBN 0-471-63028-4

Karrass, Chester L. *The Negotiating Game*. New York: Harper Business, 1994. ISBN 0-88730-709-4

Lancaster, Geoffrey and David Jobber. *Sales Techniques and Management*, 2nd ed. Philadelphia, PA: Trans-Atlantic, 1990. ISBN 0-273-03190-2

Lant, Jeffrey. *Cash Copy: How to Offer Your Products and Services so Your Prospects Buy Them*, 2nd ed. Cambridge, MA: LA Publications, 1992. ISBN 0-940374-20-X

Leonhard, Woody. *The Underground Guide to Telecommuting: Slightly Askew Advice to Leaving the Rat Race Behind.* Reading, MA: Addison Wesley Publishing Co., 1995. ISBN 0-201-48343-2

Levinson, Jay C. *Guerrilla Marketing: How to Make Big Profits in Your Small Business.* New York: Houghton Mifflin, 1985. ISBN 0-395-38314-5

Walther, George. *Phone Power.* New York: Berkley Publications Group, 1987. ISBN 0-425-10485-0

Ziglar, Zig. *Secrets of Closing the Sale.* New York: Berkley Publishing Group, 1987. ISBN 0-425-08102-8

Growing Your Business

Cohen, William A. *The Entrepreneur and Small Business Problem Solver,* 2nd ed. New York: Wiley, 1990. ISBN 0-471-50124-7

McKeever, Mike. *How to Write a Business Plan*, 4th ed. Berkeley, CA: Nolo Press, 1992. ISBN 0-87337-184-4

Nesheim, John L. *High-Tech Start-Up: The Complete How-to-Handbook for Creating Successful New High-Tech Companies.* Brett, Elaine, ed. Saratoga, CA: Electronic Trend Publications, 1992. ISBN 0-914405-71-3

Thomsett, Michael C. *The Expansion Trap: How to Make Your Business Grow Safely and Profitably.* New York: AMACOM, 1990. ISBN 0-8144-5954-4

Timmons, Jeffrey A. *New Venture Creation: Entrepreneurship in the 1990s*, 3rd ed. Homewood, IL: Irwin, 1990. ISBN 0-256-07879-3

Software Development—Business Aspects

Nisen, William G., Allan Schmidt, and Ira Alterman. *Marketing Your Software: Strategies for Success.* Reading, MA: Addison-Wesley Publishing Co., 1984. ISBN 0-201-00105-5

Schenot, Robert. *How to Sell Your Software.* New York: Wiley, 1995. ISBN 0-a471-06399-1

Software Development—Techniques

Freeman, Daniel P. and Gerald M. Weinberg. *Handbook of Walkthroughs: Inspections and Technical Reviews*, 3rd ed. New York: Dorset House, 1990. ISBN 0-932633-19-6

Jones, Capers. *Applied Software Measurement: Assuring Productivity and Quality.* New York: McGraw-Hill, 1991. ISBN 0-07-032813-7

Jones, Capers. *Programming Productivity.* New York: McGraw-Hill, 1990. ISBN 0-07-032811

Metzger, Philip and John Boddie. *Managing a Programming Project*, 3rd ed. Upper Saddle River, NJ: Prentice Hall PTR, 1996. ISBN 0-13-554239-1

Robertson, James and Suzanne Robertson. *Complete Systems Analysis*, 2 Vols. New York: Dorset House, 1994. ISBN 0-932633-25-0

Winograd, Terry and Fernando Flores. *Understanding Computers & Cognition: A New Foundation for Design.* Reading, MA: Addison Wesley, 1987. ISBN 0-201-11297-3

Training

Brandon, Bill, et al. *Computer Trainer's Personal Training Guide.* New York: Que Education and Training, 1996. ISBN: 1-57576-253-6

Clothier, Paul. *The Complete Computer Trainer.* New York: McGraw Hill, 1996. ISBN: 0-07-011639-3

Writing and Publishing

Appelbaum, Judith. *How to Get Happily Published: A Complete and Candid Guide*, 4th ed. New York: HarperCollins Publishers, 1992. ISBN 0-06-273133-5

Balkin, Richard. *How to Understand and Negotiate a Book Contract or Magazine Agreement.* Cincinnati, OH: Writer's Digest Books, 1985. ISBN 0-89879-190-1

Larsen, Michael. *How to Write a Book Proposal.* Cincinnati, OH: Writer's Digest Books, 1990. ISBN 0-89879-419-6

MAGAZINES AND NEWSLETTERS

Reselling/VAR Focus

Christian Computing Magazine
Hewlen, Inc.
P.O. Box 439
Belton, MO   64012
Phone: (816) 331-3881
BBS: (816) 331-4161

Church Bytes, Inc.
562 Brightleaf Square #9
905 West Main St.
Durham, NC   27001
Phone: (919) 472-5242

Computer Reseller News
P.O. Box 2040
Manhasset, NY   10030–4348
Phone: (516) 562-5000
FAX: (516) 562-5409

Educational Computer
Box 535
Cupertino, CA   95015

Educational Computing
730 Broadway
New York, NY   10003-9538

Medical Software Review
462 Second St.
Brooklyn, NY   11215-2503

Physicians and Computers
2333 Waukegan Road, Suite S-280
Bannockburn, IL   60015

Reseller Management
P.O. Box 650
Morris Plains, NJ   07950-0650
Phone: (201) 292-5100

Developer/Entrepreneur Focus

Consultant's News
Kennedy Publications
P.O. Box 539
Fitzwilliam, NH   03447
Phone: (603) 585-6544

Midnight Engineering
1700 Washington Ave.

Rocky Ford, CO   81067
Phone: (719) 254-4558
FAX: (719) 254-4517

Software Success
P.O. Box 9006
San Jose, CA   95157-0006

Contract Programming Focus

Computer Contractor
VNU House
32–34 Broadwick St.
London, W1A 2HG
UK
Phone: 0171-734-4567

Contract Employment Weekly
CE Publications, Inc.
P.O. Box 97000
Kirkland, WA   98083
Phone: (206) 823-2222
http://www.ceweekly.wa.com

Contract Professional
125 Walnut St.
Watertown, MA   02172-9920
Phone: (800) 529-7077

Freelance Informer
Reed Business Press
Room L206
Quadrant House, The Quadrant
Sutton, Surrey SM2 5AS
UK
Phone: 0175-356-7567

NTES Hotflash
National Technical Employment
   Services
212 West Peachtree St.
Scottsboro, AL   35768
Phone: (205) 259-1828
FAX: (205) 574-2079
http://iquest.com/~ntes

PD News
Publications & Communications,
   Inc.
P.O. Box 399
Cedar Park, TX   78613-9987
Phone: (800) 678-9724
(512) 250-8127
FAX: (512) 331-6779

The Professional Job Shopper
Alnak Publishers Incorporated
P.O. Box 465
Plainview, NY   11803-0465
Phone/FAX: (516) 921-3992

General Sales Newsletters

Competitive Advantage Newsletter
1901 N.W. 23rd Ave.
Box 10091
Portland, OR   97210
Phone: (503) 274-2953
FAX: (503) 274-4349

Personal Selling Power
1127 International Parkway
Fredericksburg, VA   22407
Phone: (703) 752-7000
FAX: (703) 752-7001

DIRECTORIES AND REFERENCE WORKS OF INTEREST TO CONSULTANTS

People

The Computer Industry Almanac
Computer Industry Almanac
Incline Village, NV   89451
ISBN 0-942107-07

Directory of Top Computer Executives
Applied Computer Research
Box 92277
Phoenix, AZ   85071-2266
Phone: (800) 234-2227

The Encyclopedia of Associations
Gale Research Company
Detroit, Michigan

Public Relations Resources

Gale's Directory of Publications and Broadcast Media
Gale Research Company
Detroit, Michigan

Media Resource Guide
The Foundation for American Communications
3800 Barnham Blvd.
Suite 409
Los Angeles, CA   90068
Phone: (213) 851-7372

Ulrich's International Periodicals Directory
R. R. Bowker Company
New York

ORGANIZATIONS OF INTEREST TO CONSULTANTS

Organizations of Consultants

Alliance of Business Consultants (ABC)
24 Hollow Lane
Shinfeld
Reading, Berks RG2 9BT
Phone: 01734 882913
clockbound@cix.compulink.co.uk

The Association of Independent Consultants (AIC)
http://www.io.org/~duke/aic/index

Independent Computer Consultants Association (ICCA)
1131 S. Towne Square
Suite F
St. Louis, MO   63123
Phone: (800) GET-ICCA
(314) 892-1675
http://www.icca.org

National Association of Computer Consultant Businesses (NACCB)
1250 Connecticut Avenue NW
Suite 700
Washington, DC   20036
Phone: (202) 637-6483

Professional and Technical Consultants Association (PATCA)
P.O. Box 4143
Mountainview, CA   94040
Phone: (415) 903-8305

Organizations for Computer Professionals and Managers

Association of Computer Professionals (ACP)
9 Forest Dr.
Plainview, NY   11803
Phone: (516) 938-8223

Association for Computing Machinery (ACM)
1515 Broadway
New York, NY   10036-5701
Phone: (212) 869-7440
http://www.acm.org

Association for Systems Management (ASM)
1933 W. Bagley Road
P.O. Box 38370
Cleveland, OH   44138-0370
Phone: (216) 243-6900

Association for Women in Computing
41 Sutter St.
Suite 1006
San Francisco, CA   94104

Black Data Processing Associates (BDPA)
1250 Connecticut Avenue NW

Suite 700
Washington, DC   20036-2603
Phone: (202) 775-4301

Data Processing Management Association (DPMA)
505 Busse Hwy.
Park Ridge, IL   60068
Phone: (708) 825-8124

Institute of Electrical and Electronic Engineers (IEEE)
345 East 47th St.
New York, NY   10017
Phone: (212) 705-7900
        (800) 678-IEEE
http://www.iece.org

Society for Information Management (SIM)
401 N. Michigan Ave.
Chicago, IL   60611-4267
Phone: (312) 644-6610

Other Computer-Related Organizations

Computer Law Association
3028 Javier Rd.
Suite 402
Fairfax, VA   27031
Phone: (703) 560-7747

Computer Software Industry Association
C/O Kaye Caldwell, President
kaye@ix.netcom.com
http://www.SoftwareIndustry.org/csia
http://www.webcom.com/software/csia

Computing Technology Industry Association (CompTIA)
450 E. 22nd St.
Suite 230
Lombard, IL   60148
Phone: (708) 268-1818

Independent National Computing Association (INCA)
The Austen Suite
Upper Street
Fleet, Hants GU13 9PE
Phone: 01252 811173
FAX: 01252 811175
nica@wiseword.demon.co.uk

Information Systems Audit and Control Association (formerly EDP
  Auditors Association)
3701 Algonquin Rd.
Suite 1010
Rolling Meadows, IL   60008
Phone: (708) 253-1545

Information Technology Association of America (ITAA)
1616 N. Fort Meyer Dr.
Suite 1300
Arlington, VA   22209
Phone: (703) 522-5055

Institute for Certification of Computer Professionals (ICCP)
2700 E. Devon St.
Suite 247
Des Plaines, IL   60018
Phone: (708) 299-4227

Society for Technical Communication (STC)
901 N. Stuart St.
Suite 904
Arlington, VA   22203
Phone: (703) 522-4114

Software Publishers Association
1703 M St. NW
Suite 700
Washington, DC   20036-4510
Phone: (202) 452-1600

Miscellaneous Organizations

American Arbitration Association
140 W. 51st St.
New York, NY   10020-1203
Phone: (212) 484-4000

Toastmasters International
P.O. Box 9052
Mission Viejo, CA   92690
Phone: (714) 858-8255

ON-LINE RESOURCES

On-line Sites of Interest to Consultants

Alternatives for Corporate Programmers
http://www.earthlink.net/~elplusan/pgmer.html

The Computer Consultant's Resource Page—Home of the Real Rate Survey
http://www.javanet.com/~technion/rate_sur.htm

Computer Contractor's Page
http://www.club.innet.be/~janjedsp/contract.htm

Computerworld Center for Professional Development
http://careers.computerworld.com

Expert Marketplace's Consultant's Resource Page
http://expert-market.com/em

Guide to Computer Vendors
http://www.ronin.com/SBA

Information Week Online Edition
http://techweb.cmp.com/iwk/current/

Local IEEE Consultant's Networks
http://www.ieee.org/DOCUMENTS/CAREERS/AICN/network.aicn.html

MBS Developer Newsletter Salary Survey
http://ourworld.compuserve.com/homepages/ken_mcarthur

The Newsletter Source
http://www.microsmithinc.com

PC Week Online
http://www.pcweek.com/

Small Business Administration
http://www.sbaonline.spa.gov

Source EDP Salary Survey
http://www.espan.com/salary/edp/edpcomp.html

Starting Your Own Business (UK)
http://www.open.gov.uk/dssca/jw/cw1.htm

Syntaxis/Web Contractor
http://www.demon.co.uk/syntaxis/

uk.consultants FAQ
http://www.lib.ox.ac.uk/internet/news/faq/archive/uk-consultants faq.html

UK Contracting
http://www.lib.ox.ac.uk/misc/contract.html

PLACES TO FIND CONTRACTS ONLINE

Newsgroups

alt.computer consultants	misc.jobs.contract
alt.computer.consultants.ads	ny.jobs.contract
ba.jobs.contract	uk.jobs. contract

Multiagency Job Search Web Sites

Contract Employment Connection—NTES
http://iquest.com/~ntes

Contract Employment Weekly Online
http://www.ceweekly.wa.com

Data Processing Independent Consultants Exchange (DICE)
Jobs Board
http://www.dice.com
telnet://dice.com

JobSafari
http://www.jobsafari.com

Net-Temps
http://www.net-temps.com

Compuserve Forums with Active Classified Sections

CLIPPER	FOXUSER	NTWORK	UNIXFORUM
CONSULT	INETCOMM	OAFORUM	VARBUSIN
DELPHI	NOVUSER	PBFORUM	VBPJFORUM
DTPFORUM	NTSERVER	UKPROF	WUGNET

BUSINESS SERVICES FOR CONSULTANTS

Software Escrow Services

Data Securities International	National Safe Depository
Phone: (617) 229-5806	Phone: (408) 243-3300
FAX: (617) 272-0558	(916) 371-5500
Fort Knox	Sourcefile
Phone: (800) 875-5669	Phone: (800) 868-4433
(404) 292-0700	

Computer Wholesalers and Distributors

Gates/Arrow Distributors
Phone: (800) 332-2222
        (800) 447-5270
http://www.gatesarrow.com

Ingram Micro
Phone: (800) 456-8000
http://www.ingrammicro.com

Merisel
Phone: (800) 252-5014
http://www.sun.merisel.com/

Tech Data
https://www.techdata.com

Providers of Generic Newsletters

Communications Briefings
http://capitol.cappubs.com/cgi-bin/tpgweb/moth.pl

Computer Update
Phone: (800) 659-0607

Executive Computing
Phone: (800) 327-9893

The Newsletter Source
Phone: (800) 642-7601
http://www.microsmithinc.com/

GOVERNMENT RESOURCES FOR CONSULTANTS

Australia

Department of Finance
Newlands Street
Parkes ACT, Australia 2600
Phone: (+61 6) 263 2222
FAX: 273 3021
Email: mark.trenerry@finance.ausgovfinance.telememo.au.

Belgium

Belgian Government Online
http://belgium.fgov.be/

Canada

Canadian Taxation Information:
International Taxation Office
Phone: (613) 952-3741

United Kingdom

CCTA Government Information Service
http://www.open.gov.uk/

Starting a Business
http://www.open.gov.uk/dssca/jw/cw1.htm

United States

To get an Employer ID from the IRS: 1-800-829-1040

IRS publications of interest to consultants:
IRS pub 334: *Tax Guide for Small Businesses*
IRS pub 463: *Travel, Entertainment and Gift Expenses*
IRS pub 1541: *Per Diem Rates* (Travel Expenses)

Office of Women's Business Ownership
409 Third St. SW, Sixth Floor
Washington, DC   20416
Phone: (202) 205-6673

SBA Information
Voice Line 1-800-827-5722
SBA BBS: (800) 859-INFO (2400 bps)
SBA BBS: (800) 697-INFO (9600 bps)
http://www.sbaonline.sba.gov

SCORE: Service Corps of Retired Executives
Contact SBA

APPENDIX B

IRS TWENTY FACTORS FOR ESTABLISHING CONTRACTOR STATUS

[The following presentation of the criteria used to test for employee status is taken from Part IV, "Audit and Investigation," of the *Internal Revenue Service Manual* dated 5/6/86.]

The factors or elements that show control are described below in the following 20 items. Any single fact or small group of facts is not conclusive evidence of the presence or absence of control.

These common law factors are not always present in every case. Some factors do not apply to certain occupations. The weight to be given each factor is not always constant. The degree of importance of each factor may vary depending on the occupation and the reason for existence. Therefore, in each case the agent will have two things to consider: First, does the factor exist; and second, what is the reason for or importance of its existence or nonexistence.

1. *Instructions.* A person who is required to comply with instructions about when, where, and how he is to work is ordinarily an employee. Some employees may work without receiving instructions because they are highly proficient and conscientious workers. However, the control factor is present if the employer has the right to require compliance with the instructions. The instructions which show how to reach the desired result may be oral or written (manuals or procedures).

2. *Training.* Training a person by an experienced employee working with him, by correspondence, by required attendance at meetings, and by other methods indicates that the employer wants the services performed in a particular method or manner. This is especially true if the training is given periodically or at frequent intervals. An independent contractor ordinarily uses his own methods and receives no training

from the purchaser of his services. In fact, it is usually his methods which bring him to the attention of the purchaser.

3. *Integration.* Integration of the person's services into the business operations generally shows that he is subject to direction and control. In applying the integration test, first determine the scope and function of the business and then whether the services of the individual are merged into it. When the success or continuation of a business depends to an appreciable degree upon the performance of certain services, the people who perform those services must necessarily be subject to a certain amount of control by the owner of the business.

4. *Services Rendered Personally.* If the services must be rendered personally, presumably the employer is interested in the methods as well as the results. He is interested in not only the result but also the worker.

5. *Hiring, Supervising, and Paying Assistants.* Hiring, supervising, and paying assistants by the employer generally shows control over the men on the job. Sometimes one worker may hire, supervise, and pay the other workmen. He may do so as the result of a contract under which he agrees to provide materials and labor and under which he is responsible for only the attainment of a result. In this case he is an independent contractor. On the other hand, if he hires, supervises, and pays workmen at the direction of the employer, he may be an employee acting in the capacity of a foreman for or representative of the employer (Rev. Rul. 70-440, 1970-2 C.B. 209).

6. *Continuing Relationship.* A continuing relationship between an individual and the person for whom he performs services is a factor which indicates that an employer–employee relationship exists. Continuing services may include work performed at frequently recurring though somewhat irregular intervals either on call of the employer or whenever the work is available. If the arrangement contemplates continuing or recurring work, the relationship is considered permanent even if the services are part-time, seasonal, or of short duration.

7. *Set Hours of Work.* The establishment of set hours of work by the employer is a factor indicating control. This condition bars the worker from being master of his own time, which is the right of the independent contractor. If the nature of the occupation makes fixed hours impractical, a requirement that the worker work at certain times is an element of control.

8. *Full Time Required.* If the worker must devote his full time to the business of the employer, the employer has control over the amount of time the worker spends working and impliedly restricts him from doing other gainful work. An independent contractor, on the other hand, is free to work when and for whom he chooses. Full time does not necessarily mean an eight-hour day or a five- or six-day week. Its meaning

may vary with the intent of the parties, the nature of the occupation, and customs in the locality. These conditions should be considered in defining "full time."

9. *Doing Work on Employer's Premises.* Doing the work on the employer's premises in itself is not control. However, it does imply that the employer has control, especially when the work is the kind that could be done elsewhere. A person working in the employer's place of business is physically within the employer's direction and supervision. The use of desk space and telephone and stenographic services provided by an employer places the worker within the employer's direction and supervision. Work done off the premises indicates some freedom from control. However, this fact by itself does not mean that the worker is not an employee. Control over the place of work is indicated when the employer has the right to compel a person to travel a designated route, to canvass a territory within a certain time, or to work at specific places as required. In some occupations services must be performed away from the premises of the employer; for example, employees of construction contractors or taxicab drivers.

10. *Order or Sequence Set.* If a person must perform services in the order or sequence set for him by the employer, it shows that the worker is not free to follow his own pattern of work but must follow the established routines and schedules of the employer. Often, because of the nature of an occupation, the employer either does not set the order of the services or sets them infrequently. It is sufficient to show control, however, if he retains the right to do so. The outside commission salesman, for example, usually is permitted latitude in mapping out his activities and may work "on his own" to a considerable degree. In many cases, however, at the direction of the employer he must report to the office at specified times, follow up on leads, and perform certain tasks at certain times. Such directions interfere with and take preference over the salesman's own routines or plans; this fact indicates control.

11. *Oral or Written Reports.* Another element of control is the requirement of submitting regular oral or written reports to the employer. This action shows that the person is compelled to account for his actions. Such reports are useful to the employer for present controls or future supervision; that is, they enable him to determine whether his instructions are being followed or, if the person has been "on his own," whether instructions should be issued.

12. *Payment by Hour, Week, Month.* Payment by the hour, week, or month generally points to an employer–employee relationship, provided that this method of payment is not just a convenient way of paying a lump sum agreed upon as the cost of doing a job. The payment by a firm of regular amounts at stated intervals to a worker strongly indicates an employer–employee relationship. (The fact that payments are

received from a third party, e.g., tips or fees, is irrelevant in determining whether an employment relationship exists.) The firm assumes the hazard that the services of the worker will be proportionate to the regular payments. This action warrants the assumption that, to protect its investment, the firm has the right to direct and control the performance of the worker. It is also assumed in absence of evidence to the contrary that the worker, by accepting payment upon such basis, has agreed that the firm shall have such right of control. Obviously, the firm expects the worker to give a day's work for a day's pay. Generally, a person is an employee if he is guaranteed a minimum salary or is given a drawing account of a specified amount at stated intervals and is not required to repay any excess drawn over commissions earned.

Payment made by the job or on a straight commission generally indicates that the person is an independent contractor. Payment by the job includes a lump sum computed by the number of hours required to do the job at a fixed rate per hour. Such a payment should not be confused with payment by the hour.

13. *Payment of Business and/or Traveling Expense.* If the employer pays the person's business and/or traveling expenses, the person is ordinarily an employee. The employer, to be able to control expenses, must retain the right to regulate and direct the person's business activities.

Conversely, a person who is paid on a job basis and who has to take care of all incidental expenses is generally an independent contractor. Since he is accountable only to himself for his expenses, he is free to work according to his own methods and means.

14. *Furnishing of Tools, Materials.* The fact that an employer furnishes tools, materials, etc., tends to show the existence of an employer–employee relationship. Such an employer can determine which tools the person is to use and, to some extent, in what order and how they shall be used.

An independent contractor ordinarily furnishes his own tools. However, in some occupational fields, e.g., skilled workmen, workers customarily furnish their own tools. They are usually small hand tools. Such a practice does not necessarily indicate a lack of control over the services of the worker.

15. *Significant Investment.* Investment by a person in facilities he uses in performing services for another is a factor which tends to establish an independent contractor status. On the other hand, lack of investment indicates dependence on the employer for such facilities and, accordingly, the existence of an employer–employee relationship.

In general, facilities include equipment or premises necessary for the work, such as office furniture, machinery, etc. This term does not include tools, instruments, clothing, etc., commonly provided by employees in their trade, nor does it include education, experience, or training.

In order for an investment to be a significant factor in establishing that an employer–employee relationship does not exist, it must be real, it must be essential, and it must be adequate.

16. *Realization of Profit or Loss.* The man who can realize a profit or suffer a loss as a result of his services is generally an independent contractor, but the individual who cannot is an employee.

"Profit or loss" implies the use of capital by the individual in an independent business of his own. Thus, opportunity for higher earnings, such as from pay on a piecework basis or the possibility of gain or loss from a commission arrangement, is not considered profit or loss.

17. *Working for More Than One Firm at a Time.* A person who works for a number of persons or firms at the same time is generally an independent contractor because he is usually free from control by any of the firms. It is possible, however, for a person to work for a number of people or firms and be an employee of one or all of them.

18. *Making Service Available to General Public.* The fact that a person makes his services available to the general public usually indicates an independent contractor relationship. An individual may hold his services out to the public in a number of ways: he may have his own office and assistants; he may hang out a "shingle" in front of his home or office; he may hold business licenses; he may be listed in business directories or maintain business listings in telephone directories; or he may advertise in newspapers, trade journals, magazines, etc.

19. *Right to Discharge.* The right to discharge is an important factor in indicating that the person possessing the right is an employer. He exercises control through the ever-present threat of dismissal, which causes the worker to obey his instructions. An independent contractor, on the other hand, cannot be fired so long as he produces a result which meets his contract specifications.

20. *Right to Terminate.* An employee has the right to end his relationship with his employer at any time he wishes without incurring liability. An independent contractor usually agrees to complete a specific job; he is responsible for its satisfactory completion or legally obligated to make good for failure to complete the job.

THE ICCA STANDARD FORM CONSULTING CONTRACT

The following is the standard form contract provided by the Independent Computer Consultants Association in 1996 as a model for the use of its membership. An up-to-date contract version and other standard form contracts are available to members of the ICCA.

This sample contract should not be used as anything other than a guide to the issues that a useful consulting contract should address. Any consulting contract you design for use in your business based on this model must be customized to conform to the requirements of state law in the state in which your business operates.

INDEPENDENT COMPUTER CONSULTANTS ASSOCIATION

STANDARD FORM CONSULTING CONTRACT

THIS AGREEMENT is made as of_____, 19_____

between _____ ("Client")

and_____ ("Consultant").

WITNESSETH, THAT:

WHEREAS, Client desires to retain the services of Consultant, and Consultant desires to provide such services; and

WHEREAS, the parties desire to enter into a Consulting Contract setting forth the terms and conditions of their agreement and their understandings.

NOW, THEREFORE, in consideration of the premises and the mutual covenants, promises, and agreements herein contained and for other good and valuable considerations, the receipt and sufficiency of which are hereby acknowledged, the parties, intending to be legally bound hereby, agree as follows:

1. Services. Consultant agrees to perform for Client the services listed in the Scope of Services as set forth on Exhibit A attached hereto and incorporated herein by reference (the "Services"). Consultant shall have access to Client's staff and resources as deemed necessary by Consultant, in Consultant's sole and absolute discretion, to perform the Services provided for by this Agreement.

2. Rate of Payment for Services. Client agrees to pay Consultant for Services in accordance with the schedule contained in Exhibit B attached hereto and incorporated herein by reference and executed by both Client and Consultant.

3. Invoicing. Consultant shall invoice Client, at Client's address as set forth in Section 15 hereof, for the Services rendered, and Client shall pay the amount set forth on such invoices to Consultant, at Consultant's address as set forth in Section 15 hereof, within ten (10) days of receipt thereof.

4. Confidential Information. (a) In the course of performing the Services referenced herein, Consultant and Client may come into possession of the other parties' financial and/or other business information pertaining to such other parties' business which is not published or readily available to the public, including, but not limited to, trade secrets, research, development, marketing concepts and plans, training, pricing information, sales techniques, lists of customers and vendors and other information pertaining to the business conducted by either Consultant or Client which is received from the agents or employees of either party ("Confidential Information"). Confidential Information shall not include information which is generally known or easily ascertainable by third parties of ordinary skill and competence in computer system design and programming, nor shall it include information already known to the receiving party or disclosed to the receiving party by a third party without violation of a duty of confidentiality to the disclosing party.

(b) Consultant and Client each acknowledge and agree that Confidential Information is important to, and greatly affects the success of, both parties in a competitive marketplace. Consultant and Client agree that during the course of their relationship and at all times thereafter, Consultant and Client shall hold in the strictest confidence, and shall not use for either parties' personal benefit, or disclose, duplicate or communicate to or use for the direct or indirect benefit of any other person, firm, corporation or entity, any Confidential Information without the prior written consent of the other party, or unless Consultant is required to do so in order to perform the Services, or pursuant to a court order or by operation of law.

5. Staff. Consultant is an independent contractor and neither Consultant nor Consultant's staff is or shall be deemed to be employed by Client. Client is hereby contracting with Consultant for the Services described on Exhibit A and Consultant reserves the right to determine the method, manner and mean by which the Services will be performed. Consultant is not required to perform the Services during a fixed hourly or daily time and if the Services are performed at the Client's premises, then Consultants time spent at the premises is to be at the discretion of the Consultant; subject to the Client's normal business hours and security requirements. Consultant hereby confirms to Client that Client will not be required to furnish or provide any training to Consultant to enable Consultant to perform Services required hereunder. The Services shall be performed by Consultant or Consultant's staff, and Client shall not be required to hire, supervise or pay any assistants to help Consultant perform the Services under this Agreement. Consultant shall not be required to devote Consultant's full time nor the full time of Consultant's staff to the performance of the Services required hereunder, and it is acknowledged that Consultant has other clients and Consultant offers services to the general public. The order or sequence in which the work is to be performed shall be under the control of Consultant. Except to the extent that the Consultant's work must be performed on or with Client's computers or Client's existing software, all materials used in providing the Services shall be provided by Consultant. Consultant's Services hereunder cannot be terminated or cancelled short of completion of the Services agreed upon except for Consultant's failure to perform the Agreement's specification as required hereunder and conversely, subject to Client's obligation to make full and timely payment(s) for Consultant's Services as set forth in Exhibit B, Consultant shall be obligated to complete the Services agreed upon and shall be liable for non-performance of the Services to the extent and as provided in Paragraph 10 hereof. Client shall not provide any insurance coverage of any kind for Consultant or Consultant's staff, and Client will not withhold any amount that would normally be withheld from an employee's pay. Consultant shall take appropriate measures to insure that Consultant's staff is competent and that they do not breach Section 4 hereof.

Each of the parties hereto agrees that while Consultant is performing Services under this Agreement and for a period six (6) months following the performance of such Services or the termination of this Agreement, whichever is later, neither party will, except with the other party's written approval, solicit or offer employment as an employee, consultant, independent contractor, or in any other capacity to the other party's employees or staff engaged in any efforts under this Agreement.

6. Use of Work Product. Except as specifically set forth in writing and signed by both Client and Consultant, Consultant shall have all copyright and patent rights with respect to all materials developed in the course of performing the Services under this Agreement, and Client is hereby granted a non-exclusive license to use and employ such materials within the Client's business.

7. Client Representative. The following individual_____ shall represent the Client during the performance of this Agreement with respect to the Services and deliverables as defined herein and has authority to execute written modifications or additions to this Agreement as defined in Section 14.

8. Disputes. Any disputes that arise between the parties with respect to the performance of this contract shall be submitted to binding arbitration by the American Arbitration Association, to be determined and resolved by said Association under its rules and procedures in effect at the time of submission and the parties hereby agree to share equally in the costs of said arbitration.

The final arbitration decision shall be enforceable through the courts of the state of Consultant's address [15(ii)] or any other state in which the Client resides or may be located. In the event that this arbitration provision is held unenforceable by any court of competent jurisdiction, then this contract shall be as binding and enforceable as if this section 8 were not a part hereof.

9. Taxes. Any and all taxes, except income taxes, imposed or assessed by reason of this Agreement or its performance, including but not limited to sales or use taxes, shall be paid by the Client.

LIMITED WARRANTY

10. LIABILITY. CONSULTANT WARRANTS TO CLIENT THAT THE MATERIAL, ANALYSIS, DATA PROGRAMS AND SERVICES TO BE DELIVERED OR RENDERED HEREUNDER, WILL BE OF THE KIND AND QUALITY DESIGNATED AND WILL BE PERFORMED BY QUALIFIED PERSONNEL. SPECIAL REQUIREMENTS FOR FORMAT OR STANDARDS TO BE FOLLOWED SHALL BE ATTACHED AS AN ADDITIONAL EXHIBIT AND EXECUTED BY BOTH CLIENT AND CONSULTANT. CONSULTANT MAKES NO OTHER WARRANTIES, WHETHER WRITTEN, ORAL OR IMPLIED, INCLUDING WITHOUT LIMITATION, WARRANTY OF FITNESS FOR A PARTICULAR PURPOSE OR MERCHANTABILITY. IN NO EVENT SHALL CONSULTANT BE LIABLE FOR SPECIAL OR CONSEQUENTIAL DAMAGES, INCLUDING, BUT NOT LIMITED TO, LOSS OF PROFITS, REVENUE, DATA, OR USE BY CLIENT OR ANY THIRD PARTY, REGARDLESS OF WHETHER A CLAIM OR ACTION IS ASSERTED IN CONTRACT OR TORT, WHETHER OR NOT THE POSSIBILITY OF SUCH DAMAGES HAS BEEN DISCLOSED TO CONSULTANT IN ADVANCE OR COULD HAVE BEEN REASONABLY FORESEEN BY CONSULTANT, AND IN THE EVENT THIS LIMITATION OF DAMAGES IS HELD UNENFORCEABLE THEN THE PARTIES AGREE THAT BY REASON OF THE DIFFICULTY IN FORESEEING POSSIBLE DAMAGES ALL LIABILITY TO CLIENT SHALL BE LIMITED TO ONE HUNDRED DOLLARS ($100.00) AS LIQUIDATED DAMAGES AND NOT AS A PENALTY.

11. Complete Agreement. This agreement contains the entire Agreement between the parties hereto with respect to the matters covered herein. No other agreements, representations, warranties or other matters, oral or written, purportedly agreed to or represented by or on behalf of Consultant by any of its employees or agents, or contained in any sales materials or brochures, shall be deemed to bind the parties hereto with respect to the subject matter hereof. Client acknowledges that it is entering into this Agreement solely on the basis of the representations contained herein. In the event of a conflict in the provisions of any attachments hereto and the provisions set forth in this Agreement, the provisions of such attachments shall govern.

12. Applicable Law. Consultant shall comply with all applicable laws in performing Services but shall be held harmless for violation of any governmental procurement regulation to which it may be subject but to which reference is not made in Exhibit A. This Agreement shall be construed in accordance with the laws of the State indicated by the Consultant's address [15(ii)].

13. Scope of Agreement. If the scope of any of the provisions of the Agreement is too broad in any respect whatsoever to permit enforcement to its full extent, then such provisions shall be enforced to the maximum extent permitted by law, and the parties hereto consent and agree that such scope may be judicially modified accordingly and that the whole of such provisions of this Agreement shall not thereby fail, but that the scope of such provisions shall be curtailed only to the extent necessary to conform to law.

14. Additional Work. After receipt of an order which adds to the Services initially provided for as set forth in Exhibit A of this Agreement, Consultant may, at its discretion, take reasonable action and expend reasonable amounts of time and money based on such order. In the event Consultant provides such additional services requested by Client, Client agrees to pay Consultant for such action and expenditure as set forth in Exhibit B of this Agreement for payments related to Services.

15. Notices. All notices, requests, demands and other communications hereunder shall be in writing and shall be deemed to have been duly given when personally delivered or two (2) business days after deposited with the United States Postal Service, certified or registered mail, postage prepaid, return receipt requested, addressed as follows (or to such other address as either party may designate by notice given in accordance with the provisions of this Section):
  (i) Notices to Client should be sent to:

  (ii) Notices to Consultant should be sent to:

16. Assignment. This Agreement may not be assigned by either party without the prior written consent of the other party. Except for the prohibition on assignment contained in the preceding sentence, this Agreement shall be binding upon and inure to the benefits of the heirs, successors and assigns of the parties hereto.

IN WITNESS WHEREOF, the parties hereto have signed this Agreement as of the date first above written. **THIS CONTRACT CONTAINS A BINDING ARBITRATION PROVISION WHICH MAY BE ENFORCED BY THE PARTIES.**

Client	Consultant

Type Name and Title

INDEX